Making Markets

Making Markets

Economic Transformation in Eastern Europe and the Post-Soviet States

Edited by Shafiqul Islam and
Michael Mandelbaum

COUNCIL ON FOREIGN RELATIONS PRESS

NEW YORK

COUNCIL ON FOREIGN RELATIONS BOOKS

The Council on Foreign Relations, Inc., is a nonprofit and nonpartisan organization devoted to promoting improved understanding of international affairs through the free exchange of ideas. The Council does not take any position on questions of foreign policy and has no affiliation with, and receives no funding from, the United States government.

From time to time, books and monographs written by members of the Council's research staff or visiting fellows, or commissioned by the Council, or written by an independent author with critical review contributed by a Council study or working group are published with the designation "Council on Foreign Relations Book." Any book or monograph bearing that designation is, in the judgment of the Committee on Studies of the Council's Board of Directors, a responsible treatment of a significant international topic worthy of presentation to the public. All statements of fact and expressions of opinion contained in Council books are, however, the sole responsibility of the author.

If you would like more information on Council publications, please write the Council on Foreign Relations, 58 East 68th Street, New York, NY 10021, or call the Publications Office at (212)734-0400.

Copyright © 1993 by the Council on Foreign Relations®, Inc.
All rights reserved.
Printed in the United States of America.

This book may not be reproduced, in whole or in part, in any form (beyond that copying permitted by Sections 107 and 108 of the U.S. Copyright Law and excerpts by reviewers for the public press), without written permission from the publishers. For information, write Publications Office, Council on Foreign Relations, 58 East 68th Street, New York, NY 10021.

Library of Congress Cataloging-in-Publication Data

Making markets : Economic transformation in Eastern Europe and the post-Soviet states / edited by Shafiqul Islam and Michael Mandelbaum.
　　p. cm.
　　Includes bibliographical references and index.
　　ISBN 0-87609-129-X : $14.95
　　1. Europe, Eastern–Economic policy–1989- 2. Former Soviet republics–Economic policy. 3. Europe, Eastern–Economic conditions–1989- 4. Former Soviet republics–Economic conditions.
　　5. Mixed economy–Europe, Eastern. 6. Mixed economy–Former Soviet republics. I. Islam, Shafiqul. II. Mandelbaum, Michael.
HC244.M256   1993   92-40676
338.947–dc20   CIP

94   95   EB   7   6   5   4   3

(Cover Design: Jon McEwen)

iv

Contents

Foreword

Making Markets addresses the formidable challenge of transforming collapsed communist economies into thriving market economies.

In this transformation, economic and political reforms are inextricably intertwined. Throughout the republics of the former Soviet Union and Eastern Europe, the state can no longer dictate economic results and the market is not yet sufficiently well established to provide the incentives necessary for vigorous or stable growth. Economic progress might not come fast enough to avoid the collapse of democratic governments, and with it a reversion to autocracy or a decline into anarchy.

Increasingly, political leaders and scholars alike will be engaging in a debate over whether countries can implement democratic reforms and market reforms at the same time. Does a nation seeking to put in place a market-oriented economy require a strong government to keep a lid on demands for inflationary wage increases and to force its citizens to adopt the institutional changes required to make the necessary economic transition? Does a government require the confidence that it can control the political evolution of its society in order to allow a substantial amount of economic autonomy for its citizens and regions? Can a government based on democratic principles survive if the populace becomes disillusioned due to insufficient improvement in living standards?

The countries of this region face an enormous set of challenges. This book provides an insight into their nature and an analysis of ways to tackle them. *Making Markets* is, in another sense, a useful guide to Americans as to how the United States can support the reform effort in formerly communist Europe. The end of the Cold War should not mean the end of America's commitment to democracy and market economics in the region. The area should not be marginalized because of America's domestic preoccupations, nor should Eastern Europe be marginalized because of our more recent preoccupation with developments in the former Soviet Union.

There are no short cuts here. The economic reform process in formerly communist Europe will require a long-term American commitment of assistance, political support, and patience—if not for the commercial benefits of success, then because of the improved security and political environment that would result from the region's prosperity and stability. Ultimately it is the moral and political authority of the United States as the leader of the democratic world that is being tested. If America fails to play a constructive and substantial role, its claim to global leadership in the 1990s will suffer. History will judge this generation of Americans harshly if at the very moment that the former communist nations of Europe sought to embrace markets and democracy, the world's major market economy and most powerful democracy failed to provide adequate assistance.

Robert D. Hormats
January 1993

Acknowledgments

This volume is part of the Council on Foreign Relations Project on East-West Relations, which is supported by the Carnegie Corporation.

The chapters were first presented as papers at a symposium on "Making Markets: Economic Transformation in Eastern Europe and the Post-Soviet Republics," held in New York on February 12 and 13, 1992. The symposium was jointly sponsored by the International Economics and Finance Program and the Project on East-West Relations. The participants in the symposium are listed in the Appendix.

The editors are grateful to all those involved in the production of the volume, especially Radha Muthiah and Theresa Weber for organizing the symposium and supervising the publication of the book.

Introduction

Michael Mandelbaum

The most important international development of the second half of the 20th century is the collapse of communism in Europe and the effort to replace it with Western political and economic systems. The heart of that effort, the most difficult and protracted part of it, is the construction of market economies on the ruins of central planning from the eastern part of Germany to the Pacific coast of Russia. That enormous task is the subject of this book.

The Nature of the Transition

Making markets where none existed before is an enterprise of daunting scale. It is far greater in scope than the parallel shift from communist to democratic governance. Government, after all, is a full-time activity for only a handful of people in any society. The economy, by contrast, is the setting in which most adults in any country spend their working lives. The transition from plan to market involves abrupt and sweeping changes in the daily routines of hundreds of millions of people—changes in how and where they work, what they buy, how they earn money to pay for their purchases, and where they live.

Western governments have never deliberately attempted to bring about such vast changes. The closest parallel to the disruption that the countries of formerly communist Europe are bringing on themselves is with natural or man-made disasters: floods, earthquakes, famines, or wars. But even those parallels understate the enormity of the social dislocation that economic transition is bound to cause. It is an easier matter to repair physical damage, even if it is extensive, than to change the beliefs, the habits, and the skills of an entire population. Rebuilding is easier than relearning.

This great transition thus has no historical precedent. To be sure, the opposite change has taken place. But it was never accomplished voluntarily or without violence. Where communists seized power, they destroyed whatever free markets they found and replaced them with central planning. Planned economies were imposed in Europe, Russia, China, Cuba, and Vietnam by brutal means, usually in the wake of wars that had already severely battered existing social arrangements, and in countries where most people still lived in villages and engaged in agriculture. The present transition, by contrast, is being undertaken peacefully and democratically, in largely urban countries with far more elaborate social and economic structures than the peasant societies that communists conquered in the course of the 20th century.

Moreover, while the communist-imposed passage from market to plan was largely an exercise in destruction, the opposite course involves creation as well, which makes it more difficult and more protracted. A Polish saying makes the point: It is easier to turn an aquarium into fish soup than the other way around. In no small part because it had never been done, moving from plan to market had, before 1989, been the subject of very little systematic thinking. Economists in communist Europe were not allowed to write about or discuss openly the full-scale conversion of their national economies to market systems. Some did write, timidly and occasionally secretly, about grafting market reforms onto their planned systems. In a few places—notably Hungary—this was actually tried, with limited success.

In the West a small group of economists, several of whom have contributed to this volume, studied the economies of socialist countries. These economists, however, were generally interested in how planned economies worked and how they were similar to and, for the most part, different from the economies of the West, not in how to get from one to the other.

Yet, despite the lack of experience with a transition of this sort, a consensus has emerged in both East and West on what it involves. It may be divided into three principal parts. The first is stabilization—bringing the balance of payments into rough equilibrium and above all correcting economic imbalances that are ordinarily expressed as overt or suppressed inflation. Inflation is not a necessary consequence of central planning, but some of the economies of formerly communist Europe—notably Poland's and Russia's—have suffered from it at the outset of their transitions. Various methods of stabilization are available. Correcting for repressed inflation requires that prices be allowed to rise to market-clearing levels. The challenge is to permit only a once-and-for-all increase in prices, not recurrent bouts of inflation. Preventing the inevitable price increases from turning into an inflationary spiral demands that the profligate issuance of money stop, the state budget be kept in reasonable balance, and rises in wages and incomes remain below the initial rate of inflation. Selling state assets to domestic holders of money can also help to fight inflation. Stabilization programs are, of course, familiar features of the economic policies of noncommunist countries as well, often prescribed by the International Monetary Fund.

A second set of changes necessary for the transition from plan to market comes under the rubric "liberalization." All involve dissolving state controls of economic activity and substituting market rules and practices. They include such measures as breaking up the monopolistic structure of industries to foster competition and putting economic relations with other countries on a market basis, an important element of which is making local currencies convertible.

The third set of changes involves building the institutions necessary to sustain a market economy. Perhaps the most important is private property. Ownership must be transferred from the state to private hands. Also important is the establishment of a legal framework within which private economic activity can take place, contracts are enforced, and private property is protected. Important as well is the development of a financial system that can channel capital, in the form of private savings, to profitable uses. And perhaps most important of all is the accumulation of the skills—managerial, legal, and entrepreneurial, among others—that are necessary to make free markets work.

The Book

The purpose of *Making Markets* is to introduce the subject of economic transition to a non-specialist audience. The authors of the essays that follow approach the large, complicated, difficult, and mostly untried changes that the transition involves from different perspectives. Richard Portes provides an overview of the transition, based chiefly on the experiences of Hungary, Poland, and Czechoslovakia, because it is in these countries that the transformation of planned into market economies is thus far most advanced. He describes the nature of the economic systems under communism and the failure of the various efforts to reform them in Central Europe. He outlines the main features and problems that the transition from plan to market involves. He discusses the lessons for formerly communist Europe of comparable, although not identical, economic changes in Western Europe after World War II and Latin America in the 1980s. Finally, he assesses the results to date of the process of transition.

Moving from this overview, Paul Marer gives a more detailed account of the economic transition in the three major countries of Central Europe, as well as his own summary of the principal features of this process. He sketches the economic histories of Poland, Hungary, and Czechoslovakia under communist rule and discusses how these countries' histories shaped their different approaches to the postcommunist period. He assesses what has been achieved so far and what may lie ahead for these three countries, as well as for the former East Germany, Romania, Bulgaria, and the independent states that have emerged from what was Yugoslavia.

The chapter by Robert W. Campbell covers the uncertain prospects for the now sovereign pieces of the former Soviet Union, especially the largest piece—Russia. The author describes the economic system that Stalin imposed and shows how the efforts to reform it during the Gorbachev era worsened its performance, particularly as growing budget deficits were financed by the printing of more and more rubles. He offers some thoughts on the daunting task of converting the successor states of the Soviet Union to market economies, which is all the more difficult because they must cope with the division of what was once a single economic unit into several countries, each with its own laws, governments, currencies, and economic policies.

Jeffrey Sachs's essay on the Western role in the transition complements Campbell's: Sachs takes as his illustrative case Russia, the most important politically, if not the most promising economically, of all the formerly communist countries. Sachs discusses the sources of popular opposition to the values the transition involves. To reinforce his case that Western assistance is crucial, he cites episodes in economic history in which external support made ultimate success possible. And he explains the different types of assistance the West can provide, noting how the emphasis can change as the transition proceeds.

Economic Problems

It is already apparent that this great transition will be difficult, protracted, and unevenly achieved throughout formerly communist Europe. Some of the difficulties stem from what economists call the problem of sequencing. The problem arises from the fact that in an economy, everything affects everything else. The best way to implement the various changes required is thus to do everything at once. But this is simply not possible. The varying schedules for the different aspects of the transition create bottlenecks and delay the benefits of the changes that are made.

Stabilization can be accomplished soonest. In theory, prices can be raised, subsidies stopped, the currency-printing presses shut down overnight. In practice, immediate, full-scale stabilization is likely to be so disruptive as to be politically infeasible. Boris Yeltsin shrank from freeing all Russian prices at a stroke. To reap fully the benefits of stabilization, however, requires substantial privatization, and that is necessarily a more gradual process.

Privatization is essential because macroeconomic stability—that is, stable prices—does not by itself bring prosperity. It provides a setting in which farms, factories, and firms can operate efficiently, knowing that the costs tomorrow will be roughly what they are today. To be productive, people need incentives. The principal economic incentive is the accumulation of wealth, which requires that individuals own enterprises rather than merely work for them.

Some economic thinkers once considered private ownership unnecessary for productive economic activity. "Market socialism," in which the state owns society's productive assets but operates them according to market rules, was thought to be a viable form of economic organization. Now almost no economist believes that; the consensus is that, for a society to derive the greatest economic benefit from market rules, individuals, not the state, must own the sources of wealth.

Transferring productive assets from the state to private hands in formerly communist Europe is bound to take a long time. Privatization proved a protracted undertaking in Britain and Mexico, where a far smaller part of the total economy was in the hands of the state. In the formerly communist countries, moreover, there is no easy way to assign a price to the assets to be sold because there is no point of reference: all prices under communism were set by administrative fiat rather than by the market.

In addition to the logistical obstacles, financial problems impede rapid privatization. Whatever prices are put on state properties, few citizens will be able to pay them; this reality leads to the observation that privatization consists in selling assets with no value to people with no money. One way to get around this problem is to distribute vouchers to everyone, which can be used to acquire stock in newly privatized assets. Several countries, notably Czechoslovakia and Poland, have launched programs to do so. But designing and carrying out a voucher scheme is itself complicated and time-consuming.

Foreigners can purchase state property, and foreign capital can assist the transition. But the specter of a country's assets falling into foreign hands, however legally, has the potential to trigger a nationalist backlash. This has already happened in Poland and Hungary.

Some state property has passed to members of the former communist elite, who have used their positions, contacts, and information from the old system to take advantage of the opportunities the new one offers. This "capitalization of the *nomenklatura*" provides some benefits to these societies. By giving the old elite a stake in a market economy, it undercuts what would otherwise be a strong incentive to keep one from being created. And some of the members of the *nomenklatura* have skills and experience that are useful in managing enterprises under market conditions. But if those who prospered under communism use their positions to enrich themselves under capitalism on a large scale, those who were less privileged under the old regime are bound to be distressed, and popular faith in a market economy could be destroyed.

Nor is it necessarily proper to give shares of enterprises to those who happen to work in them. This would favor workers in profitable concerns and penalize those in unprofitable ones; people will find themselves in one group or the other purely by chance.

Privatization thus provokes a broad political issue. Involving as it does the redistribution of virtually all of a society's productive assets, it raises a fundamental question that is political, economic, and ultimately moral in character: What is fair? What is a just distribution of wealth in a society? It is a question that philosophers have explored for centuries. No answer has ever commanded universal assent.

In the West this is an academic, hypothetical question. Changes in the distribution of wealth that are subject to collective action—that is, to government policy—are marginal. Whatever distribution history and the workings of the market have provided is widely accepted, at least tacitly, as more or less just. Not everyone everywhere is satisfied with it, of course, but in no Western society is dissatisfaction great enough to provoke a sweeping rearrangement. In the East today, by contrast, the question is a profoundly practical one, the ultimate answer to which cannot help being controversial.

The impossibility of putting all productive assets in private hands rapidly has created growing sentiment among those involved in the transition for something partway between state and private ownership. It is called "commercialization," and it involves states turning enterprises into joint stock companies. In the first instance the shares of these companies are generally owned by the government, which means that commercialization creates many of the features of what economists used to think of as market socialism. Ironically, it was the conviction that market socialism was not, in the long term, a basis for prosperity that led the countries of formerly communist Europe to the conclusion that privatization was imperative in the first place.

A successful market economy requires not only stable economic conditions and the necessary economic institutions, including a well-established private sector, but also an adequate distribution throughout the society of the appropriate attitudes, skills, and patterns of behavior. Just how rapidly these will develop is unclear. If the distribution of virtually all property through privatization is a central event in the rather sketchy history of applied political philosophy, the growth of the personal qualities a market requires offers a rare empirical test of what might be called—with some exaggeration—two contending approaches to the understanding of social behavior: the economic and the sociological.

Economists believe—or assume—that human beings are rational maximizers. Individuals, according to this view, do what is best for themselves within the confines of the social or economic system in which they are placed. Managers, workers, and consumers in centrally planned communist economies behaved rationally. If the result was unsatisfactory, this was because the system was poorly designed. It follows that a better-designed system will yield better results from the same people. Put Poles, Czechs, or Russians in a market economy, and they will become as productive as Swedes, Swiss, or Canadians.

Sociologists consider human behavior more variable, determined by a wide range of cultural, historical, and psychological forces. Behavior is the product of attitudes and beliefs that develop slowly. It can and does change, but not as rapidly as economic models sometimes suggest; and change does not come simply from altering the social and political systems in which people live. Economists generally believe in adaptation; sociologists in learning.

Plainly, both interpretations are at least partly accurate (and neither profession denies the validity of what the other emphasizes). People do adapt. The citizens of formerly communist Europe are responding to market reforms. Visible evidence of commercial and entrepreneurial activity is appearing there. (Such activity even took place during the communist period, although it was far less visible because it was illegal.) But not everyone can adapt easily. And if attitudes can change quickly, skills take time to acquire. No one can learn to be an accountant or a banker overnight. It is not possible to produce quickly large enough numbers of accountants or lawyers for an advanced capitalist economy.

Political Problems

The transition from plan to market is an economic process of uniquely broad scope and enormous difficulty. It is difficult because it is so sweeping; because it has never before been attempted; and because, despite a general consensus on what must be done, everything cannot be done quickly enough to avoid bottlenecks and breakdowns. The transition is complicated as well for political reasons. Although it is an economic process, it is enmeshed in politics.

For all the countries of formerly communist Europe, political considerations are part of the answers to the two major questions that the transition raises: Why embark on it at all? And what are the chances for success?

There are, to be sure, purely economic reasons for seeking to establish a market economy. The evidence of the last 40 years, and especially the last decade, proves that market mechanisms are more efficient and productive than central planning. Since people generally prefer wealth to poverty, it is not surprising that when free to choose, they opt for economic institutions and practices with a record of creating prosperity.

There is also, however, a political rationale for embarking on this transition. The market is compatible with the new democratic political systems that almost all of Europe's formerly communist countries are trying to establish; a centrally controlled economic system is not. Not all market economies are democracies; but no centrally planned economic system is democratic and it is not plausible that any could be.

The system of central planning was created by communist political power for the purpose of perpetuating communist political power. Communists were tiny minorities without popular support when they seized power in Europe and in Russia. They sought to control every aspect of social life—hence the term "totalitarian" that came to describe their rule—among other reasons, to make certain that no challenge to their authority could arise.

Communist officials aspired not simply to hold power but also to steer the societies they governed in particular directions. Gathering all power over economic affairs into their own hands not only helped to ensure that they would continue to rule, it also gave them the means to impose their own economic preferences: investment over consumption; industry over agriculture; heavy over light industry; and, particularly in the Soviet Union, military over civilian production.

Central planning thus goes hand in hand with authoritarian rule. The market system, by contrast, is compatible with democratic politics. At the heart of both the market and democracy is individual freedom—to engage in economic and political activity, respectively. Both embody the principle of popular sovereignty: just as democratic governments are chosen by popular vote, so market economies are partly driven by the decisions of individual consumers.

Democratic rule is incompatible with central control of the economy because democracy requires a large sphere of activity independent of the government, known to students of politics as "civil society," whose mainstay is a private economy. A planned economy thus smothers the social basis of democracy, as communists intended that it should. For the transition from plan to market, however, this presents a paradox: a private economy is necessary to sustain the kind of political order in which a private economy can flourish. Therefore, political support for the early stages of a transition is likely to be fragile, and this bears on the second great question the transition raises: What are its chances for success?

The answer to that question, like the answer to the question of why countries have embarked on the transition in the first place, is partly an economic one. How soon the formerly communist countries begin to reap the benefits of market practices, and how substantial those benefits will be, will depend on economic conditions at the outset of the transition and the skill with which the program is designed and implemented. But the chances for its ultimate success will depend, as well, on the depth of public support for the measures involved: that is, on how long and how consistently the policies can be sustained. Public support is bound to be shaky, at least in the initial stages of the transition, and perhaps even for years, because the necessary policies inevitably bring hardship.

Things get worse before they get better. When prices rise and subsidies are abolished while salaries remain constant, almost everyone becomes poorer. When firms and factories cannot meet the market test of profitability and must close, many workers lose their jobs. Ultimately these measures help to create a more productive economy than the old one, an economy that makes virtually everyone richer. The transition may be seen as history's largest example of what the economist Joseph Schumpeter called "gales of creative destruction," the periodic upheavals that kept capitalism vital by sweeping away obsolete and inefficient businesses and industries to make room for new, healthier, more vibrant ones.

But the cycle takes time to run its course. At the outset of the one through which formerly communist Europe is passing, there is considerable destruction and very little creation. Between the beginning of the transition and the ultimate payoff runs what the sociologist Ralf Dahrendorf has called the "valley of tears."

In that valley more people will feel worse than better off. At the beginning there are likely to be more losers than winners.

Even when winners outnumber losers, those who will lose the most can do considerable political damage to the governments trying to steer their societies toward market economies. Workers in large, obsolete enterprises are numerous in formerly communist Europe. They have already staged demonstrations in Poland, gone out on strike in Russia, and rioted in Romania.

In the long run the transition will succeed. But to get to the long run, the appropriate policies and the governments committed to them must survive the short run, and there is no guarantee that they will. The valley of tears is turning out to be longer and deeper than expected. This jeopardizes the governments trying to guide their countries through it.

Economic distress drains the popularity of the elected officials who are responsible for it. The architects of stabilization, liberalization, and institution-building have seen their policies generate discontent wherever they have been implemented—in Central Europe, the Balkans, the Baltic, and Russia. Democratic politicians in these countries thus face a dilemma. They are torn between economic wisdom and political necessity. Voters are not kind to politicians whose policies inflict hardship, even if those policies are necessary for long-term prosperity.

There is some danger that discontent and resentment will sweep away not only particular governments but even democracy itself. It has even been suggested that authoritarian rule is necessary to sustain a transition from plan to market. Like Ulysses lashing himself to the mast of his ship to resist the call of the sirens, goes this argument, formerly communist countries can sustain the appropriate economic policies only by depriving their citizens of the power to change them. Often invoked in support of such a scenario is the experience of Chile under General Augusto Pinochet, whose combination of political repression and economic liberalization achieved salutary economic, if not political, results.

Pinochet was an embarrassment to the United States and the West. A Russian version of the Chilean general, armed with thousands of nuclear weapons and perhaps embroiled in border disputes with Russia's neighbors, would be considerably worse than that.

Nor would a Central European or Russian authoritarian ruler necessarily carry out liberal economic policies. The alternative is not a return to full-fledged communist planning, but the retention of some communist practices also found in many countries of the Third World, practices that may be called "populist." They include the maintenance of a sizable state industrial sector, the provision of consumer subsidies on a large scale, the granting of inflationary wage increases for groups such as workers in key industries, and the imposition of selected price controls—all leading to severe macroeconomic imbalances. Populist economic policies would make things worse, not better. Printing money to continue subsidies would ignite hyperinflation unless price controls were broadly applied, but controls would perpetuate the shortages and stagnation of the communist period. The hardship of the transition thus could encumber some or even all of formerly communist Europe with the worst of both worlds: authoritarian politics and populist economics.

The long-term prospects for these countries depend on their establishing, and keeping, the opposite combination: democratic politics and liberal economics. The West can help them do so.

The West supports the creation of Western-style politics and economics in formerly communist Europe even without launching any specific initiatives, simply by the example that it sets. Many of the people who lived under communism wish to remake their countries in the image of the West. It has been a political asset for leaders like Jorzef Antall in Hungary, Václav Havel in Czechoslovakia, Lech Walesa in Poland, and Boris Yeltsin in Russia to be able to say that their policies, no matter how painful, are necessary to create the kind of economic system in which Western Europe and North America have prospered. That assertion is particularly powerful because, with the dissolution of the Iron Curtain, Western prosperity can be seen—on television, if not in person—by everyone from Berlin to Vladivostok.

To be sure, a reputation for adhering to policies that meet Western approval is an asset of variable worth. It is strongest where the commitment to Western political and economic forms is most intense, which is to say in Central Europe. Hungarians,

Czechs, and Poles are the most certain that they wish to be European, by which they mean Western European; Russians are probably the least; and the peoples of the Baltic, Ukraine, and the Balkans fall somewhere in between.

These countries are looking to the West for more than symbolic reassurance. They seek specific forms of assistance: food and medicine; Western cash to buy Western products; and training programs to impart the skills needed to operate market economies, such as banking, accounting, management, and legal counsel. (The peoples of these countries need no instruction in the art of trading and in the underdeveloped practice of consuming.) Over the long term perhaps the most important economic contribution the West can make to the East is not assistance at all, but access to Western markets.

Western aid, however much is provided, will affect the economic prospects for transition programs in each country. Particularly useful will be balance-of-payments assistance that can be used to purchase imports necessary to keep production going, and money to establish modest social safety nets for people suffering from the dislocations of the transition. But economic aid has a political impact as well. It imparts credibility to the transition itself. It is a vote of confidence in the process by Western governments that often command more respect among the peoples of formerly communist Europe than do the local authorities, even though almost all of these have now been democratically elected. Western support provides Eastern governments with the political equivalent of one particular form of economic assistance: a reserve fund to support currency convertibility.

A national currency is convertible when others are willing to hold it. Convertibility requires confidence. Standing by themselves, the currencies of formerly communist Europe do not, on the whole, command confidence. A reserve fund provides the basis for it. People were willing to hold Polish zlotys when they knew that, if they wished, they could exchange those zlotys for dollars in the reserve fund. Knowing this, they did not exercise the option of exchanging their zlotys.

Similarly, what the new governments of formerly communist Europe need is the confidence of their people, who, especially at the outset of this wrenching series of changes, will be harried, confused, ignorant, and occasionally desperate. The new governments need popular confidence that the transition will ultimately bring prosperity. To be sure, the most important basis for confidence in countries in the midst of transition is not what others do for them, but what they do for themselves. The better the results of the policies, the broader the support for them will be. The genius of the Chinese program of economic liberalization was that it brought better economic times quickly to the countryside, creating an enormous reservoir of support in rural China for market reforms. The same pattern of success is not possible in formerly communist Europe, where most people live in cities rather than villages. But in Poland, for example, the appearance of previously unavailable goods in the stores soon after the beginning of reform had a similar, if more modest, effect. Few Poles had the means to buy what was on display, but at least they could see what they might someday acquire by taking advantage of the new opportunities to earn money.

Success will be slow in coming and modest at first. Thus, tangible Western support also has a political role to play by contributing to public confidence in the prospects for a successful transition. And without confidence, the policies of political authoritarianism and economic populism will have their day.

With confidence, on the other hand, comes patience. This, too, will be in short supply. Communism required patience in abundance, for communist rule promised a radiant future, if those subject to it would only wait. They waited for four decades, and what was promised never came; communist economics simply did not work. But free markets will work. That is why patience is vital. The harsh economic medicine will ultimately have the desired effect. So if the people of formerly communist Europe can endure the hardship that the policies of stabilization, liberalization, and institution-building inflict, they will emerge at the end of the greatest upheaval and dislocation that any democratic government has ever brought deliberately upon its own people, at the other end of the valley of tears, into the sunlight of Western freedom and prosperity.

1

From Central Planning to a Market Economy

Richard Portes

The current economic transformation of Central and Eastern Europe (CEE) and the former Soviet Union is qualitatively different from other historical or current examples of major changes in the structure of economic institutions. The initial conditions, the scope and desired speed of the undertaking, the guidance offered by economic analysis, all distinguish this process from economic change elsewhere.

Because of the depth and difficulty of the transformation process, it is imperative to seek lessons from economic theory, from history, and from other countries. Decision makers in both the East and the West need to examine such lessons, because the process is not going well.

There is no question about the objective: it is market capitalism. There is no plausible "third way" to economic progress. We have no blueprint for a coherent, stable, and successful model in between capitalism with markets and communism with central planning. One legacy of the many failed reform programs from the late 1950s onward was to discredit all models of "market socialism." The market is necessary to organize production and exchange, and private ownership is necessary to motivate economic agents.

Market capitalism comes in many versions, however, and we may see a variety of outcomes in Eastern Europe (including CEE and the former Soviet Union), perhaps as different as the United States from Japan. Whichever one a given East European country chooses, there must be a better way of getting there than the current path.

The costs of the policies followed since 1989 have proven to be excessive and excessively protracted, economically and politically. So far, even talk of a "J-curve" of economic transformation—in which the economy first goes downhill, then recovers to a higher level—seems too optimistic. We have seen an "L-curve," with no upturn in sight. The enthusiasm, high expectations, and political renewal of the revolutions of 1989 have given way to widespread disillusion. So far, there are not enough obvious, important successes to justify the sacrifices. Filling the shelves is easy but unhelpful if most people cannot afford to buy, so the main effect is to heighten perceptions of the inegalitarian redistribution of income.

CEE is in a deep depression. In Poland, gross national product fell 21 percent in 1990–1991; in Hungary, 12 percent; in Czechoslovakia, 16 percent in the single year 1991. Industrial production in these countries is down by at least one-quarter. Václav Klaus, Czechoslovakia's minister of finance, quipped that the "third way" leads to the Third World; at this rate, the Western way will get there quicker.

Whatever the ravages of communist central planning, these were not Third World countries at the outset. They have high educational levels. Poland is not badly endowed with natural resources, and parts of the former Soviet Union are very rich. Over several decades, they invested tremendous amounts—very badly, to be sure, and much of it in military industries. Still, the human and physical capital provided a decent level of consumption, despite the high levels of domestic savings.

There was hidden unemployment, some hidden inflation, and substantial environmental damage. But the depression is not merely a result of making these visible. The problem is not so much revealing unemployment—that has been gradual—as it is a precipitous fall in output, with little sign of recovery or redeployment of resources.

With a view toward exploring alternative ways, this chapter assesses the lessons of history and theory and the experience of the transformation to late 1992. First it reviews the key features of the old central planning system and discusses previous economic reforms in Eastern Europe from 1956–1957 to the 1980s (excluding Yugoslavia, because of its unique workers' management system and its current political disintegration). The discussion illustrates that reform was indeed "reform," as many had always insisted: the old system was very stable, and a necessary condition for a self-sustaining shift to a market economy was a radical change in the geopolitical environment.

Next, the essay sets out what has to be done for economic transformation and the contribution that economic analysis— our existing tool kit—can make to the design of the transformation programs. The basic elements are uncontroversial: macroeconomic stabilization, where necessary; liberalization of prices and elimination of pervasive direct controls; restructuring of production; and systemic change—new laws and institutions, including wide-ranging privatization.

We know quite a lot about the macroeconomics of stabilization and the microeconomics of institutions, but much less about the interplay between the two. One important aspect of that interaction is the order in which various measures should be implemented: the problem of sequencing. It is here that we enter the often exaggerated debate between partisans of a a "big bang," "global shock therapy," or "gradualism."

In practice, everything is urgent, but some measures are more important than others. It is simply not feasible to do everything at once. Yet some policies, like currency convertibility, may not make sense if others, like price liberalization, are not in place. There may be a minimum coherent initial package—which is not to say that it would be administratively and politically feasible to implement it simultaneously, especially if it includes large-scale privatization.

What about the lessons from other countries and regions and from other historical periods? The next part of the chapter considers two major examples: postwar reconstruction in Western Europe and recent economic reform programs implemented in Latin America. Despite differences in initial conditions, some generalizations of wide relevance are fairly clear: about establishing macroeconomic equilibrium, reforming public finances, liberalizing the financial sector, dealing with foreign debt, and implementing appropriate conditionality for foreign assistance.

There are no straightforward blueprints, however, and indeed there are evident pitfalls in seeking the German Wirtschaftswunder of the early 1950s or the Mexican miracle of 1988–1992 with a standard International Monetary Fund (IMF) program. Quoting Ludwig Erhard and his Ordnungspolitik may be a serious misuse of history, as is suggested by the way today's Germany is using the highly interventionist Treuhandanstalt to restructure the Eastern lands.

The essay goes on to consider the results of East European economic transformation to date. Some quite positive phenomena are apparent: the unexpectedly rapid expansion of exports to the West that some countries have achieved, the dynamism of very small-scale private economic activity, some significant foreign direct investment, and the longer-term prospects opened up by the conclusion of association agreements between the three Central European countries and the European Community. Yet despite major institutional changes, progress seems painfully slow. Even more painful is the fall in output and living standards throughout the region. The chapter reviews at this point the obstacles encountered by reform. It discusses in some detail the most difficult puzzle: Why has the economic contraction in the region so far been so deep, generalized, and persistent?

The economic and political consequences of a major depression will hit even those countries where the situation appears best so far, while the prospects for Poland and especially Russia—to take just two examples—are extremely worrying. And our preoccupation with them has unduly taken our attention away from other countries for which we might actually be able to do more, and with more positive results, than we can for those large nations with even larger and more complex problems. The concluding section proposes policies, both for Eastern Europe and for the West, to deal now with the obstacles to economic transformation.

Central Planning and Economic Reforms
in Eastern Europe

The "standard system" of central planning was installed in the Soviet Union at the end of the 1920s and in CEE two decades later. As a system of economic organization, its key feature was the central allocation of resources *in natura*, by rationing of quantities of inputs among users, with plans for production specified in physical terms. The central planners also set the distribution of these outputs quantitatively, with specific addressees for all output. The only role for decentralized allocation with price signals was on the supply side of the labor market, where workers were broadly free to respond to wages in choosing among jobs determined by the planners, and on the demand side of the consumer goods market, where given their incomes, households were broadly free to respond to prices in buying whatever the planners made available.

Most goods and services were produced by state-owned enterprises (SOEs), with some cooperatives in agriculture. Private production in industry and agriculture was minimal, most services were provided by the state, and private property as such (for example, housing) was severely restricted.

These key features implied certain other characteristics of the system. Quantitative planning was much easier with prices fixed for long periods, so that monetary aggregates could be planned, too; and since prices were not used as signals, they did not need to follow supply-and-demand conditions. Output targets took priority in the system of incentives facing managers and workers; minimizing costs and maximizing profits were subordinate to (over)fulfillment of the output plans. The combined central and commercial bank ("monobank") also implemented the plans, through "control by the ruble" (*khozraschet*); the bank ensured that expenditures matched the planned purchases of inputs, in particular wage payments. But the planners have overriden these budget constraints in the interest of fulfillment of the output plans. The system made no provisions for bankruptcy of state enterprises.

The complete separation of domestic producers and users from foreign trade also facilitated planning. Central importing and exporting organizations carried out all trade transactions according to the plans. Domestic prices, too, were totally insulated from foreign prices by the "price equalization" system. The domestic currency was totally inconvertible into foreign exchange, but this system went even further by subsidizing or taxing away the difference between the prices paid and received abroad and those at home.

Indeed, there was "commodity inconvertibility": neither foreign nor domestic currency would entitle a buyer at home or abroad to purchase domestically produced goods unless the plan so provided. This was necessary not merely to avoid disruption of the quantitative plans. Since the domestic price system was totally irrational, what such a buyer would pay would not reflect the resource costs of production, so buyers could not be allowed to purchase freely.

The simplicity of the macroeconomic, monetary, and fiscal systems reflected the dominance of central allocation at the microeconomic level.[1] To be sure, there were plans for aggregate investment and consumption, but the only important macroeconomic planning tool was the "balance of incomes and expenditures of the population." The planners compared the volume of consumer goods they would supply with their estimates of household demand, to avoid inflationary pressures and "forced saving."

Monetary policy was simply the consequence of policies that regulated incomes ("incomes policies"): given the quantitative plans for consumption, the key was to control wages. The monobank monopolized credit provision, and it administratively fixed interest rates for working capital loans and household deposits; these interest rates were not varied to affect economic decision making. Indeed, the system permitted no capital market—no stocks or bonds, no way to borrow or lend except through the monobank.

The fiscal system was extremely complex, insofar as the rates of tax and subsidy varied widely across goods and enterprises. The "turnover tax" made up the difference between producer and consumer prices on each product. Since these prices were set quite independently of each other, this tax could in principle be assessed at a different rate (positive or negative) for each product. The main source of budget revenue was a "tax" on the profits of SOEs. This in fact simply siphoned into the state budget all profits over and above those that the plan had specified the enterprise could use for predetermined purposes. Since centralized setting of wages and consumer prices could be used to determine both the level and the distribution of household incomes, an income tax was unnecessary, except on private-sector activity.

This economic system both reflected and reinforced the priorities of economic policy: the growth of industrial output, especially in heavy industry; full employment; no inflation; rapid capital accumulation; and self-sufficiency, if not autarky. But obvious internal contradictions pervaded both these policies and the system itself. For example, whereas some degree of autarky may have been possible for the large and resource-rich USSR, it clearly was not for the smaller countries of Eastern Europe that did not possess raw material reserves like those of the Soviet Union. As the size and diversity of their industrial sectors grew, so did their dependence on the USSR as a source of raw material imports and a market for industrial output.

The problems that began to appear in the mid-1950s first seemed to be the consequences of an overcentralization whose origins were bureaucratic and administrative. Only later did it become clear that overcentralization itself was a manifestation of the internal logic of the system *and* of the policies it was intended to implement. The enterprises had incentives to distort the information they gave to the planners. Moreover, the vertical relationships of a hierarchical administrative allocation system conflicted with the horizontal relationships dictated by direct contacts between enterprises, needed to organize the flows of output to users. And plan and market clashed directly in the markets for labor and consumer goods: even if the planners could achieve macroeconomic balance, they were unable to adjust wages and consumer prices to achieve micro-level balance between demand and supply.

The multiple priorities of the planners—all, of course, important—led to multiple objectives for managers. The quantitative plans themselves could never be perfectly consistent, and SOE decision makers therefore could not satisfy them all. With their choices thus overdetermined, they did have to choose. Since in principle the plan was to have dictated all micro-level choices, the managers' decisions were bound to violate some of the planners' priorities.

At the macroeconomic level, in the productive sector, the emphasis on output growth and the consequent pressure to invest led to substantial excess aggregate demand, in real terms. This was not of monetary origin, but it had monetary consequences: inflationary pressures in the producer goods and labor markets. If the monobank's controls had failed, these pressures could have pushed up wages and caused open or hidden inflation in consumer markets. In fact, however, such inflation (and the "monetary overhang") was in most Eastern countries unimportant until the mid-1980s; even thereafter, it was not significant in Czechoslovakia and Hungary.

It is clear, however, that shortages and bottlenecks were pervasive in the SOE sector. These created a dominance of supplier over user with widespread negative consequences, such as uncontrollable neglect of quality and delivery times. The system and the generalized excess demand led enterprise managers to adopt very short-run horizons and defensive behavior like hoarding inventories of scarce inputs.

Other "legacies" of the system hindered all reform efforts—and still do. The very success in controlling consumer price inflation, in maintaining full employment, and in generating a fairly egalitarian income distribution had a strong impact on the population: they became hypersensitive to open inflation, to unemployment, and to inequality. The structure of prices, production, and the capital stock are grossly distorted relative to any market equilibrium.

The intricate tax-subsidy system had an overall "leveling" thrust that eliminated differences among the after-tax results of SOEs. Ministries bargained with enterprises over taxes and subsidies and simultaneously sought favorable treatment for their enterprises. This system of ministerial responsibility for the performance of firms was a form of "tutelage" that effectively eliminated competition within the bureaucratic system and gave patronage to the *nomenklatura* at every level. They therefore fiercely resist attempts to destroy it, and this is a major behavioral and institutional constraint that still hinders progress toward a market environment.

By the early 1960s the authorities throughout Eastern Europe perceived grave problems, first with overcentralization itself, then with what they interpreted as its consequences: a slowing of aggregate growth; increasing disparities at the micro level between the structures of supply and of demand, with consequent shortages and unsalable goods; inefficiency of investment, with sharp investment cycles and accumulation of unfinished projects at the macroeconomic level; deteriorating product quality; and slow technical progress. One conclusion was that it was necessary to switch from "extensive" growth, relying on heavy investment and massive transfer of labor, to "intensive" growth, which would require greater efficiency, higher capital-labor ratios, and much more adaptation to demand from consumers and trade partners. This was always a facile explanation that ignored the quantity-driven logic of the system and pretended that decentralization without real markets—in particular without a capital market—would suffice.

Direct attempts to deal with overcentralization came first in Hungary and Poland in 1957, then in Czechoslovakia in 1958–1959. The essential measure was to reduce the number of quantitative indices transmitted through the hierarchy—the number of goods centrally planned, the range of targets and success indicators communicated to enterprises. Some decisions were no longer dictated by plan targets; others were now governed by aggregate indices rather than specific instructions.

This approach failed. Initially the overall level of pressure—the aggregate growth objectives—was relaxed, but as soon as it rose again, excess demand created bottlenecks that compelled the planners to intervene, at an increasingly detailed level. Decentralization without markets and with excessively expansionary macroeconomic policies was not viable, as Mikhail Gorbachev discovered thirty years later. This was the first clear demonstration that the distinction between economic system and economic policy was untenable: it was impossible to decentralize while maintaining heavy pressure for rapid growth.

Meanwhile, in 1957 Nikita Khrushchev launched a quite different alternative, which, in view of the breakup of the Soviet Union into its republics, bears great contemporary relevance. His notion of decentralization was, indeed, to transfer authority away from the Moscow ministries to the republic level. This led to vertical integration and efforts towards self-sufficiency in the republics; a fall in interrepublic exchanges; and inefficiencies of small-scale production that substituted for the previous inefficiencies of long supply lines between highly specialized, horizontally integrated enterprises. This also failed, and the reorganization was reversed in 1963.

Subsequent reform efforts fell into two categories: "technocratic" and "managerial." The technocratic reforms called for administrative decentralization but retained fixed prices (subject to administrative "reform") and disaggregated, quantitative plans that continued to function as the primary success indicators for managers. The managerial reforms replaced central physical allocation and obligatory quantitative plans with a highly regulated market that had some price flexibility, but a complex system of "indirect regulators," mainly taxes and subsidies affecting profitability, which became the main objective of the enterprise.

The prototype of the former was East Germany, starting in 1964; other examples were the USSR in 1965 and again in 1971, Poland frequently, and subsequently Bulgaria. In both the German and the Soviet cases, amalgamating the enterprises into vertically integrated combines compensated for some of the redistribution of authority from ministries to enterprises.

Meanwhile, Hungary preceded its managerial reforms by an industrial reorganization in 1963 that yielded an extraordinarily high degree of horizontal integration—at the time, only 800 enterprises in all of state industry, with remarkable concentration on very large firms. Indeed, excessive industrial concentration is to this day a major obstacle to the creation of competitive markets in Eastern Europe.

The Hungarian Communist Party decided in November 1964 to launch preparations for a truly comprehensive reform, ultimately destined to create a "socialist market economy." These changes were implemented en bloc on January 1, 1968. Meanwhile, a more spontaneous reform movement with wider political implications had taken hold in Czechoslovakia. The direction of movement there in 1967–1968 was similar to that in Hungary, with more emphasis on workers' self-management. Doubtless, the political tensions between the USSR and Yugoslavia contributed to the Soviet ideological animosity toward workers' control. This was one provocation for the Soviet intervention; more serious, no doubt, were the challenge to the party's "leading role" in Czechoslovakia, and the tendency there to turn away from the Council for Mutual Economic Assistance (CMEA) in trade relations (with the fear that this would generalize to Warsaw Pact relations).

After August 1968 Czechoslovakia returned to extreme economic orthodoxy. The Hungarian case was thus the leading example of reforms in the East until 1990; a substantial literature on the reform process describes why it was ultimately blocked.[2] Hungary followed the managerial model outlined above as far as it could, adding substantial decentralization of investment decisions (financed from retained earnings and bank credits), as well as considerable decentralization of foreign trade and direct links of the domestic price structure to foreign prices. It also introduced an incomes policy tool that has since been widely imitated, including in the current transformation programs: the "tax on wage increases," under which profits were hit with penal taxation once the enterprise's wage increase exceeded a given percentage. The authorities also retained power to apply differentiated taxes and subsidies, which eventually led to the reassertion of tutelage.

The reluctance of any other CMEA economies to take the same path, and the consequent survival of a substantial nonmarket set of transactions with these trade partners, impeded Hungary's early reform effort. The 1973 oil shock and subsequent deterioration of world market conditions also contributed to the pressure for recentralization. But two more important obstacles blocked the reforms: First, the inability to control the demand for investment, and general inexperience with macro-economic management, led to excess demand and pressures for the center to intervene. Second, some politically threatening developments in income distribution occurred: average incomes among peasants rose above those of the urban proletariat; the large industrial SOEs were the least efficient and least able to increase wages, so their workers—the vanguard of the proletariat and stalwarts of the party—fell behind; and successful entrepreneurs in the private and cooperative sectors were doing excessively and visibly well.

In November 1972 the party called a halt. Not much was rolled back, but the development of the "socialist market" was blocked. Nevertheless, the early reforms and a new wave of institutional changes in 1979 and in the 1980s have made Hungary into the only example of a "gradualist" transformation.

Poland was an important and quite different case.[3] After the December 1970 fall of Wladislaw Gomulka, a victim of resistance to an attempt to raise meat prices, his successor, Edward Gierek, launched a new strategy: a dash for growth that relied not on decentralization and markets, but on a simultaneous increase of real wages and investment. The former was intended to stimulate effort and productivity, the latter to expand exportable output on the basis of technology imported from the West. But implementation of this program required a substantial current-account deficit financed by borrowing from the West, and Poland rapidly accumulated debt that already appeared threatening by early 1977.[4]

Meanwhile, the strategy was not working: the rate of investment exceeded absorptive capacity; much of the imported plan and equipment was precisely that made uneconomic by the sharp relative price changes of the early 1970s; harvests were bad. When interest rates rose and recession hit at the end of the decade, Poland was the first to feel the pressure. Attempts to cut consumption led to political reaction, Solidarity, the "Polish crisis" of 1981, economic disintegration, and ultimately the military coup in December of that year.

The 1980s are better known and less interesting. The fate of efforts to achieve market socialism by reforming central planning was already clear. But the Soviet case is illuminating insofar as it reinforces our main conclusions: the combination of partial decentralization with the loss of macroeconomic control is not merely untenable as a reform program; it can be economically and politically devastating.[5]

There was no dangerous macroeconomic disequilibrium or monetary overhang in the USSR in 1985.[6] But Gorbachev's antialcohol campaign (which cut excise tax revenues) and the fall in oil prices then combined with *perestroika*, which, economically, meant partial and inconsistent decentralization. This eroded the enterprise tax base and weakened central (and bank) control over enterprise expenditures, particularly wages. The efforts to "accelerate" growth in 1987–1988 pushed the accumulating budgetary disequilibrium completely out of control. The culmination of this process was Valentin Pavlov's pathetic "currency reform." Even in the absence of republican separatism, economic reform could never have succeeded in the Soviet Union; economic transformation became essential once *perestroika* had done its work. Partial decentralization is inconsistent, and reforms are not feasible in extreme macroeconomic disequilibrium.

The culprit was not the absence of financial discipline over SOEs—the so-called soft budget constraint. Imposing such discipline on enterprises is neither necessary nor sufficient for macroeconomic equilibrium. It is not sufficient, since the government budget can remain in deficit for all sorts of other reasons that keep revenues low and expenditures high. Nor is it necessary, as long as the planners and the monobank do their jobs: the monetary position in most of these countries, including the USSR, was sustainable until the mid-1980s. If the soft budget constraint and all its supposed nefarious consequences had been characteristic of the centrally planned economies from the outset (early postwar), the macroeconomic denouement and rapid open inflation would have come much earlier.[7]

Overall, the main lesson of this brief history of economic reforms in Eastern Europe is the remarkable stability of the old central planning system and its resistance to fundamental change. The once-vaunted managerial revolution and change of generations in the East had little effect on economic organization or performance. The legacies of the old system—deep-rooted distortions of the structure of production and prices and of the behavior of managers, workers, and households—were too strong and pervasive. Many of those distortions survive—even the revolutions of 1989 could not eliminate them in CEE, and they are doubtless even more important in the former Soviet Union. Nor could Hungary's gradualism gradually ameliorate them. The Hungarian case may suggest not that the original Hungarian goal of market socialism was inherently unworkable, but rather that it required political changes, and they were then infeasible. By the time they came, the goal had clearly changed. Partly because of the nature of the political revolutions, the objective everywhere in the region became market capitalism.

Economic Analysis and Economic Transformation

The East European challenge quickly brought a consensus among economists on what had to be done in the economic transformation of a socialist, centrally planned economy into a capitalist market economy: macroeconomic stabilization (where necessary), liberalization, restructuring, and systemic change. Liberalization refers to prices, including the exchange rate and interest rate, as well as the physical allocation mechanism and foreign trade. Restructuring covers both production and trade. Systemic change involves a wide range of new laws and institutions, in areas such as tax, social security, legal, accounting, bankruptcy, and banking systems; cleaning up the balance sheets of banks and enterprises; and privatization.

East Germany offers the only example of true global shock therapy. It was not necessary to do it that way, but the political choice was made to import the entire program—including a new currency—and implement it simultaneously. The disadvantages of this approach are now clear in the precipitous fall of output since July 1990, high and rising unemployment, and huge financial transfers required from the West. Even those transfers, as well as massive administrative and technical assistance, have not yet been sufficient to banish the specter of a German Mezzogiorno. Perhaps the global shock would have worked if the East had not also imported the West's high wage rates, or if there were no demands for restitution of nationalized properties to their previous owners; but perhaps such an abrupt and comprehensive set of socioeconomic changes simply cannot be absorbed properly.

This is an extreme case. It is unlikely to be replicated elsewhere (except Korea), and it does not determine the choice between gradualism and a "big bang." Evidently the initial conditions determine some decisions: if the economy is sliding into hyperinflation, a full stabilization package may appear urgent. Yet its chances of lasting success may be slim if a sound tax base cannot be created quickly, or if supply will not respond to a more stable macroeconomic environment. It may then seem that even the full stabilization bang, perhaps including currency convertibility, will not be sufficient as an initial step.

One can indeed argue that it is necessary to do almost everything simultaneously, because of the well-known principle that in economics, everything depends on everything else. That is what we learn from general equilibrium theory. Dynamics is difficult, the more so when the outcome depends on the path chosen as well as the speed; the easiest strategy, it may seem, is just to ignore the path and jump quickly.

But it may be impossible to jump far enough to get all the way across the crevasse. The hypothesis that a "big bang" is the most effective road is not testable, simply because it is administratively, institutionally, and probably politically infeasible to implement all the required reforms at once, except in the German mode. It is always possible, however, to blame the failure of any program on what it left out or implemented inadequately. Thus the negative results of the Polish package are attributed to the delay of privatization, since without it large firms did not have the incentive to respond to the new environment. Yet one might say that the preoccupation with macroeconomic issues even after the stabilization itself drew attention and momentum away from privatization.

The initial conditions did not put forward many candidates for a gradualist approach. East Germany was clearly one. Czechoslovakia did take its time, insofar as nothing was really decided until after the elections of May 1990, and then the program did not go into effect until January 1991, with fairly extensive preparations. But then it was introduced as a sharp, general discontinuity. In view of circumstances elsewhere, Hungary appears to be the only feasible example of gradualism. And that has been the choice of the government elected in April 1990, although the opposition would probably have tried much faster implementation of a comprehensive blueprint.

Hungary's history is special. For the others, there may be a necessary "minimum bang."[8] But in some cases no feasible set of measures is likely to be sufficient to achieve stabilization without unsustainable output falls. In such circumstances—perhaps Russia in 1993—it might be wise not to play for high stakes with an ambitious stabilization program, but rather to focus on sectors that may be fairly independent of the macroeconomy, like agriculture and energy. Meanwhile, one can pursue the somewhat more limited goal of implementing a set of measures necessary to establish a "regime change"—a definitive and irreversible exit from the socialist planned economy, sufficient to change expectations.[9] This, I believe, has now been achieved in all the countries of Central Europe, and perhaps in Bulgaria and Romania, as well.

In considering the application of the economist's tool kit at a more detailed level, we start with macroeconomic stabilization, as it was necessary to do in Poland. Here we do know rather a lot.[10] There is ample practical experience of stabilization programs.[11] Controversy over IMF stabilization packages has led to a new literature on "heterodox" stabilizations that include wage and price controls.[12]

For example, we know to distinguish between an excess initial stock of money (the monetary overhang) and the flow disequilibrium, in the form of a continuing budget deficit, that might reproduce the stock problem even if it were eliminated at the outset. A monetary overhang might be eliminated by engineering a discrete jump in the price level (normally associated with a sharp devaluation of the exchange rate); confiscating some part of money balances with a currency reform; selling state assets to households; or suddenly bringing in substantial volumes of imports, financed from abroad. Historically, the currency reform has been most popular; but Poland chose the sharp devaluation.

Methods for cutting a budget deficit are well known, too. In Eastern Europe, eliminating most of the web of subsidies will go part of the way, and that will improve efficiency greatly, as well.

On the tax side, a strong professional consensus favors the value-added tax as the most effective measure. It is especially urgent because SOE profits are likely to fall, and with them the main existing tax base, while rising unemployment will raise the cost of the social safety net. Revenue from seigniorage (the "inflation tax" derived from the government's monopoly over issuing money) will also fall with stabilization.

Macroeconomic equilibrium does not depend only on the state, however, and it is important to analyze enterprise and household behavior. Here, too, we can make some generalizations: investment demand will be weak at the outset of a program, and precautionary household savings are likely to increase sharply, in both cases because of the very high uncertainty associated with radical transformation from planned full employment to markets and the vagaries of supply and demand.

There is some disagreement about the desirable extent of indexation, especially whether wages should be linked closely to prices to avoid sharp movements in the real wage. It is nevertheless important to do everything possible to make expectations forward-looking rather than backward-looking, in order to escape inflationary habits. We have also learned to stress the credibility of macroeconomic policy and how that affects the behavior of households and firms. This is especially important in the East European context, where economic agents have learned over decades to mistrust the authorities totally, to expect arbitrary actions, and to take appropriate defensive measures.

This applies equally in devising microeconomic policies and institutional change: it is essential to choose solutions that offer maximum credibility—for example, by tying policies to externally imposed conditionality. The IMF, World Bank, and European Bank for Reconstruction and Development can be extremely useful in this way. So can obligations such as those regarding competition policy and "approximation of laws" embodied in the new association agreements between the Central European countries and the European Community.

One or more "nominal anchors" may support the credibility of a stabilization program. The main purpose of wage controls or pegging the nominal exchange rate is to tie down the price level; because of the major changes in monetary institutions, they may be better for this purpose than targeting the money supply. But the exchange rate is also a particularly visible target, and adherence to it is a powerful symbol of policy credibility. By the same token, credibility can suffer deeply if the authorities choose an exchange rate target they cannot defend.

The behavior of the real interest rate and its effects—on savings, investment, inventory holding, output, and the budget—are less well understood. We appreciate the importance of this key variable, but we are still learning about how high real interest rates and a "credit squeeze" may effect SOEs, households, and the new private sector in the initial phases of a stabilization.[13]

For the most part, these macroeconomic and monetary phenomena do admit analysis that gives a framework applicable to the Eastern economies in transition, as well as to market capitalist countries. The "real" economy—the determinants of production, consumption, and trade at a micro level—reflects much more its specific institutional basis. There are, of course, qualifications: the absence of markets for government securities in Eastern Europe, for example, is a major factor in determining the relation between fiscal and monetary policies.

One extraordinary example of microeconomic theory in action is the procedure now being used for voucher privatization in Czechoslovakia. This is as pure an application of the 19th-century French economist Léon Walras's iterative price-setting procedure (*tâtonnement*) on as large a scale as we are likely to see in economic policy—and correspondingly risky. Alternative procedures might use recent modeling of different kinds of (smaller-scale) auctions.[14]

Designers of the institutional framework for the privatized firms and remaining SOEs should pay close attention to recent work on incentives and corporate governance.[15] For example, there are strong objections to mass privatization that would distribute shares of any given firm among many individuals and thus so disperse control as to leave the existing management in charge. Whether or not the authorities choose to break up giant firms before they are privatized, setting up competition policy can benefit not only from experience in the European Community, but also from recent work in industrial economics.[16]

We also know a good deal both in theory and on a comparative cross-country basis about financial institutions, financial structure, and financial repression.[17] In somewhat controversial applications to Eastern Europe, Jenny Corbett and Colin Mayer[18] argue for a much more German-style financial system and corporate control than Eastern Europe has chosen so far, whereas Ronald McKinnon[19] proposes that banks not be permitted to lend at all to "liberalized" SOEs and the private sector until a wide range of other institutional changes have taken place.

The academic and policy discussion of the sequencing of economic reforms started with the order of financial liberalization and then turned to a discussion of the right order in which to liberalize international trade and capital flows (the current and capital accounts). This analysis has arrived at a conventionally preferred sequencing for less developed countries: the current account of the balance of payments should normally precede the capital account, and removing distortions in goods markets should take priority over factor markets (in particular, capital markets).

This literature has not addressed in detail some specific issues for Eastern Europe. For example, should privatization accompany stabilization, or must it await the restoration of macroeconomic equilibrium and the arrival at reasonable relative prices? There seems no reason why "small privatization" of service establishments cannot go very quickly, except for any obstacles that restitution laws pose. One can make a strong case, however, that privatization of the larger SOEs should follow financial restructuring ("cleaning out the books")[20] and demonopolization, a centrally directed breaking up of large firms.[21] Yet others argue that without privatization, there will be no supply response to lift the economy out of the depression that macroeconomic stabilization and price liberalization will induce.[22]

The sequencing literature is now quite extensive.[23] Some consensus exists, but in addition to the place of privatization, that of convertibility (on current-account transactions) is also widely debated. John Williamson, Andrew Berg and Jeffrey Sachs, and myself all push on somewhat different grounds for an early move to convertibility.[24] Berg and Sachs take the strongest view here, arguing in a monetarist framework that convertibility is always achievable with a nominal exchange rate sufficiently devalued relative to the money supply. Technically this is true; in practice, however, the required devaluation may be so deep as to give a real wage too low to be sustained. I stress the role of convertibility in establishing credibility and in permitting the use of the exchange rate as both a nominal anchor for the price level and a fixed point for the relative price structure. But a country like Hungary, with a tremendously heavy debt service burden, is justifiably cautious—despite its excellent performance in exporting to the West—about going to full convertibility, even only on current account.

Sequencing involves maintaining credibility. It must also take account of the balance of political forces. Some writers have viewed the choice of an optimal sequence as an issue of political economy that can be analyzed in the framework of building and sustaining coalitions sufficient to ensure adequate political support for the program. Individuals have built up special advantages ("situation rents") associated with their roles in the old system; if all such rents were eliminated simultaneously, the government would fall as soon as voters could get rid of it. The trick is to take measures at the beginning that will benefit a sufficient proportion of voters, then to maintain dominant though shifting coalitions.[25]

These examples should illustrate how much economic analysis can already contribute to the design and implementation of economic transformation programs. But there can be no single blueprint, and the proposals offered at the end of this chapter are not intended to create one.

Lessons from Postwar Reconstruction and Latin American Reforms

The situation of the East European economies today is very different from that of Western Europe just after the war. Firms and households can interact productively in a modern economy only if a structured environment, an appropriate institutional framework, is in place. Postwar catch-up with the previous trend would not have been feasible without a suitable legal system, properly trained accountants and bankers, and so forth.

Moreover, not only the initial conditions but also the previous history is significantly different. The system that prevailed before the collapse of communism was qualitatively different from the examples of the wartime command economy. Central physical allocation in Eastern Europe and the absence of meaningful prices were much more extreme than wartime rationing and materials allocation in Western Europe. Nor was central planning at all like the postwar Swedish or British socialism. The long history of command planning and failed efforts to reform threatened the credibility of policymakers from 1989 onward, even if they were a new team under a popularly elected government (and not all were); they had to establish that credibility with their new policies. Some found it harder because their extreme laissez-faire ideology and public positions were not in practice feasible; compromises were necessary, from administratively fixing the exchange rate to keeping energy prices below world market levels.

Thus the case for a rapid move to convertibility in the East European economies is qualitatively different from that of postwar Western Europe. The West European countries did not need convertibility for reconstruction in the same way that Eastern Europe does for transformation. A direct link of domestic to foreign prices as a fundamental building block of the market economy is essential in Eastern Europe now; it was not after the war, for the reconstruction of a preexisting market economy with a capital stock that had suffered damage and depreciation but whose structure was not highly distorted.

Instant convertibility would make any form of payments union superfluous. Instead, the last section of this chapter suggests a settlements mechanism to deal with the chaos in trade within the former Soviet Union and with its CEE trading partners. The postwar European Payments Union would not be an appropriate analogy.[26]

One clear lesson from the immediate postwar period is that convertibility with exchange rate stability will require foreign support and debt consolidation. Even the Anglo-American loan and the Marshall Plan were not sufficient for sterling convertibility. One of the most striking—and productive—historical examples of debt relief is that given to Germany in 1953. Why can our policymakers not take such an enlightened initiative now to ease the burden on Hungary and Bulgaria?

The Korean War rescued Ludwig Erhard's program of nonintervention in both macroeconomic and microeconomic policies. If foreign demand had not increased sharply in 1950, it is likely that the Erhard program for German reconstruction would have failed. No supply-side response can last without markets for the output. For Eastern Europe forty years later, the key is access to European Community markets. The new association agreements between the Community and Czechoslovakia, Hungary, and Poland are rather better than expected, but they are still restrictive on agriculture and incorporate potentially dangerous "safeguards" and antidumping provisions. There should be continuous pressure to implement these liberally and to extend similar agreements to the other countries of Eastern Europe, so as to give them all the foreign markets that underpinned the German Wirtschaftswunder.[27]

A final lesson from the postwar period is in the role of the Marshall Plan. It did make a difference, if only because of the conditionality it imposed.[28] That conditionality was perfectly clear: market allocation and no communists in government. In Eastern Europe now, there are so many donors, so many international organizations wandering about, and so many missions that it is close to an occupation army, especially if we add the merchant bankers and the management consultants (not to mention the academics). The consequence is multiple and inconsistent conditionality: they are hearing too many kinds of advice, much of it related to aid. As discussed in the concluding section, there must be more coordination in this conditionality and in the aid itself.

The postward period is mute on some of the key issues. It tells us nothing about mass privatization, about the sequencing of privatization and restructuring, or about the choice among financial systems and the speed of financial liberalization. To be sure, privatization in Latin America is nowhere as extensive as that envisaged in Eastern Europe, but the Mexican program, for example, is quite substantial in terms of the volume of assets sold. And on sequencing and financial liberalization, as well as several other issues, Latin America offers many lessons. We consider Chile and Mexico, which Sebastian Edwards[29] and José Cordoba,[30] respectively, have studied from this viewpoint.

The Chilean economic reform program that began in the 1970s had two clear advantages relative to Eastern Europe: a preexisting set of market institutions, and a dictatorial government to enforce unpopular measures. The key relevant conclusions appear to be the following. First, Chile chose to eliminate its monetary overhang with a discrete jump in prices. The evidence indicates that this created high and widely varying inflationary expectations, hence both inflation inertia and uncertainty. Stabilization took several years. A monetary reform might have been preferable. Second, the Chilean experience suggests it is very important to eliminate indexation of wages and of financial assets as much and as fast as possible, while it is equally essential to index the tax system so as to avoid losing real revenue through inflation. Third, Chile's use of the exchange rate as a nominal anchor in a stabilization program led to overvaluation as inflation proceeded, with the consequent loss of competitiveness and an unsustainable trade deficit. The exchange rate rule did not sufficiently moderate the inertial forces in the system, perhaps because it was not accompanied by an incomes policy.

Several lessons from the Mexican case are directly relevant to Eastern Europe. For stabilization, the prescriptions are straightforward and important: give absolute priority to fiscal consolidation, making all expenditures and the inflation tax revenue totally transparent, with proper monitoring of the accounts of state enterprises; as in Chile, avoid wage or financial indexation, but index the fiscal system; and use direct controls for key prices and wages.

In sequencing, trade liberalization should come very quickly, though it must be credible, or a speculative import boom will occur in advance of expected new restrictions; financial liberalization should be delayed until there is fiscal consolidation and adequate supervision; and public revenues will be maximized if privatization takes place in stages. Finally, Mexico has benefited from creating special conditions for foreign direct investment; yet capital inflows did not really take off until after the 1989 debt settlement. Its success is a brilliant example— clearly relevant to Hungary—of how debt reduction supported by the United States and the IMF can build on a previous foundation of reforms and lay the basis for sustained growth.

All these generalizations from postwar Europe and contemporary Latin America are interesting, important, and potentially useful. Yet one cannot help feeling that too much of the foreign advice to Eastern Europe transfers this experience without full understanding of the specific characteristics of these economies and the institutional and behavioral legacies of central planning.

It is clear that the extent of privatization required is an order of magnitude greater than anywhere else; that totally new legal, accounting, regulatory, and other institutional frameworks are needed; and that the industrial structure is exceptionally concentrated. To those without experience in the region, however, it may not be equally evident that deeply irrational incentives, prices, and investment go back forty years and more. The resulting patterns of production and capital stock are immeasurably further from an "equilibrium" than in any middle-income developing country contemplating liberalization, and the behavior of managers in a liberalized environment may not accord with experience elsewhere.

Thus freeing prices and unifying the exchange rate will make many product lines, plants, and enterprises appear hopelessly uneconomic. That will result simply from bringing energy prices close to world prices, rationalizing the enterprise tax-subsidy system, and establishing a positive real interest rate. But structural change will have to go much further.

In the ensuing adjustment, it is important to distinguish temporarily unprofitable from permanently unviable activities. Price distortions are both cause and effect of baroque tax-subsidy systems, and simultaneous efforts to rationalize both will interact. Moreover, the inherited debts of enterprises were accumulated more or less randomly under the old system and have no relation to their future profitability. So workers should not be sacked, capital stock scrapped, nor enterprises closed in the short run unless it is transparently clear that they are unviable in the long run. And these considerations, as well as the inadequacy of accounting systems and data, suggest how difficult it will be for anyone (including "the market") to value the assets of firms to be privatized.

Lessons from the Transformation Process

The results of economic transformation so far have been remarkably similar. The stabilizations have been relatively successful. The initial jump in the price level is always greater than expected, sometimes so much that significant inflation persists; but the rate does come down rather than taking off into hyperinflation. This is mainly because of a large improvement in the state budget, but after some months, the fiscal position tends to deteriorate. Initially the balance of payments shows strong improvement, but that, again, may be partly transitory. Typically, a dynamic development of new small-scale private enterprise occurs, mainly in services.

This is far from counterbalancing the deep and persistent contraction of activity elsewhere. The collapse of output is not just a short-run signal of "creative destruction." Investment and consumption both fall sharply. Except perhaps for exports, responses to the new prices and incentives are weak. Foreign investment is less than expected, partly because of uncertainty about the future rules of the game. Privatization of medium- and large-scale firms is very slow. It is technically difficult, but there has also been policy hesitation. On the other hand, this is one area where it is not obvious that the optimal policy was full speed ahead regardless.[31] Tax reform is delayed, and collection is difficult.

Industrial restructuring from the center—that is, deconcentration—has made little progress. Privatization will not cure that, so it will be necessary to improve conditions for entry and encourage new small and medium enterprises (not just one-person service establishments). The transformation still has not fully eliminated tutelage and established enterprise autonomy for the SOEs.

Restitution laws have been a major obstacle to privatization and foreign direct investment. But the problems of legal framework, monopoly, and the difficulty of valuation under distortions have hindered conventional privatization and have led to giveaway schemes. Spontaneous privatization—at the initiative of managers (sometimes in collaboration with the workers)—was initially prone to abuses; but since the introduction of regulation, it is back in some favor, and it actually gives results.

The authorities have been unable to impose financial discipline on firms. Much SOE debt goes back to the pretransformation period; for that and other reasons, the distribution of debt among SOEs has little relation to their likely future performance without debt. They have accumulated arrears to the banks and among themselves (forced supplier credit). The banks themselves could not survive a serious squeeze. They do not have a capital base that could withstand significant bankruptcies.

Where the program has included convertibility, strong arguments favored initially pegging the exchange rate rather than floating. There is a considerable danger, however, of choosing a seriously undervalued rate. Whatever marginal auction, "black" or legal free market for foreign currency may be operating in the prereform economy, it will always and everywhere undervalue the domestic currency. Buyers of foreign currency in an economy with pervasive micro-level shortages will want it in order to buy the goods in greatest excess demand, like "luxury" consumer goods, bottleneck inputs, and foreign travel; and they will be on the upper tail of the income (or liquid asset) distributions of households and firms.

Excessive devaluation will bring cost-push inflation and a strong negative supply shock to import-dependent firms. It will vitiate one of the most important reasons for convertibility: with a severely undervalued currency, domestic firms feel no competitive pressure, and the world price structure does not exercise sufficient influence on domestic relative prices, since without competition, prices may move to clear home markets but not approach world relative prices. The "anchor" will not hold anything down.

Speculation against an overvalued rate could threaten the entire program. But it is unrealistic and damaging to try to eliminate any such downside risk, as shown by the excessive devaluation in Poland on January 1, 1990. The bold move to convertibility was absolutely right, and after the initial jump in the price level, it did appear that inertial inflation had been cut radically. Subsequently, however, the inflation rate picked up despite the switch to budget surplus and a tough monetary policy. Much of this must be interpreted as catching up to the undervalued exchange rate, in a process in which competitive pressure from abroad did not check the monopoly power of domestic firms. Even the elimination of the monetary overhang by the initial price jump went too far.

Some observers have argued that the massive devaluation at least brought many firms into exporting for the first time; but the rise in convertible currency exports may have been primarily a consequence of the collapse of domestic and CMEA markets. In any case, the real exchange rate appreciation since January 1, 1990, has already pushed the convertible currency trade balance into deficit.

Credibility of exchange rate policy and convertibility itself requires specifying ex ante the rule by which the exchange rate peg will be adjusted if it is driven out of line (in particular, by inflation). Not setting a rule for parity changes is likely to generate uncertainty and speculation in due course. More important, economic agents will recognize that it is unrealistic to maintain that the peg will hold indefinitely. In the absence of further information about policy, they are likely to conclude that eventually the authorities will be forced to devalue sufficiently to accommodate inflation fully. This will vitiate the ex ante pressure for adaptation and delay credibility. In the event, Poland did have to devalue in May 1991 and again in October 1991, when it shifted to a crawling peg.

The speed and extent of collapse of intra-CMEA trade is remarkable. Much if not most of this is attributable to economic chaos in the former Soviet Union and to German unification. Nevertheless, the disintegration of this trade has gone far beyond elimination of that part of it without any short-run economic justification.

This is one major reason for the fall in output throughout the region. We should not forget, however, that the trade breakdown was partly self-inflicted, at the initiative of the CEE countries: they knew the shift to world market prices and the disintegration of CMEA were coming, and they made little effort to mitigate the shock. Moreover, some who use this as a rationale for the contraction in output also say that this trade was undesirable anyway, that the exports to the former Soviet Union in particular were the output from the dinosaur firms that ought to go as soon as possible.

One argument holds that some of the apparent fall in output reflects measurement errors. Managers had incentives to overstate production targets and were forced to report fulfillment of those plans even if actual production was less. And now the private sector is underreported. Moreover, measured output is not closely related to welfare—quality and composition and availability are all up. Some of the output was simply unwanted.

But under central planning, there were incentives to underreport output in some circumstances. Overfulfillment of the plan this period would lead to a very tough plan for the next period (the ratchet effect). Moreover, the increase in private-sector output is primarily in services. These countries do *need* some transfer of labor into services, but perhaps more of it should come from agriculture than from industry. Do we want them eventually to look more like Germany or the United States?

In the extreme, "unwanted output" is production generating negative value added at world prices.[32] In that case, stopping it should show gross domestic product *up* at world prices. So is this just a measurement problem? No: in many cases the value-subtracting activities had appeared profitable because they were supported by other sectors, such as underpriced primary product or intermediate good output. The switch to world market prices should raise measured value added in those sectors. The question then arises whether the market has worked: whether it is eliminating the unwanted, value-subtracting production, or whether the contraction is more random, less rational. Unfortunately, recent research suggests the latter.[33]

Excessively tight macroeconomic policies are another explanation of the contraction in Eastern Europe. In Czechoslovakia as well as in Poland, the policymakers overestimated the extent of devaluation required. The excessive devaluation gave an unnecessarily large inflationary shock, which then did indeed require severely restrictive policies to stop propagation. Macroeconomic policy was therefore much too tight in Czechoslovakia.[34] And as David Begg and I argue,[35] a credit squeeze cannot really restrict many firms that can effectively force their banks or suppliers to lend, so for a given degree of required macro tightness, the squeeze has to go further and differentially hits the small firms and the private sector.

We must definitively reject the rationalization that macroeconomic stabilization typically does have a temporary cost in terms of lost output.[36] This is simply false. Survey papers from the World Bank[37] and the IMF[38] covering over a dozen major stabilization efforts show that "hyperinflation has been stopped almost instantaneously with no major output costs, while stabilization programs in chronic-inflation countries have resulted in an initial expansion followed by a later recession.[39] So either CEE is very different or policies are doing something wrong—or, indeed, policies are wrong because those who are guiding them do not realize that CEE is very different.

Much of the problem lies in the inadequate microeconomic foundations for production and investment in these economies. Structural reform—in property rights, lending discipline, managerial motivation, and much else—has been inadequate. These are key factors addressed in the next section.

All these explanations doubtless have some role. There is certainly no acceptable monocausal interpretation. Moreover, the initial contraction of output and its persistence may have different primary causes, with correspondingly different policy implications for the former Soviet Union and for CEE now.

Policies to Accelerate Economic Transformation Today

The principles of economic transformation evoke little disagreement. The issues are thus matters of sequencing, emphasis, and choice of specific policies. These are not technical quibbles— serious, operational policy is about detail. Certain pragmatic measures could substantially improve the standard program. These measures involve exchange rate policy, tariffs, industrial policy, and financial restructuring. They are both important and urgent.

It is impossible to do everything at once. There must be priorities: sequencing does matter. Although macroeconomic stabilization, where necessary, comes first, it received excessive attention in Poland and elsewhere. The required measures are well understood—once they are implemented, the policymakers should pass on to other, more important problems. Preoccupation with monthly inflation rates and interest rates diverted Polish policymakers from privatization and financial reform. The delay lost precious political momentum, and large-scale privatization in Poland is still not off the ground.

There was also a serious macroeconomic policy error in both Poland and Czechoslovakia: initial excessive devaluation of the currency and unwillingness to choose and announce an exchange rate policy. A move to convertibility must be accompanied by a sensible exchange rate policy: do not devalue excessively; peg initially; then go to a crawling peg. Some of the output loss in Poland and Czechoslovakia is due, directly or indirectly, to violation of one or more of those principles.

The opening to trade with the West—with convertibility, low tariffs, and few quantitative restrictions—was too abrupt. Despite the initial, protective devaluations, many important industrial branches became vulnerable. And it will be politically impossible to keep the real exchange rate at a level that gives these countries Third World wages. Nor is that justified. A uniform (or possibly cascading) tariff at a significant level would give more time to adjust, for senile even more than for infant industries. It could also be an important source of budgetary revenue. (A transitional wage subsidy would also help to keep production going temporarily with relatively little distortion, but the fiscal constraint may rule this out.)

Large-scale privatization is difficult and slow. Giveaway schemes (free distribution of shares) are surprisingly difficult to implement and would sacrifice scarce budgetary revenue. And strong arguments favor breaking up the big firms before privatizing them. Hence the need for an immediate major effort to "commercialize" the big state firms and to introduce incentives and controls that will improve their management now, long before privatization. For the most part, "state desertion" in the name of laissez-faire has instead left them floundering without any guidance in a radically new environment.

Many of these firms are unprofitable, and a significant proportion may actually produce negative value added at world prices. It is politically impossible to shut them all down, and economically unjustifiable, too, in the short run if they are adding value and creating employment: there are no alternative uses for these resources. Yet extensive closures are clearly necessary, and they are not happening. Meanwhile, there may be substantial scope for raising efficiency with reorganization and limited investment. All this argues for an active policy for the kind of industrial restructuring that cannot be left to the market, judging by experience so far.[40] The market cannot and will not restructure the large SOEs—and they are too big to fail, until they are broken up and some expansion appears elsewhere in the economy. But we cannot trust the old *nomenklatura* to guide the restructuring any more than the market. This is therefore a major challenge for foreign advice and advisers.[41]

Enterprise debt inherited from the premarket era has no economic rationale, and partly for this reason it is not serviced. Neither the market nor the government can guide restructuring successfully, however, if firms' financial obligations are not enforced; monetary policy, too, will not operate properly if its microeconomic foundations are undermined. A market economy simply cannot function in these circumstances. The first, long-overdue step is to recapitalize the banks. The second is to develop workable rules for canceling debts of enterprises that are privatized. The third is to substitute explicit "cash-limited" fiscal subsidies to SOEs that are currently being kept going with covert rollovers of credit and accumulation of arrears. All this would not create a fiscal problem, but would rather make explicit what is currently being concealed. This financial restructuring should have been near the top of the sequence—it is even higher priority now.[42]

Finally, some of the lost Eastern trade could and should be re-created. Within the former Soviet Union, and between it and its former CMEA partners, a substantial part of the problem is that the switch to the market has been *incomplete*. After the initial shock of liberalization, there has been a serious coordination failure—markets are not yet functioning. The enforced move to barter has created great inefficiency and has brought a dramatic fall in the volume of transactions and consequently of output. The most urgent measure is to create the simplest institutional framework for monetary exchange—a payments or settlements *mechanism* with a mutually acceptable means of exchange and facilities for organizing transactions. Grand schemes for payments unions are a distraction; they are not feasible (and perhaps not desirable). But if we believe in the market, the least we can do is to create the institutional framework for it to function. This is the quickest way to raise output in the short run, or at least to stop it from falling yet further. Meanwhile, there are encouraging moves toward a free trade area in Central Europe.

Beyond advice, we can give market access and financial and technical assistance to support the transformation effort. The European Community countries and other members of the Organization for Economic Cooperation and Development should be pressed to liberalize their imports from CEE. Aid should be less tied to trade (export credits), and include more grants, with debt reduction where appropriate. Aid efforts should be complementary, not competitive. Stanley Fischer confirms that the donors are "already competing for influence . . . most [of the competition] will be counterproductive, leading to duplication of effort, bureaucratic infighting, and turf battles. . . . Experience in Eastern Europe has shown that competition confuses policymakers in the recipient country."[43]

The Group of 7 governments have resisted coordination. The multilateral organizations meet to exchange information, but that is quite inadequate. Little public discussion has focused on serious coordination; most of it has been mixed up with proposals for a "Marshall Plan" for CEE. That is too easy to dismiss with suggestions of American dominance (despite the absence of American money), vague notions of massive scale, and legitimate argument about the economic impact of the Marshall Plan.

The effort must continue, in both the East and the West. It will be more difficult than many originally believed, both economically and psychologically. The latter is perhaps more important: We do know many of the economic answers and the right measures to take. But the politically untidy consequences of revolution have hindered their implementation. Now the aftermath of a revolutionary enthusiasm that has encountered tough obstacles and disappointments may be politically very unpleasant and hence economically dangerous, too.

Some of the disappointments arise from policy errors: in particular, from ignoring or misapplying some of the lessons of history and of economic analysis that are suggested here. Some arise from exaggerated expectations—often of Western help that in the event was not forthcoming or not well delivered or coordinated. We should not further inflate those expectations. But we should nevertheless do our utmost to justify them, always bearing in mind the constraints of political feasibility in both the East and the West.

Notes

1. Richard Portes, "Central Planning and Monetarism: Fellow Travellers?" in Padma Desai, ed., *Marxism, Central Planning, and the Soviet Economy* (Cambridge, Mass.: MIT Press, 1983).
2. See, for example, Bela Balassa, "Economic Reform in Hungary," *Economica* 37 (February 1970), pp. 1–22; Janos Kornai, "The Hungarian Reform Process: Visions, Hopes and Reality," *Journal of Economic Literature* 24 (December 1986), pp. 1687–737; Richard Portes, "Economic Reforms in Hungary," *American Economic Review* 60 (May 1970), pp. 307–13; Portes, "The Strategy and Tactics of Economic Decentralization," *Soviet Studies* (April 1972); and Portes, "Hungary: Economic Performance, Policy and Prospects," in Joint Economic Committee, United States Congress, *East European Economies Post-Helsinki* (Washington, D.C.: GPO, 1977).
3. Richard Portes, *The Polish Crisis* (London: Royal Institute of International Affairs, 1981).
4. Richard Portes, "East Europe's Debt to the West: Interdependence Is a Two-Way Street," *Foreign Affairs* 55 (1977).
5. Anders Aslund, "Prospects for Economic Reform in the USSR" (Paper for World Bank Conference on Development Economics, Washington, D.C., 1992); *European Economy* 45 (December 1991); Gerard Roland, "The Political Economy of Transition in the Soviet Union," Centre for Economic Policy Research Discussion Paper, no. 628 (London, 1991).
6. Gur Ofer, "Macroeconomic Issues of Soviet Reform," *NBER Macroeconomics Annual 1990* (Cambridge, Mass.: MIT Press, 1990).
7. Richard Portes, "The Theory and Measurement of Macroeconomic Disequilibrium in CPEs," in Wojciech Charemza and Christopher Davis, eds., *Models of Disequilibrium and Shortage for Centrally Planned Economies* (London: Chapman and Hall, 1989).
8. John Williamson, *The Economic Opening of Eastern Europe and the USSR* (Washington, D.C.: Institute for International Economics, 1991).
9. Richard Portes, "Introduction" to "Economic Transformation of Hungary and Poland," *European Economy* 43 (1990).
10. Michael Bruno, Guido Di Tella, Rudiger Dornbusch, and Stanley Fischer, eds., *Inflation Stabilization: The Experience of Israel, Argentina, Brazil, Bolivia, and Mexico* (Cambridge, Mass.: MIT Press, 1988); and Michael Bruno, Stanley Fischer, Elchenan Helpman, and Nissan Liviatan, eds., *Lessons of Economic Stabilization and Its Aftermath* (Cambridge, Mass.: MIT Press, 1991).
11. See Carlos Vegh, "Stopping High Inflation: An Analytical Overview," IMF Working Paper, no. 107 (Washington, D.C., 1991).
12. See Miguel Kiguel and Nissan Liviatan, "The Old and the New in Heterodox Stabilization Programmes," World Bank Working Paper, no. 323 (Washington, D.C., 1989).

13. Guillermo Calvo and Fabrizio Coricelli, "Stabilizing a Previously Centrally Planned Economy," *Economic Policy* 14 (1992).

14. Philippe Aghion, Oliver Hart, and John Moore, "The Economics of Bankruptcy Reform," in Olivier Blanchard, Ken Froot, and Jeffrey Sachs, eds., *Transition in Eastern Europe*. (Chicago: University of Chicago Press, forthcoming 1993).

15. Philippe Aghion and Irena Grosfeld, "De la desetatisation en Europe de l'Est," in Jean-Paul Fitoussi, ed., *A l'Est en Europe* (Paris: Presses de la FNSP, 1990); Irena Grosfeld and Paul Hare, "Privatization in Poland, Hungary, and Czechoslovakia," in Richard Portes, ed., *European Economy*, special issue no. 2 (1991); Colin Mayer and Julian Franks, "Capital Markets and Corporate Control: A Study of France, Germany and the UK," *Economic Policy* 10 (1990); Jean Tirole, "Privatization in Eastern Europe," *NBER Macroeconomics Annual 1991* (Cambridge, Mass.: MIT Press, 1991); and Tirole, "Ownership and Incentives in a Transitional Economy," Centre for Economic Policy Research Working Paper, no. 104 (Toulouse, France, 1991).

16. Kai-Uwe Kuhn, Paul Seabright, and Alasdair Smith, "Competition Policy Research: Where Do We Stand?" Centre for Economic Policy Research Occasional Paper, no. 8 (London, 1992).

17. Jenny Corbett, "Policy Issues in the Design of Banking and Financial Systems for Industrial Finance," *European Economy* 43 (March 1990).

18. Jenny Corbett and Colin Mayer, "Financial Reform in Eastern Europe: Progress with the Wrong Model?" Centre for Economic Policy Research Discussion Paper, no. 603 (London, 1991).

19. Ronald McKinnon, "Macroeconomic Control in the Transition," in Alberto Giovanninni, ed., *Finance and Development in Europe* (Cambridge, U.K.: Cambridge University Press, 1993).

20. David Begg and Richard Portes, "Enterprise Debt and Economic Transformation," Centre for Economic Policy Research Discussion Paper, no. 695 (London, 1992).

21. David Newberry, "Reform in Hungary: Sequencing and Privatization," *European Economic Review* 35 (1991); Newberry, "Sequencing the Transition," Centre for Economic Policy Research Discussion Paper, no. 575 (London, 1991).

22. David Lipton and Jeffrey Sachs, "Creating a Market Economy in Eastern Europe: The Case of Poland," Brookings Papers on Economic Activity (Washington, D.C.: Brookings Institute, 1990).

23. For general summaries, see Stanley Fischer and Alan Gelb, "Issues in the Reform of Socialist Economies," in Vittorio Corbo et al., eds., *Reforming Central and East European Economies* (Washington, D.C.: World Bank, 1991); Hans Genberg, "On the Sequencing of Reforms in Eastern Europe," IMF Working Paper, no. 91/13 (Washington, D.C., 1991); D.M. Nuti, "Stabilization and Sequencing in the Reform of Socialist Economies," in S. Commander, ed., *Managing Inflation in Socialist Economies in Transition* (Washington, D.C.: World Bank, 1991); and R. Dornbusch, "Priorities of Economic Reform in Eastern Europe and the Soviet Union," Centre for Economic Policy Research Occasional Paper, no. 5 (London, 1991).

24. Richard Portes, "The Transition to Convertibility for Eastern Europe and the Soviet Union," in Anthony Atkinson and Renato Brunetta, eds., *Economics for a New Europe* (London: Macmillan, 1991); John Williamson, *The Economic Opening of Eastern Europe and the USSR* (Washington, D.C.: Institute for International Economics, 1991); and Andrew Berg and Jeffrey Sachs, "Structural Adjustment and International Trade in Eastern Europe: The Case of Poland," *Economic Policy* 14 (1992).

25. Gerard Roland, "Political Economy of Sequencing Tactics in the Transition Period," in Laszlo Csaba, ed., *Systemic Change and Stabilization in Eastern Europe* (Aldershot: Dartmouth, 1991); and Mathias Dewatripont and Gerard Roland, "The Virtues of Gradualism and Legitimacy in the Transition to a Market Economy," Centre for Economic Policy Research Discussion Paper, no. 538 (London, 1991).

26. See Peter Kenen, "Transitional Arrangements for Trade and Payments among the CMEA Countries," IMF Staff Paper (Washington, D.C., 1991); Dariousz Rosati, "Problems of Post-CMEA Trade and Payments," Centre for Economic Policy Research Discussion Paper, no. 650 (London, 1992).

27. Richard Portes, "The European Community's Response to Eastern Europe," in P. Bofinger, ed., *Economic Consequences of the East* (London: Centre for Economic Policy Research, 1992).

28. Barry Eichengreen and Marc Uzan, "The Marshall Plan: Economic Effects and Implications for Eastern Europe and the Former USSR," *Economic Policy* 14 (1992).

29. Sebastian Edwards, "Stabilization and Liberalization Policies in Central and Eastern Europe: Lessons from Latin America," National Bureau of Economic Research, Working Paper no. 3816 (Cambridge, 1991).

30. Jose Cordoba, "Ten Lessons From Mexico's Economic Reform," mimeo (1990).

31. Irena Grosfeld and Paul Hare, "Privatization in Poland, Hungary and Czechoslovakia," *European Economy*, special edition no. 2 (1991).

32. Paul Hare and Gordon Hughes, "Competitiveness and Industrial Restructuring in Czechoslovakia, Hungary and Poland," *European Economy*, special edition no. 2 (1991).

33. Gordon Hughes and Paul Hare, "Industrial Policy and Restructuring in Eastern Europe," Centre for Economic Policy Research Discussion Paper, no. 653 (London, 1992).

34. David Begg, "Economic Reform in Czechoslovakia: Should We Believe in Santa Klaus?" *Economic Policy* 13 (1991). Begg also suggests that Czechoslovakia could and should have borrowed abroad to cushion the shock.

35. Begg and Portes, "Enterprise Debt and Economic Transformation."

36. Michael Burde, "Discussion of Berg and Sachs," *Economic Policy* 14 (1992).

37. Kiguel and Liviatan, "The Old and the New in Heterodox Stabilization Programmes."

38. Vegh, "Stopping High Inflation."

39. Ibid.

40. Gordon Hughes and Paul Hare, "Industrial Policy and Restructuring in Eastern Europe," Centre for Economic Policy Research Discussion Paper, no. 653 (1992); and Michael Dooley and Peter Isard, "Establishing Incen-

tive Structures and Planning Agencies That Support Market-Oriented Transformations," IMF Working Paper, no. 91/113 (Washington, D.C., 1991).

41. Consider the experience of the Treuhandanstalt. See Wendy Carlin and Colin Mayer, "Restructuring Enterprises in Eastern Europe," *Economic Policy* 15 (October 1992).

42. Begg and Portes, "Enterprise Debt and Economic Transformation."

43. Stanley Fischer, "Economic Reform in the USSR and the Role of Aid," Brookings Papers on Economic Activity, no. 2 (Washington, D.C.: Brookings Institute, 1991).

2

Economic Transformation in Central and Eastern Europe

Paul Marer

As the countries of Central and Eastern Europe proceed with market-oriented reforms, a complex set of factors—historical, political, economic, and social—determine the pace and results of their efforts. This essay focuses on the political economy of systemic transformation in these countries, including a detailed examination of the three that are clearly in the lead in the transition: Hungary, Poland, and Czechoslovakia.

A Capsule History

Prior to 1990 "Central and Eastern Europe" (CEE) was a geopolitical term, defining eight small and medium-size communist countries: Albania, Bulgaria, Czechoslovakia, the German Democratic Republic (GDR), Hungary, Poland, Romania, and Yugoslavia. The CEE-8 had a total population of about 140 million and a total gross national product (GNP) roughly the same as that of France or the People's Republic of China.

Today the definition of CEE is unclear, given the disappearance, disintegration, birth, or rebirth of countries in the area. A dramatic, multidimensional process of nation-state transformation has been taking place since 1989.

The CEE region has been a mosaic of peoples and ancient cultures of different origins whose varied historical experiences were often marked by bitter conflicts. This is a region of the world where the idea of a *people* has rarely been synonymous with a nation-state. For centuries, states and like entities have come and gone, often being superimposed on the peoples of the region by various historical forces.

World War I brought the demise of the region's three great monarchies—the Austro-Hungarian, the German, and the Russian—which had directly or indirectly controlled all of the peoples in CEE. The victorious allies—the United States, Britain, and France—then created or sanctified new states and boundaries. Although the truncation of some and the creation of other independent states was, on balance, an improvement over the prewar situation, the job was not done well because large ethnic minorities were left with or attached to states dominated by other ethnic groups. This created or perpetuated ancient rivalries and tensions, which were repressed under communism but today are among the fundamental forces shaping the present and the future in several countries.

In spite of immense historical, cultural, ethnic, political, and economic differences among the countries of CEE, this region can be considered a historical entity in the sense that ever since the Middle Ages, its economic development has lagged behind Western Europe's (for the Czech lands and what is now the eastern part of Germany, the gap was created after World War II). It has been a long-standing and deeply felt desire of the peoples in the region to "catch up" with the developed West, a yearning that Russia shared also. In fact, it was at least in part this yearning that motivated some members of the intelligentsia to initially support, or at least tolerate, a Soviet-type economic and political system, as a quick way to overcome underdevelopment. For a time, some believed that the pursuit of this goal justified large sacrifices, even repression.

The realization that communism meant not only alien domination (except in Albania and Yugoslavia) but also economic backsliding vis-à-vis the industrialized and the newly industrializing countries added to the disappointments and frustrations of the peoples of CEE and contributed to the loss of faith, delegitimization, and eventual collapse of communist rule.

Pretransformation Differences Among Hungary, Poland, and Czechoslovakia

Examination of four variables—past systemic reforms (defined as a meaningful change in the operating principles of the system); domestic macroeconomic balance; foreign debt and debt management; and the domestic political situation just prior to transformation—may reveal differences among the CEE-3 in the situations that their postcommunist governments inherited. Each of these variables has implications for designing a transformation program, for evaluating a country's economic performance and prospects, and for foreign economic assistance.

The reasons for differences among the countries are varied. Historians will have to explain why, even under Soviet domination, the extent of economic or political system reform was substantial in certain countries and practically absent in others— also, why certain regimes bequeathed a small macroeconomic imbalance, others a large one; and why some managed to accumulate only a modest foreign debt, while others took on debt burdens that eventually became unmanageable. Table 1 (page 56) summarizes the differences described below.

Hungary

Systemic Reforms. In a region of the world where many of the old and new nation-states that are in economic transformation measure their reform efforts in months or at most a few years, Hungary has had a program of economic change under way since the 1960s. To be sure, the reform effort had many stops and restarts and occasional reversals. But, on balance, the movement was forward.

Hungary's reforms can be traced to the Revolution of 1956, which the Soviets ruthlessly suppressed. A half dozen years later the party leader, Janos Kadar, changed the Stalinist strategy of exercising political power. Gradually, he instituted a set of policies that increased the personal security of the citizenry and made life in Hungary more tolerable than that elsewhere in CEE, if we consider jointly the political, social, and economic aspects. Domestic political and economic reforms were, in Kadar's judgment, the best way to ensure that 1956 would not be repeated. But power remained firmly the monopoly of the party—or, more accurately, of those self-selected to exercise it. The West referred to the political changes in Hungary as liberalization, although it would be more accurate to label Kadar's policies "enlightened absolutism."

TABLE 1. HUNGARY, POLAND, AND CZECHOSLOVAKIA: PRETRANSFORMATION DIFFERENCES

Factor	Hungary	Poland	Czechoslovakia
Systemic reforms (1980s)			
Political (defined as tolerance for and co-opting of opposition groups and methods, even though human and political rights may not have been codified)	Substantial and growing	Ambivalent and cyclical; in the lead by 1989	Little or none
Economic			
State sector	Substantial	Modest	None
Private sector	Substantial	Substantial	Very little
Macroeconomic balance	Reasonable	Poor	Good
Foreign debt			
Size	Very large	Very large	Moderate
Was serviced fully	Yes	No	Yes
Political situation just prior to transformation			
Significant ethnic or border conflict:			
Within the country's borders	No	No	Yes
Outside the borders	Yes	No	No
Relationship between the authorities and opposition	Cooperation/ confrontation	Confrontation/ cooperation	Confrontation
Date of democratic election	4/90	6/89*; 11/90†; 10/91‡	6/90
Term of government	4 yrs.	Variable	2 yrs.
Beginning of major transformation program	None	1/1/90	1/1/91
Initial domestic support for the new government	Moderate	High	High

*Senate: freely elected; House: one-third freely elected.
† Presidential election.
‡ Free elections to the House.

Kadar, in effect, told the Hungarian people: "The Soviet Union and its basic policies are here to stay. Cooperate with me by not challenging the political system, and I'll make life as tolerable for you as it can possibly be under our geopolitical circumstances." To the Soviet leaders Kadar said: "Hungarians are unhappy with your rule, as you saw in 1956. Give me a free hand in domestic affairs, so I can calm this explosive situation, and my management will be to your advantage."

Economic system reforms were introduced in the socialist and the private sectors.

In the *socialist sector,* central planning was retained under the New Economic Mechanism (NEM), introduced in 1968, but mandatory plan directives to enterprises and central resource allocation were replaced by financial and administrative regulations—that is, by indirect planning.

Between 1972 and 1978 the reforms stalled and the actions taken reversed some of the reform steps. Opposition to reforms by vested interests, foreign policy considerations, and attempts to insulate the economy from external economic shocks were the main reasons the reforms could not go forward.

Between 1979 and 1989 the government undertook a new series of reforms, prompted by the need to improve economic efficiency and the balance of payments. These created some of the institutional preconditions of a market system. In approximate chronological order, they were as follows:

- The domestic prices of energy and raw materials were linked to world market levels, and the price system was made more flexible and somewhat responsive to market forces.

- Some of the large, monopolistic producers and distributors were broken up.

- "Production profile" restrictions—that is, controls on the output mix that are typical under central planning—were eased and then eliminated.

- Foreign trade decisions became more and more decentralized, and in some areas competition between traders replaced the monopoly of foreign trade.

- A system of tenders for managerial positions was introduced, and "enterprise councils" were given some say in the appointment of managers and in other strategic business affairs.

- Enterprises were given the right to issue bonds, which could be traded on a seedling financial market, newly established.

- A bankruptcy law (weak as it was) was enacted.

- A two-tier banking system was established, in the absence, however, of all the conditions necessary to make the newly independent commercial banks able to function as banks do in market economies.

- A new law allowed the conversion of an enterprise's ownership structure from one based on a vague form of state ownership to one based on shares (stock) that are divisible and salable, which was a necessary precursor to privatization.

- A law eased many restrictions on foreign investment, guaranteed profit repatriation, and treated joint ventures and foreign subsidiaries the same as local business.

- A value-added tax, a personal income tax, and an enterprise profit tax were instituted, creating a tax system similar to those found in market economies.

More or less parallel with reforms in the *socialist sector*, a series of limited but cumulatively significant reforms were also introduced in the *private sector*. The NEM gave workers the right to change jobs. Agricultural and retail cooperatives were granted increased autonomy of operations. They, in turn, established subsidiaries in industry and construction that became the first important forms of semiprivate activity, characterized by strong profit orientation and de facto independence from the authorities.

Reforms between 1979 and 1989 encouraged the private sector for economic reasons, but only halfheartedly, because expansion went against the ideological-political objective that the socialist sector remain predominant. Increased opportunities arose—as did pressures (on account of the austerity program that has been in place since 1979)—for people to have two jobs: one in the socialist sector, for the sake of security and its entitlements; and one in the private sector, for money or creative satisfaction. By the late 1980s about half of the workforce had at least two jobs.

Although the private sector generated much of the economy's modest growth in the 1980s, the many restrictions that shackled such activities caused the sector's efficiency to remain low. And since many of its participants took on such activities as second and third jobs, the growth of this sector coincided with a significant deterioration in stress-related national health indicators.

The reforms—partial and inconsistent as they were—nevertheless had a positive impact on the economy's performance and today are helpful for the transformation process.

First, by 1990 the reforms enabled about one-quarter to one-third of Hungary's adjusted gross domestic product (GDP)—official GDP, corrected in a rough-and-ready way for the underreporting of private activities—to originate in the private sector. (The share of the means of production in private hands was much smaller.) Thus, at the beginning of the transformation, the nonagricultural private sector in Hungary was much larger than that in the other CEE countries. The significance of this for transformation is threefold: it is easing somewhat the huge task of structural transformation; it is contributing to the reduction of shortage, which in turn has helped keep inflationary pressures in check; and it is helping to prop up the economy's performance.

Second, state enterprises in Hungary are somewhat more flexible, certainly more market-oriented, and a great deal more familiar with the ways of doing business in the West than their counterparts in the other CEE countries. One reason for this is the relative high share of foreign trade in the GDP.

Third, the systemic changes that were introduced between the mid-1960s and the late 1980s moved the country some way toward creating the institutional and psychological foundations of a market economy.

This is not to say that several fundamental and mutually reinforcing problems of the economic system had not remained.

Ill-defined ownership, the continued dominance of the "social-ist" over the private sector, the absence of a market for the factors of production, and weak financial discipline on enterprises were some of the essential problems that transformation had to tackle.

Macroeconomic Balance. As a result of earlier reforms, Hungary was able to move away from the classical shortage economy. The supply, assortment, and quality of food and many other con-sumer and industrial products became significantly better than elsewhere in the region. Queuing in retail stores was eliminated, although it continued for a segment of the housing market, cars, and major repairs.[1] Money and credit creation were never hugely excessive. Moreover, earlier reforms gradually freed more and more prices. For approximately this combination of reasons, the new government did not inherit severe repressed inflation. Al-though open inflation accelerated through 1991 to 36%, it re-mained much lower than in Poland, where it declined from more than 600 percent in 1990 to about 75 percent in 1991 (Figure 1).

Thus, in the critical years before transformation, the combi-nation of repressed inflation (on which empirical evidence is difficult to obtain) and open inflation (on which Hungary's statis-tics are reasonably accurate) did not present an unusually diffi-cult situation. This had two implications for transition. One, the program did not have to place an overriding emphasis on macro-economic stabilization via shock treatment, as was the case, for example, in Poland. Two, ceteris paribus, program implementa-tion has been easier—from the social and political points of view—because the very large costs usually associated with dra-matic macroeconomic stabilization programs could be avoided.

Foreign Debt and Debt Management. Hungary's new government inherited a huge debt to the West—$20 billion (Figure 2), repre-senting roughly two-thirds of the country's GDP and a $2,000 burden per inhabitant (Figure 3). Debt servicing took 57 percent of merchandise export earnings in 1990, but only 40 percent in 1991, as trade with the former Council for Mutual Economic Assistance (CMEA) countries moved to convertible-currency

FIGURE 1.   INFLATION, 1980–1991 (ANNUAL PERCENTAGE CHANGE
IN RETAIL PRICE INDEX)

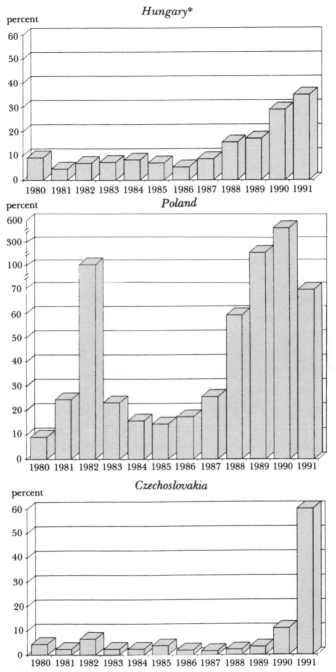

Sources: *PlanEcon Reports*, various issues; author's estimate.

*Consumer price index.

basis and the denominator of the debt-service ratio (the ratio of annual debt service to convertible exports) thus took a large jump.

In the 1970s Hungary borrowed to increase the standard of living, to pay for the import costs of what often turned out to be misguided investments, and to buffer itself from the effects of a large deterioration in its terms of trade after the oil price shock of 1973–1975. In the 1980s Hungary borrowed to refinance the payment of principal and a portion of the interest on the debt. The other portion of the interest was paid by squeezing domestic investment (mostly) and consumption (somewhat), which contributed to the economic stagnation of the 1980s.

Hungary is one of a small number of heavily indebted countries that have continued to service their debts fully, no matter how severe the conditions under which their economies have labored. The views of policymakers who have argued that the adverse consequences of not meeting debt obligations would be greater than those of punctual debt servicing have prevailed. Moreover, since most of Hungary's debt has been to private, not official, lenders, at best only a partial postponent of payment, not debt forgiveness, could be negotiated. Rescheduling would have caused the unavailability for some time of new private money; the necessity to pay for imports in cash, which would upset the normal operation of the economy; and the need for the country to give up a valuable "intangible" asset, namely, the good international reputation it has earned by being for years in the forefront of political and economic reform and by not rescheduling.[2]

Politics. The apparent stability of Hungary's economic and political situation from the 1960s till the late 1980s rested on two pillars: steady improvements in the standard of living through the late 1970s (the carrot); and the Brezhnev Doctrine, which was in effect until the late 1980s (the stick).[3] But around 1980, living standards began to stagnate, owing to the accumulated legacies of a centrally planned system, economic deterioration in the Soviet Union and in the CEE countries (Hungary's main trade partners), and major mistakes in economic policy, of which taking on a large foreign debt and being ambivalent about re-

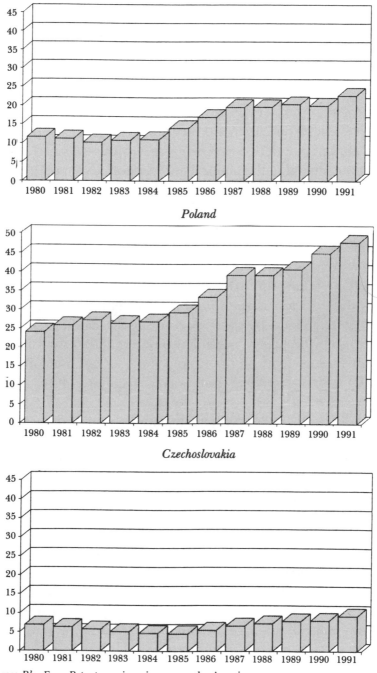

FIGURE 2. GROSS DOLLAR DEBT, 1980–1991
(BILLIONS OF 1992 U.S. DOLLARS)

Hungary

Poland

Czechoslovakia

Sources: *PlanEcon Reports*, various issues; author's estimate.

forms had the most significant negative consequences. Although no sudden economic crisis occurred, the economy had in effect stagnated all through the 1980s, so the carrot was lost. And during 1988–1989, when it became clear that Gorbachev had repudiated the Brezhnev Doctrine, Hungary's leaders lost the stick also and became uncertain and divided as to how to exercise power.

These developments prompted Hungary's politically attuned population to express long-suppressed views and desires about changing the political and economic system. Party leaders responded by making whatever domestic political concessions they thought would be sufficient "to keep the lid on," given the potentially explosive political situation. Many of the political liberalization measures the party introduced or accepted were intended as lightning rods for the pent-up tensions of the populations: taking down the barbed-wire fortifications on the border with Austria; allowing unlimited travel to that country; giving citizens a global passport; permitting increased press freedoms; revising the party's previous condemnation of events and persons connected with the Revolution of 1956; and—the ultimate concession—agreeing to allow free elections in 1990 and to abide by the results.

After the government dismantled the barbed wire on the border with Austria—a symbol of the Iron Curtain—tens of thousands of East Germans escaped to the West through Hungary. When East Germany closed travel to Hungary, the escape continued through Czechoslovakia and Poland. Within a few months 200,000 East Germans found this new way around the Wall; in November 1989 the Berlin Wall came down, and the fate of the East German communist regime was sealed. The actions of a liberal communist government in Hungary thus contributed to the domino-like fall of all communist regimes in CEE.

The transfer of political power was peaceful, and the economy was not disrupted. A majority of the voters preferred the center-right parties, enabling three of them to form a coalition government. The next general election will be in 1994; until then the first postcommunist government will likely remain at the

FIGURE 3.   PER CAPITA GROSS DEBT,* 1980–1991 (1992 U.S. DOLLARS)

Hungary

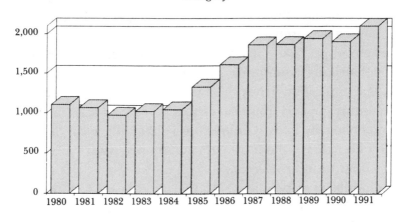

Poland

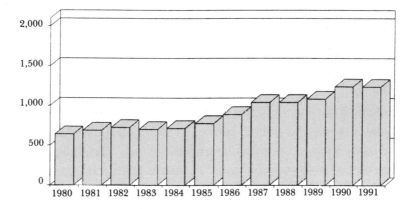

Czechoslovakia

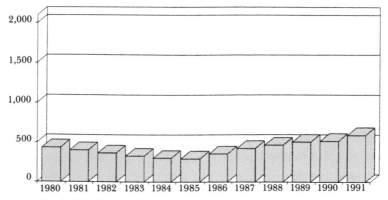

*Gross debt divided by population.

helm. Although the government is not popular, the constitution—wisely—makes replacing it difficult, so Hungary has a greater degree of political stability than Czechoslovakia or Poland.

Since the Communist Party voluntarily gave up power, none of the opposition groups could take exclusive credit for ending communism, and thus claim the kind of legitimacy and support that Solidarity *initially* enjoyed in Poland. This was one factor in why Hungary's initial transformation program was more gradual than those of Czechoslovakia and Poland.

Millions of people of Hungarian descent live in the neighboring countries. For example, the largest ethnic minority in all of Europe is the approximately two million Hungarians who reside in Transylvania, in a region that at the end of World War I was attached to Romania. The treatment of the Hungarian minorities by the host governments is, for Hungary, a very important domestic as well as foreign policy issue.

Poland

Systemic Reforms. Reforms in Poland had been linked to major social unrests and political crises in 1956, 1970, and 1980–1981. Each crisis led to the promise and then halfhearted implementation of political and economic reforms, followed by stabilization of the economic and political situation, and abandonment of much or all of what was promised, especially in the economic realm.

The crisis of 1956 brought to power Wladislaw Gomulka, a liberal communist who allowed collective farms to disband. Since then, 75 percent of Poland's agriculture has remained private, even though the sector was discriminated against in favor of the smaller but ideologically preferable socialist sector. The church, the artists, the intellectuals, and the press gained a degree of freedom, which subsequent cycles of retreat clipped but never fully rescinded. In 1956 Gomulka appointed a reform commission of distinguished economists who came up with an innovative proposal for decentralized management. However, the reforms were not implemented at the time. Some decentralization and limited economic reforms were introduced during the 1970s.

The events that led to the formation in August 1980 of the independent trade union Solidarity were familiar: violent responses to the price increases that were needed to reduce both the state budget deficits and repressed inflation. The increasingly strong worker movement made it possible to have the strikes on economic issues culminate in political demands for independent trade unions, the right to strike, freedom of speech and end to censorship, release of all political prisoners, full public disclosure, and formal consultations with social groups about economic and political reforms. During 1980–1981 Solidarity gained ten million members, not counting rural Solidarity, which represented the country's three million private farmers. The increasing popularity and boldness of Solidarity in challenging the regime led to continued threats of military intervention by the Soviets, and ended with the imposition of martial law in December 1981.

In January 1982 the government introduced an economic reform program, whose design was similar to that proposed in 1956–1957 and resembled in many ways Hungary's 1968 NEM. It abolished directive planning and brought some decentralization in production, investment, wage and price setting, and international trade. During the 1980s economic regulations changed frequently and remained exceedingly complex. Direct central control was replaced with a plethora of indirect policy instruments that came to be exercised with growing arbitrariness. Enterprises bargained for credit, subsidies, tax reliefs, and access to foreign exchange. The rules changed so frequently that in practice there were no rules. Decentralization in the end turned out to be a poor substitute for the creation of real markets.[4]

While this assessment is very similar to the standard criticism levied against Hungary's reforms, Poland's reforms apparently did not go as far as Hungary's, because the state in Poland retained a much larger direct role and implementation was more patchy.

One recurring theme that distinguishes Poland's reform proposals, going all the way back to the immediate postwar period, is an emphasis on worker self-management, desired for economic and for political reasons. Worker self-management became a centerpiece of Solidarity's 1981 reform proposals and was also incorporated into the government's reform program.

As in Hungary, the authorities' ultimate criterion in choosing a course of action was the preservation of power. This led to seemingly contradictory actions: supporting a reform to avert a political crisis or in response to external pressures by Western creditors and later by the International Monetary Fund (IMF), but also opposing reform because it would curtail the regime's span of control and hurt vested interests. This ambivalence was the main reason each reform attempt went through a predictable cycle of crisis, reform, stabilization, and partial or complete abandonment. Foreign policy considerations, of course, played a role also.

Whether reforms had a large positive significance for transformation, as they did in Hungary, is less clear in the case of Poland. For example, decentralization's being a cause of Poland's persisting macroeconomic imbalances may have offset reform's positive impact.

Macroeconomic Balance. Beginning in the late 1960s Poland faced strong inflationary pressures that its authorities were unable to bring under permanent control. The two fundamental causes were the systemic legacies and the populist policies pursued by successive and politically weak governments trying to contain political crises. The main systemic causes were the soft budget constraint, cost-plus pricing, and decentralization carried out before market discipline could be imposed. The main populist policies were engaging in unsustainably large foreign borrowing (discussed below); granting wage increases much in excess of productivity improvements; and placing controls on prices at much below equilibrium levels. In the final year of the communist regime, the financial system, including the state budget, practically collapsed, leading to runaway inflation (Figure 1).

Poland's persistent lack of success in fighting strong inflationary pressures can be traced to the authorities' failure to gain political support for government policies. Time and again, measures designed to reduce the yawning gap between the purchasing power of the population and the value of goods and services were thwarted by the need to placate the public in order to avoid or overcome political crises.[5]

The main implication of this legacy was that the first order of priority in designing a transformation program had to be stabilization—that is, eliminating shortages and reducing open inflation. In a situation of hyperinflation, a decisive, quick, and comprehensive program is probably the most effective.

Foreign Debt and Debt Management. During the 1960s economic performance deteriorated and personal incomes stagnated. To reestablish macroeconomic equilibrium, in December 1970 the authorities declared large price increases, which brought down the government. The new leader, Edward Gierek, staked the country's future on an economic strategy of import- and consumption-led growth. The goal was an immediate improvement in living standards, financed by Western credits. Technology was imported on a large scale to increase the production of modern manufactures, to accelerate economic growth, to improve living standards, and to generate the exports needed to service the foreign credits. However, exports to the West did not materialize on the scale envisioned. The economy's galloping expansion worsened inflationary pressures and inefficiencies, and created an inauspicious environment for market-oriented reforms.[6] Because by the end of the decade the supply of foreign capital had dried up while debt service approached 100 percent of exports, imports had to be cut sharply and real investment slashed. This led to a one-third drop in industrial production between 1979 and 1982 (up to then a European economy's worst performance since the Great Depression) and unsatisfactory economic performance throughout the 1980s (Figure 4).

Poland became the first CEE country to reschedule its debts in 1981. (Romania followed in 1982, Yugoslavia in 1983, Bulgaria and Albania in 1990, and the Soviet Union in 1991.) During the 1980s Poland was unable to generate sufficient foreign exchange to pay all of the interest on its debt. As a result, its total debt rose from about $25 billion in 1980 to more than $40 billion by 1989 (Figure 2), as interest arrears (primarily to government

FIGURE 4.   INDUSTRIAL PRODUCTION AND INVESTMENT, 1980–1991
(ANNUAL PERCENTAGE CHANGE)

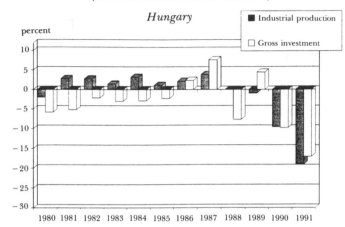

Hungary

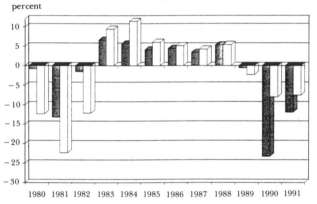

Poland

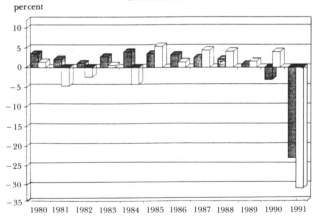

Czechoslovakia

Sources: *PlanEcon Reports*, various issues; author's estimate.

creditors, holding the largest part of Poland's debt) accumulated and were automatically converted into new loans. Although until September 1989 Poland continued to pay interest on debt owed to commercial banks, new credits from the West were not forthcoming. To shock the creditors into some action on debt relief, in September 1989 the Solidarity-led government formally defaulted.

The large foreign debt, and the fact that Poland was not servicing it fully, caused the country to lose creditworthiness.[7] This, in turn, has hindered the inflow of foreign investment since 1986, when it became legally permitted and desired for economic and political reasons. The need to reestablish foreign confidence in Poland's economy, and to help justify debt forgiveness by foreign governments (even though such an act is always largely politically motivated), reinforced the need for a "big-bang" type of transformation program.

Politics. After the martial law crackdown on Solidarity in 1981, Poland faced not only severe economic problems but also political stalemate. In 1988 attempted price increases sparked a new round of massive protests and strikes. In August the government offered to discuss the legalization of Solidarity if the strikers would go back to work. After lengthy negotiations, in January 1989 the party legalized Solidarity and political pluralism. This action led to a series of "roundtable" negotiations among representatives of the government, Solidarity, and the Catholic church. The talks ended with several path-breaking agreements in April 1989, including the promise of free elections to the Senate and limited free elections to the lower house—the Sejm—for up to 35 percent of the seats, to be held in two months.

The Solidarity-led opposition scored a stunning victory in the election, capturing *all* the contested seats in the Sejm and 99 of the 100 seats in the Senate. When the parties that up to then were collaborating with the communists swung their support to Solidarity, the opposition was able to form a government, led by Tadeusz Mazowiecki. Poland thus became the first country in CEE to overthrow communism and to establish a noncommunist government.

In late 1989 and early 1990 Poland was in a unique political situation: the Solidarity-led government was *initially* very popular because Solidarity received much of the credit for ending communism. This popular enthusiasm and support made it politically possible for the new government to introduce harsh economic measures,[8] for which Poland's macroeconomic and foreign debt situations greatly reinforced the need.

Czechoslovakia

Systemic Reforms. Czechoslovakia remained a Stalinist country even after Khrushchev introduced reforms in the Soviet Union. Politically and economically, the country was tied closely to the Soviet Union. By the early 1960s Czechoslovakia was experiencing economic stagnation. That brought to power Alexander Dubček, who initiated the policies known as the Prague Spring. He intended to create a more democratic type of socialism, one that would respect human rights, while retaining the leading role of the Communist Party. The economy was to be reformed by somehow combining central planning and the market.

The Soviet Union worried that allowing the Prague Spring reforms to proceed would "infect" the rest of CEE. Therefore, it intervened militarily, using the Brezhnev Doctrine to justify it.

Dubček was replaced by Gustáv Husák, who for the next 20 years followed an unswerving policy of "consolidation," designed to erase all personnel, institutional, and policy traces of the 1968 reforms and to restore the status quo ante.[9] Historians will have to find out why Husák proceeded differently than Kadar did in Hungary after the Revolution of 1956. Personality differences may have played a role: Husák was reportedly harsh and vindictive; Kadar had a preference for consensus, within limits.

The almost complete absence of reforms for two decades meant that the new government inherited a largely traditional centrally planned system. This suggested the need for a quick and radical transformation program.

Macroeconomic Balance. During 1969–1989 Czech authorities were able to maintain better macroeconomic balance than their counterparts in either Hungary or Poland. Several factors explain why. Most fundamental, perhaps, is the cautious, sober nature of the Czechs, their preference for avoiding risk.[10]

Between 1967 and 1988 the official wholesale price indices in industry and construction remained unchanged, although a modest degree of inflation remained hidden. Nevertheless, increases in consumer prices were small. A comparison between personal consumption in Austria and Czechoslovakia on the basis of purchasing power parity yields an implicit rise of consumer prices of just over 3 percent per annum, versus under 2 percent in the official index, indicating hidden inflation of only around 2 percent a year.[11]

Whichever set of data one focuses on, no large global disequilibrium is detectable for the two decades prior to transformation, owing to the relatively strict control over increases in the money income of the population. However, persistent shortages occurred at microeconomic levels because the structure, availability, and quality of goods and services did not match fully the structure of effective demand. Nominal purchasing power increased more rapidly than supply and prices in the late 1980s, so repressed inflation was getting modestly worse.

Foreign Debt and Debt Management. In the late 1980s, next to Romania, Czechoslovakia was the least indebted CEE country in both absolute and relative terms. At the end of 1988 its gross hard-currency debt was less than $7 billion (Figure 2); net debt (gross debt minus foreign-exchange reserves) was about $5 billion. On a per capita basis Czechoslovakia's gross debt was $430, less than a quarter that of Hungary and less than half that of Poland (Figure 3).

Czechoslovakia accumulated much of its debt during the second half of the 1970s; it followed a very cautious borrowing policy during the 1980s (Figure 2). Throughout the period the debt was serviced fully. The strategy on foreign debt, as on macroeconomic policy, reflected the cautious temperament of the decision makers and a desire to avoid the severe problems faced by Poland and the other countries that had borrowed imprudently.

The relatively favorable domestic and foreign macro-economic situation that Czechoslovakia's new government inherited had three "offsets." First, Czechoslovakia had modernized at a slower pace than either Hungary or Poland. Second, it had granted a large volume of outstanding trade credits (loans) to Third World countries, a considerable part of which has become "nonperforming." Third, compared with Hungary and Poland, Czechoslovakia conducted a much higher share of its total foreign trade during the 1980s with the CMEA countries, especially the USSR. Although the arbitrariness of exchange rates and prices in intra-CMEA trade makes an accurate computation of trade shares impossible, a ballpark estimate for 1985–1988 is that 60 percent of the country's total trade was with the socialist group, whereas for Hungary and Poland the shares were 10–20 percent lower.

Politics. Czechoslovakia's leadership, which for two decades worked tirelessly to eradicate earlier reforms, did not welcome *glasnost* and reforms in the Soviet Union and elsewhere in CEE. During the two decades following the Prague Spring, controls were so pervasive and penalties for nonconformity so harsh that very few persons dared to voice open dissent. One of the few who did was playwright and Charter 77 founding member Václav Havel. He argued that ordinary people should challenge a totalitarian system by rejecting the lies and the rituals of officialdom, by not participating in any activities that were establishment-sponsored.

Encouraged by the events in the USSR and the other CEE countries, during 1988–1989 the people of Czechoslovakia staged ever larger public demonstrations demanding reforms. The authorities, at a loss as to what to do, alternated repression with concessions. Havel's earlier principled position, eloquent writings, incarceration during the dark years, and being jailed anew during the 1989 demonstrations galvanized the opposition and made him a national hero. When demonstrations freed him, Havel and other opposition leaders organized the Civic Forum to coordinate the strikes and protests. (Civic Forum's counterpart in Slovakia was Public Against Violence.) In November 1989 a general strike paralyzed the country and forced the party to agree to a coalition government and to free elections. A month later Havel replaced Husák as president, in one of history's most stunningly quick and symbolic reversals. In Havel's phrase: while the system change took ten weeks in East Germany, ten months in Hungary, and ten years in Poland, Czechoslovakia's "velvet revolution" overturned the system in ten days.[12]

Complicating domestic politics and economics is the relationship between the Czech and Slovak lands. The background, briefly, is this. After the creation of a unified Czechoslovakia in 1918, Slovakia specialized in producing raw materials and food; the Czech lands, in strengthening the industrial base. After World War II Slovakia became a processor of raw materials and a producer of military hardware. By the late 1980s one-third of Slovak industry was defense-related, and 80 percent of trade was with the USSR.

In the first two years after the political transformation, 1990–1991, the people in the Czech land took a right-of-center political position; those in Slovakia, left-of-center. For example, politicians in the Czech land favor quick privatization from below, via a voucher system, whereas the Slovaks prefer a slower pace and look to the state to manage the process.

Slovak demands for greater autonomy were acknowledged in the April 1990 change of the country's name to the Czech and Slovak Federal Republic, and in a constitutional amendment at the end of the year that ceded many of the central government's powers to the republics.[13] Although initially the majority in each land reportedly wanted some sort of continued relationship between the republics, movements for complete independence have been gaining ground. At the July 1992 elections the split between the Czechs and the Slovaks had become sharper and, owing to the opposition by Slovakia's newly elected leader, Vladimír Meciar, Havel was not reelected. Although the split between the two parts of Czechoslovakia now seems to be a fait accompli, the conflict in that country has none of the viciousness that characterizes the conflicts in the former Yugoslavia, so civil war is not even a remote possibility.

The Political Economy of Transformation

The essay by Richard Portes in this volume provides an overview of how centrally planned economies functioned and the legacies they bequeathed, and discusses many of the strategic issues of transition to a market-driven system. Here we add only a few thoughts.

The essential tasks of system transformation can be grouped into two main categories: tasks that require decisive implementation early in the transition (say, during approximately the first two years), and those that require an early start but take longer to implement (say, somewhere between three and ten years). Although agreement among the experts on which are the key tasks and how to sequence their introduction is not 100 percent,[14] Table 2 summarizes this author's views, which are probably not too far from what may be called the economists' consensus.

One of the most urgent tasks is to establish a social safety net. This refers to government programs that provide a minimum level of support to the poor and assistance to the unemployed to enhance their chances of becoming gainfully employed. The old system did not include unemployment compensation because there was no unemployment. The inherited welfare programs (pensions, health care, child care, years of paid maternity leave, disability) were targeted to the general population, not to the needy. Deteriorating economic conditions and the dramatically shrinking tax base have caused the funding levels of existing programs to erode to the point that the design and financing of a welfare program must be rethought.

Decisive action is also needed to create a well-functioning price system and to achieve macroeconomic stabilization. A market economy can function well only if it has appropriate "signals"—prices—for making buying, selling, saving, and investing decisions. The price system encompasses the prices of all goods and services, as well as of factors of production (land, labor, capital), plus the exchange rate. For small and medium-size economies especially, such as those of CEE, governments must liberalize import prices by opening up trade and by making the currency convertible, at least for the enterprise sector.

TABLE 2.   ESSENTIAL TASKS OF ECONOMIC TRANSFORMATION

Tasks requiring early and decisive implementation

Establish a social safety net
Reform the price system and marketize
  • Free the prices of most goods and services
  • Reduce subsidies
  • Free entry and exit; strengthen other competition policies
  • Significantly liberalize imports
  • Introduce convertibility at realistic exchange rates
  • Reform the interest rate
  • Liberalize labor compensation in the private sector and create a labor market
  • Grant substantial autonomy to enterprises
Promote macroeconomic stabilization
  • Pursue tight monetary policy
  • Maintain responsible fiscal policy
  • Introduce temporary incomes policy
  • Consider using the exchange rate as an "anchor" for prices (consistent with introducing convertibility at realistic exchange rates)

Tasks requiring early start, longer implementation

Create or strengthen the institutional framework
  • Revise and codify the legal system and pass new laws on economic activities and institutions
  • Establish or redefine the role of financial institutions and create financial instruments
  • Set up new and modify existing economic information systems, such as statistical and accounting systems
  • Modify the tax system and strengthen tax administration
Restructure the economy
  • Promote the establishment and growth of private business
  • Deconcentrate production and distribution
  • Restructure loan portfolios and recapitalize the banks
  • Privatize state enterprises and involuntary cooperatives
  • Restructure other state enterprises
  • Build up the infrastructure
  • Promote the growth of the service sector
  • Restructure and reorient foreign trade
Make additional strategic policy choices on
  • other aspects of industrial policy
  • long-term policy on agriculture
  • foreign trade (degree of protection)
  • exchange rate (how to set exchange rates to support economic policy priorities)
  • foreign debt (how large, whether to reschedule, debt-equity conversion)
  • foreign investment (to favor it, to discriminate against it, or to be "neutral")
  • regional integration (whether to join and on what terms)
  • agriculture (whether to protect the sector, as the EC does)

Macroeconomic stabilization means bringing under control a high level of repressed or open inflation, including the inflationary pressures that are generated by reforming the price system, when many prices suddenly become market-determined. Failure to bring high inflation under control has three important consequences. First, with high inflation, incomes and wealth are redistributed arbitrarily, which is a cause of economic inefficiency, as well as social and political resentment. Second, when inflation is high, prices cannot perform well their signaling role, because it is difficult for the actors in the economy to interpret a price change as simply catching up or leading inflation or as a change in relative prices. Third, during periods of high inflation, enterprises and households concentrate their economic activities on taking short-term (often speculative) measures to protect their incomes and assets, rather than on such longer-term decisions as saving and productive investing, which are essential for achieving sustainable economic growth.

A transition economy requires "shock therapy" if it inherits a highly distorted structure of relative prices or a large macroeconomic disequilibrium. If both of these conditions prevail, then shock therapy is almost certainly necessary, though not sufficient, to get the economy back on its feet.

In Hungary, owing to gradual reforms of the price system since the late 1960s and the substantial trade liberalization that began in the late 1980s, the new government inherited a price system that was already by and large market-based. And inflation, although it accelerated and peaked in 1991 at around 35 percent, has remained under control; no drastic action was required to curb it. Thus, Hungary had no need for shock therapy.

Poland, by contrast, inherited a large domestic and external disequilibrium and a price system that was more distorted than Hungary's. These legacies made it plausible for Poland's new government to try shock therapy; whether the program was designed and implemented well is another question, discussed in the next section.

Czechoslovakia did not inherit a large macroeconomic disequilibrium. But one of its legacies was a highly distorted set of relative prices. This prompted the authorities to allow most prices to become market-determined on January 1, 1991; in many cases this meant significant price increases. To make sure that the resulting jump in the price level will be once and for all, and not the beginning of permanent high inflation, the authorities had to clamp down with very tight monetary and fiscal policies. This was a key aspect of Czechoslovakia's "big-bang" program. Economic logic underlay the strategy; whether the approach's design and implementation were appropriate is a different question.

The main point of the three-country comparison is that it is much too simplistic to focus on the presence or absence of shock therapy for dividing countries into those that are making rapid progress versus those that are dragging their feet on economic transition.

Fundamental transformation of the kind under way in CEE is a very difficult task. Shock therapy is especially painful. Early during the transition, initial price increases will outpace the growth in the incomes of many people. Living standards will thus fall, in a significant number of cases below the poverty line. But compensating people fully for price increases would undermine stabilization because it would trigger a cost-price spiral.

Together, tight monetary and fiscal policies, the imposition of hard budget constraints on enterprises, the declining purchasing power of households, and the impact of the collapse of intraregional trade are causing production to decline, profits and tax payments to plummet, and unemployment to climb. Job insecurity is suddenly becoming a fact of life for many, as blue- and white-collar workers alike wonder when and on whom the ax will fall. Such worries are all the more difficult to put up with in economies where open inflation and unemployment were long considered capitalist ills and where the distribution of income and wealth is suddenly becoming much more unequal, often because of corruption and tax cheating. The elimination of shortage and the creation of new opportunities in the private sector are compensations. But at least during transition's early years, a segment of the population will be net losers, and uncertainty about many things will become a cause of worry for many.

The declines in output and employment that accompany transformation and stabilization have three causes: imports from the West, which suddenly become available as the transition economies open up foreign trade, satisfy the pent-up demand for high-quality products, and displace some domestic products; the collapse of the economies and trade of the former CMEA countries; and the impact of macroeconomic stabilization policies, including the reduction of subsidies to producers. The flexibility and adaptiveness of the economy on the supply side and general economic conditions in the markets of the main trade partner countries will influence the length and depth of the decline in production. Since one of the legacies of central planning is enterprise inflexibility and poor adaptiveness (low "supply response"), the cost of stabilization tends to be higher than in market economies facing similar circumstances. And the collapse of trade with the former CMEA countries—comparable in magnitude to the contraction of trade during the Great Depression—may be viewed either as an economic disaster or as a welcome pressure on producers to reorient their trade to the West.

Compounding the trade shock and the legacy of low supply responses are the economic and political uncertainties during early transition. What will be the rules and practices of compensating the former owners of nationalized property? What will be the strategy of privatization, and how will it work in practice? Who will ultimately own and dispose of property? Who will be legally responsible for the inherited environmental damage? What will the new tax system be like? How will the authorities respond to gaping new budget deficits? What will be the division of responsibility between the central and local governments? In which areas will foreign investors receive preferential or discriminatory treatment? Will the policies announced remain unchanged, or will they be modified as political conditions change?

These and other imponderables create immense uncertainties and risks, but also unprecedented opportunities for private gain. Until substantial progress is made on practically all the tasks of transformation, an environment of uncertainty will prevail. This can paralyze the managers of state enterprises, as well as many prospective domestic and foreign private investors. It also can encourage short-termism. Both impede recovery, thus exacerbating political tensions. These are some of the reasons the economics and politics of transition are so difficult.

Pressures on managers and workers in the state sector and opportunities that open up in the private sector will cause a rapid expansion of the private sector—both by establishing or expanding private businesses and by privatizing state operations. Initially favored areas will be those that do not require much capital. It will take time for the private sector to become profitable. In any event, the true level of output and profitability of private-sector activities will be substantially underreported to reduce the tax burden, which remains very high in all these countries.

The trends just sketched are evident in every transition economy. What differentiates the countries is how quickly and effectively the new governments are able to address the many interdependent tasks of transition. That, in turn, is contingent on such variables as the traditions of precommunist economic, political, and social systems; the legacies of communism, including how far economic and political reforms have progressed before the transition; and the nature and scope of ethnic and political problems. Such objective factors, together with the unpredictable accidents of history, determine the pace of economic progress and transformation's eventual outcomes.

Progress in CEE Through Mid-1992

The eight countries that used to constitute the region of CEE have made varying degrees of progress toward economic transformation. A brief summary of each one's important developments follows.

Hungary

Hungary's new government is continuing many of the systemic reforms and economic policies of the previous regime. It has been benefiting from the head start it inherited; from a constitution that provides a reasonable degree of political stability, including elections every four years; from the presence of an entrepreneurial spirit that is evident throughout the country; and from the preliminary judgment of the international community that the transformation in Hungary is by and large proceeding on course.

The main new economic program element is the government's pledge to achieve a rapid increase in the *share* of the private sector within several years. Implementation is proceeding, but perhaps at a slower-than-optimum pace; the same is true of progress on the many other tasks of transformation. For example, each year Parliament must hold a debate on the government's objectives and strategies of privatization, to approve as a law the proposed policy guidelines. This gives an element of impermanence to the policies.

Privatization may be initiated by management (the most frequent case), by the state, or by the investor. In all cases, however, only the State Property Agency (SPA)—which, for all practical purposes, is the sole legal owner of all state property—has the right to make a sale. The SPA periodically organizes privatization "programs," under which it prepares a group of state-owned enterprises for sale and proactively seeks investor offers.

The law specifies that a sale must be decided through competitive tender. However good an investor's initial offer may be, a serious attempt must be made to find more than one offer. This is not common practice in the West, so this requirement has discouraged some investors. The justification is that, given Hungary's underdeveloped market for assets, the SPA cannot effectively evaluate the merits of a single bid. But the real reason is probably to deflect criticism by showing that the SPA has made a proper decision in disposing of public assets. The stated criterion for choosing among the offers is not the highest price but the best business plan. While this makes economic sense, it also opens the door to political influence.

Hungary's basic strategy is to sell, not give away, state property. The government believes that only this approach creates real owners who will care about improving the efficiency of asset use; the authorities are also counting on a steady revenue flow.

To be sure, approximately 25 percent of the shares of state enterprises being privatized are scheduled to be transferred on other than market terms: to employees, to the social security fund, and to other public entities; and as compensation to citizens whose property was confiscated earlier or who suffered other kinds of injustices.

Because the purchasing power of the population is still modest, under present policies most firms of significant size are likely to be purchased by foreign investors. This is one reason why privatization has been proceeding slowly; another is that the SPA is overburdened; and still another is that it takes time to get a firm ready for sale and to negotiate a deal, even when foreign advisers do much of the preparatory work. The substantial risks and uncertainties that are present in any transition economy are also factors.

As for economic performance, although since 1988 the economy has been going through a severe contraction, the decline in output has been significantly less in Hungary than in the other CEE countries (see Figures 4 and 5 for a comparison with Poland and Czechoslovakia). That output did not decline more steeply is due to the cumulative effects of earlier partial reforms, the notable success in reorienting trade from East to West, and the substantial inflow of foreign direct investment. The last two achievements brought an impressive turnaround in the balance of payments. Through 1991 Hungary had obtained more foreign investment than all the other CEE countries combined (the eastern part of Germany excluded). Further on the plus side is that inflation probably peaked in 1991, at 35 percent.

On the negative side: the economy seems to be too "boxed in" to experience the kind of impressive economic takeoff that could exploit its considerable potential. Marginal business and personal taxes are very high, in part because tax evasion is so widespread. Severe tensions in the budget seem to preclude the kinds of tax reductions that could jump-start the economy. Servicing the large foreign debt requires a significant net outflow of resources, which constrains investment, whose expansion should serve as a catalyst for an economic boom. Problems of the infra-

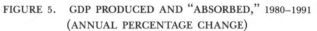

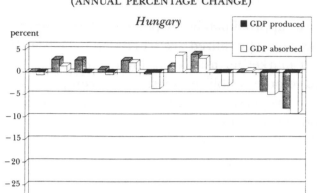

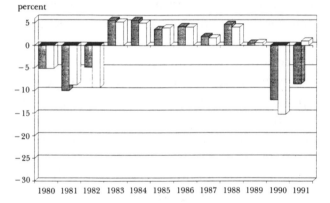

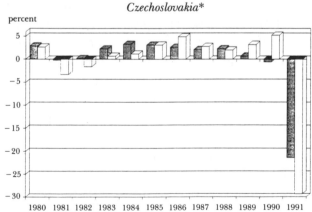

Sources: *PlanEcon Reports*, various issues; author's estimate.

*NMP.

structure, the environment, and the need to restructure state enterprises with good prospects will persist for many years.

Of some concern is public disillusionment with the performance of the economy, which may have unsettling political consequences. Much of the public believes that living standards have been declining, or at least stagnating, for years. Neither the government nor any of the opposition parties has been able to offer a convincing program of economic renewal.

In sum, the economic and political performance of Hungary during these early years of transformation looks much better from outside the country, when it is compared with that of other CEE nations, than when it is experienced and judged from the inside, by the population. The main concerns are the decline in the standard of living, the increased inequality of income and wealth, growing unemployment and uncertainty of life, the slow implementation of the package of transformation measures (which is not the same as the absence of a big-bang program), and the perceived absence of a plausible economic strategy.

Poland

On January 1, 1990, the new government introduced a radical package of measures, known as shock therapy or big bang, whose main objective was to simultaneously open up the economy to market forces and stabilize the macroeconomic situation characterized by high open and repressed inflation. The government took such drastic measures because the economy was in a crisis; because of the belief that only drastic actions would change inflationary expectations; because the new government had an opportunity to take advantage of the considerable political support it initially enjoyed, which made the population more willing to tolerate pain; and because it had to convince the international community, including the IMF, that Poland deserved support, such as debt relief.

Regrettably, many of the complementary reforms, especially privatization and other types of restructuring, received inadequate attention. This has reduced the supply response and thus lowered the beneficial impacts of the shock therapy.

While the privatization of many small service establishments occurred quickly and effectively, the demonopolization, restructuring, and privatization of industrial enterprises got bogged down because of political disagreements about how to implement these tasks and resistance by some of the main parties who would be affected. Politics has been causing the authorities to switch from one privatization scheme to another and then still to another. The privatization programs that have gotten under way have encountered strong resistance—from labor, which claims property rights, especially since the 1981 establishment of the workers' councils; from managers, who worry about their sinecures; and from those in politics and in government who wish to limit the scope of the private sector or who advocate their own schemes.[15] In other cases privatization is hindered by weaknesses in the legal, banking, accounting, and information infrastructure.

The economy's performance during 1990–1991 was mixed. On the positive side, the program quickly eliminated shortages and made the currency convertible. At the same time, production declined much more steeply and the decline has persisted much longer than anyone expected, even in the face of the external shocks experienced during 1990–1991.

Between 1989 and October 1991 Poland had three elections, each bringing in a new government and significant discontinuity in economic policy. In June 1992 the fourth postcommunist government was formed after Parliament voted no confidence in the prime minister, who had been feuding with President Lech Walesa.

Poland faces the danger that as popular dissatisfaction with the economic situation fells governments, each successive government changes policies. The greatest danger is populism, which means pursuing short-term palliatives to economic problems even though they tend to undermine the economy's prospects in the long term. Such policies (for example, the widespread bailing out of failing enterprises and the financing of large budget deficits by printing money) inevitably lead to new bouts of inflation and to conflict with foreign trade partners, creditors, and prospective investors. Poland must avoid cycles of policy reversals, which can lead to the same kind of long-term stagnation or decline as was experienced, until recently, by Argentina.

Political paralysis, a deep recession in the old state-owned sector, and buoyant growth in the new private sector are the dominant realities of today's Poland.

Czechoslovakia

The highest priority *near-term objectives* of the transformation program that the Czech and Slovak Federal Republic launched exactly one year after Poland's were to liberalize domestic prices and foreign trade and to contain the inflationary pressures triggered by marketization. The instruments of this policy were similar to those employed by the big-bang program of Poland: very tight monetary and fiscal policies, a highly restrictive incomes policy (levying high taxes on wage increases), and import liberalization. As expected, the liberalization of prices caused a burst in prices during the first quarter of 1991, following a 10 percent rise during 1990. But by midyear, annual inflation was reduced to single digits. For all of 1991 inflation was 60 percent, much of it concentrated in the first half.

The highest priority *medium-term objective* is to carry out a quick and massive privatization, using the voucher system. Many small properties, such as restaurants and workshops, were privatized quickly; finding new owners who can effectively manage large firms will clearly take much longer.

In the voucher scheme currently in place, every citizen over the age of eighteen has the right to acquire a voucher book, which has 1,000 investment points. These can be used to bid for shares of enterprises being auctioned or tendered in exchange for shares in mutual funds.

Not all large enterprises will be privatized through this method. Among those excluded from the first round are ones for which there is a foreign offer to purchase. This is done because the government wishes to attract foreign investment and accompanying capital, technology, and expertise. Nevertheless, the scale of voucher privatization will be massive. By early 1992 about 8.4 million citizens had bought coupons. The coupons may be pooled in any of 437 sanctioned mutual funds (which foreigners are also allowed to establish), or traded for shares in about 800 large firms, with total book value of around $9 billion. The medium-term results of the country's pioneering privatization program are awaited eagerly not only by people in Czechoslovakia and in the other transition economies, but also by the international community.

During 1990–1991 production declined precipitously, for very much the same reasons as in Hungary and Poland. Among the three, Czechoslovakia has been the most successful in putting in place quickly a strong social safety net, intended to mitigate the economic and social consequences of rapidly climbing unemployment.

As to economic prospects, Czechoslovakia is in a more favorable position than Poland in two respects: it is better able to control inflation, and it has a much smaller burden of foreign debt service. On the other hand, Czechoslovakia has had a much smaller private sector and a much heavier dependence on the USSR and on the other trade partners in Eastern Europe than either Hungary or Poland.

Politically, the fact that elections must be held every two years gives the government too short a time to implement its programs. In the June 1992 elections the political split between the Czech lands and Slovakia sharpened and now appears to have become a fait accompli. In the former, the right-of-center party, led by Minister of Finance Václav Klaus, won a plurality of votes, whereas in the latter, left-of-center and separatist Vladimír Meciar was victorious. The splitting of the country will cause severe new economic problems, probably more in Slovakia than in the Czech lands. A period of political uncertainty is a strong possibility.

Eastern Germany

The eastern part of Germany had the biggest big-bang program imaginable, given that everything was done at once, immediately after reunification, and to an economy that was, for all practical purposes, a traditional, Soviet-type, centrally planned system. Practically all prices were liberalized, and hitherto protected firms and farms were exposed to international competition, literally overnight. A decision has been made to reach wage parity with the western part of Germany within a few years, even though average productivity in the East is only a fraction of that in the West. The introduction of the West German currency in the East meant that the exchange rate was discarded as a policy tool that could otherwise have protected producers in eastern Germany.

The result has been a very sharp drop in production—more than 50 percent in three years—and a huge rise in unemployment. This would have been catastrophic were it not for the estimated 400 billion deutsche mark ($250 billion) transfer from the western to the eastern part of Germany in three years, 1990–1992.[16] As important as the money is the transfer and adoption of West Germany's legal, financial, and accounting systems; public administration; and social safety net.

The dominant institution that is transforming the eastern part into a market economy and integrating it with the rest of Germany is Treuhandanstalt. Founded in March 1990 by the interim Modrow government as a state body to hold the shares to the to-be-commercialized state enterprises, Treuhand was transformed in June 1990 into a huge, Western-style holding company. At the time, it "owned" 8,000 enterprises with 45,000 plants, tens of thousands of other commercial establishments, and land representing 27 percent of the agricultural area of the former GDR. In industry and construction alone, firms under Treuhand's control had 3.5 million employees.[17]

Treuhand was given two interdependent tasks: to privatize as many businesses as quickly as possible and to operate firms until they could be privatized or closed down. In the meantime firms are subsidized or restructured, as Treuhand deems necessary. Initially, the value of the assets entrusted to Treuhand was estimated to be 600 billion deutsche marks; the figure has successively been revised down to 200 billion deutsche marks.[18] When privatizing, Treuhand bargains with one or more buyers, not necessarily accepting the highest bid, but preferring an investor (who may pay to, or receive payment from Treuhand to, take over operations) who provides competent management and new investments, and guarantees a negotiated level of employment for an agreed period. Treuhand encourages practically all methods of privatization, including management and employee buyouts. It does not discriminate against foreign investors. Treuhand's motto is to privatize quickly, to restructure thoroughly, and to close down cautiously.[19]

In spite of the political backlash in the West by 1992 against the financial burden of subsidizing the East—a burden that is taking the form of higher inflation, higher taxes, and lower real wages—it is almost certain that the immense tasks will be accomplished successfully within approximately ten years. It is more than likely that by the turn of the century, the public infrastructure in the eastern part of Germany (excluding housing) will be the most modern in Europe, and the economy one of the most dynamic.

Eastern Germany's transformation is unique in many respects. First, the task is much greater and more urgent than anywhere else in CEE. The task is not just to reverse economic decline, but also to bring this region on par with the rest of Germany, in terms of productivity and the standard of living, and to do it in a hurry. The political urgency of the job stemmed initially from a desire to make the process of reunification quickly irreversible, in case politics in the former Soviet Union closed the window of opportunity that the policies of Mikhail Gorbachev opened. Later, the imperative to move quickly stemmed from a fear of mass migration from the eastern to the western part of the country. Second, eastern Germany is unique also because it has a big brother that is able and willing to finance rapid transformation and has the political will and administrative capability to get the job done.

Romania

Between 1949 and 1989 Romania had gone through 40 years of intensive, semiautarkic industrialization, with a stress on heavy industry that, even by the standards of communist countries, was extreme. The country's absolute leader between 1965 and 1989 was Nicolae Ceausescu, whose predilection was to build exorbitantly expensive pharaonic projects that made little economic sense. The caliber of his economic stewardship is illustrated by his personal decision to repay all of Romania's total convertible-currency debt of $10 billion, an immense task he had just about accomplished by the time he was executed, following a palace coup d'état in 1989. To pay back the debt, producer and consumer goods were mobilized for exports, at any cost. Enterprises were starved of inputs; households of foods and other economic goods. During the 1980s deliveries of foodstuffs to the domestic market were cut, on average, by half, from already low levels. Households were allowed to consume electricity that was enough only for one lightbulb per room for two or three hours a day.[20]

The postrevolutionary government's first order of business was to bring some relief to hard-pressed consumers by putting on the market consumer goods stored in government warehouses, and by increasing imports. But the new government also granted large wage increases, transfer payments, and lowered taxes. These actions boosted inflation during 1991 to more than 200 percent; inflation was still not under control during the first half of 1992.

Although Romania has made some headway toward democratization and marketization since 1989, progress has been slow. The changes appear to be more cosmetic than substantive. Many of the people in charge are quick-change artists who served the ancien régime. The current leaders have continued an old formula: to try to legitimate themselves by using the mantle of nationalism. And as the economy continues to decline, ethnic tensions are increasing; the large Hungarian minority is a notable case in point.

Lack of experience with anything like a competitive democracy is an important legacy. Far more than, say, the Hungarians or the Poles, the Romanians have lived in a truly totalitarian state for decades. Few people have had unsupervised contact with the West, so there has been little opportunity to learn modern economics or business.

Bulgaria

The political situation in Bulgaria is uncertain. No party has a majority, and the ability of the government to implement economic policies is weak.

In 1991 the government instituted an almost complete liberalization of prices (except for energy) and a large reduction of subsidies to enterprises. But, given the continued high monopolization of production and distribution, this has so far led more to higher prices than to increased output; as of year-end 1991 no large Bulgarian producer had gone bankrupt.[21]

The intention of the government was to undertake large-scale privatization, deconcentration, commercialization, tax reform, and banking reform, and to erect a social safety net. Unfortunately, it implemented few of these plans, owing to political disruptions and the absence of a reasonably well functioning civil service.

Bulgaria owes about $10 billion to 300 commercial banks and is in de facto default to them. Consequently, it has no access to foreign credits, except from international financial institutions, on which it has become highly dependent.

No European country, not even wartorn Yugoslavia, had as poor an economic performance as Bulgaria had in 1991: output declined by 23 percent, inflation soared to more than 500 percent, and unemployment grew sevenfold and imports declined by two-thirds in real terms. Whether Bulgaria reached the trough in 1991 or whether output will continue to spin downward is an open question. The country's economic future depends on domestic economic and political stabilization and on effective international economic help.

Yugoslavia

The decomposition of Yugoslavia began in the 1980s and accelerated in the early 1990s. The disruptions were made worse by the wars Serbia and its allies waged, first in Slovenia, then in Croatia and later in Bosnia-Hercegovina. Although the carving up of Yugoslavia and the war are obviously slowing systemic transition, it has become evident that the path of transition in the successor states will not be identical, owing to differences in the legacies, some of which predate communism.

Slovenia and *Croatia* are relatively well endowed with capacity to manufacture consumer goods. This should ease their restructuring and trade reorientation toward the world market.

Bosnia-Hercegovina has many large and outmoded heavy industries, which (together with the country's isolated location) will cause the most massive economic adjustment problems. *Macedonia* has staked heavily on producing agricultural and other raw materials and semifinished products. Its economic prospects will thus be influenced by world market developments and by its ability to find markets for those products and ways to transport them there.

Montenegro—economically highly dependent on Serbia, very poor, and having staked on tourism, which has been disrupted—has decided by referendum to remain joined with Serbia. *Serbia* proper will have to contend with tensions arising from large differences among its regions—for example, between the formerly autonomous regions of Vojvodina and Kosovo. The primarily agricultural and relatively rich and sparsely populated Vojvodina, with a large Hungarian minority, is not likely to push for the same policies as the very poor, densely populated, largely Albanian, energy- and raw-material-producing Kosovo. Also, Serbia took over a much larger government bureaucracy and armed forces than it needs or can possibly support. This, too, will remain a source of economic and political tension.

For Croatia, Bosnia-Hercegovina, and Serbia, the costs of the war have been enormous, although in different ways. In Croatia, by mid-1992 physical damage had reached an estimated $20 billion, and the number of displaced persons 800,000—this in a country with a GNP of about $15 billion (around $3,000 per capita in 1989) and 4.7 million people. The fighting that has spread to the territory of Bosnia-Hercegovina has caused even greater damage and disruption there. Serbia's financing of the war via the massive printing of money has led to four-digit hyperinflation, and the government had no plans (as of June 1992) for economic stabilization. This, too, is sure to cause economic and political instability.

Slovenia, Croatia, Macedonia, and Bosnia-Hercegovina have decided to abandon reform socialism and to transform to mixed market economies. They also hope to become associated with the European Community. This means that their institutional changes and economic policies will have to be guided by the need to become compatible with those of the member countries of the Community. Serbia and Montenegro are much more of a question mark in this regard. They have made no decisive break with reform socialism. As of mid-1992 former communists (with changed labels) were still in power and the vague concept of "social ownership" of the means of production had not been eliminated, as it has been, constitutionally, in several of the other republics.

Albania

One of Europe's smallest countries, and perhaps its poorest, Albania has remained isolated from the rest of the world for almost two generations. Elections in March 1992, won by the Democratic Party, which has promised democracy and a market economy, hold out the hope that Albania will join the rest of Europe. However, it faces immense economic problems in the short run. For example, forecasters predict that agricultural output in 1992 will have declined by 75 percent, because of arguments over how to carve up the collective farms into private plots.

As Yugoslavia continues to fall apart, tensions over the fate of the large number of Albanians in Kosovo will likely complicate politics in Albania also.

Conclusions and Implications for the Soviet Successor States

In place of the eight former CEE countries, today there are eleven; the number would rise to twelve when the Czech and Slovak federal republics divorce. The change in the number of countries came about by the German Democratic Republic's joining the Federal Republic of Germany, which left seven, and by Yugoslavia's breaking up into five independent countries.

Even the brief country profiles in this essay reveal the immense diversity among the countries and the peoples in this region, in terms of their history, pretransformation policies, and transformation programs.

As regards progress already achieved and prospects for successful transformation into a market economy, I would place Hungary, Czechoslovakia, Slovenia, and Poland into one group, and all the others into another (the eastern part of Germany is not included). Although in certain respects the differences may be larger among some countries within a group than between pairs of countries from the two groups, those in the first group have certain advantages that, in combination, are particularly important for successful transformation. These advantages include considerable historical experiences with a market economy. Moreover, all have achieved a level of development that makes it inappropriate to classify them as *poor countries,* although the legacies of the recent past make them *poor economies.* (The distinction lies in the quality of the inherited physical and human capital, which is more developed than their current dollar per capita GNP would suggest.) None of the countries in the first group have domestic ethnic conflicts that are likely to culminate in civil strife. And all of them are oriented toward and are conditionally welcomed by the European Community. An example is the associate member status in the Community that Czechoslovakia, Hungary, and Poland had negotiated by year-end 1991, separately but on practically identical terms.

The experiences of the CEE economies thus far yield a number of lessons for transition economies:

(1) In countries that inherit a large macroeconomic imbalance, macroeconomic stabilization must receive high priority, for the reasons stated in this essay. But for such stabilization to succeed—within a reasonable time frame and without too great a cost in declining production and increased unemployment—government leaders must concentrate attention not only on reining in demand (via traditional IMF policies) but also on stimulating supply. That, in turn, requires significant progress on practically all the tasks of transformation, since they are so interdependent. This statement, of course, holds true for all transition economies. Generating a strong supply response is the key to sustained economic recovery.

(2) In view of the insufficient effectiveness during transition of tight monetary and fiscal policies to control inflation, owing to

underdeveloped institutions and the old patterns of enterprise behavior, governments should entertain the introduction of temporary incomes policies. This means imposing temporary administrative controls on compensation, first and foremost in the state sector.

(3) Market forces alone cannot be counted upon to restructure and fundamentally improve productivity in large state enterprises. Whereas the right policies can privatize trade, other services, and small manufacturing quickly, even the most liberal laws and procedures are likely to be less than fully effective in rapidly privatizing large state-owned enterprises; that task will take many years, if not decades. In the meantime, the state will have to find ways to simultaneously improve the operation of these firms and get them ready for privatization.

(4) Many channels of privatization should be allowed. But any policy on privatization should adhere to two main guidelines. First, for each unit being privatized, effective control should be concentrated in the hands of an individual or an entrepreneurial group of owners. Privatization that disperses ownership too widely and on a permanent basis will not give the owners the practical means to motivate managers to make good business decisions and thus to maximize the rate of return on investment. Second, the main objective of privatization should be to obtain a contractual pledge to undertake the needed restructuring and new investment. Privatization that focuses exclusively on generating revenue will soak up too much capital—especially the little domestic capital that is available—that would be better put for new business investment.

(5) Attracting foreign investment requires a reasonable degree of political, legal, and economic stability, including clear and transparent rules and regulations that are not frequently altered. In their absence, speeches by politicians and bureaucrats have no lasting impact on prospective investors.

(6) Confidence in the political order is crucial; otherwise, the electorate is unlikely to be willing to continue making the sacrifices necessary for a successful transition. But to maintain political confidence, elected leaders must trust the people and must be bluntly honest with them regarding the difficult road

ahead and explain to them what the proposed policies will accomplish and why any alternative would yield less desirable outcomes.

(7) Effective implementation of policies is as important as having the right policies. Strengthening public administration should be a very high priority for the new governments and should also be a target of foreign assistance.

Notes

The author acknowledges, with thanks, comments on an earlier version or country-specific interpretations provided by Ivo Bicanic, Aurel Braun, Shafiqul Islam, Owen Johnson, Michael Mandelbaum, Michael Montias, Dusan Mramor, and Rychard Rapacki. None of these individuals should be held responsible for any of the facts or interpretations presented.

1. Janos Kornai, "The Hungarian Reform Process: Visions, Hopes, and Reality," *Journal of Economic Literature*, vol. 24, no. 4 (1986), pp. 1687–737.
2. Andras Inotai and Mihaly Patai, "Hungarian Debt Management Strategy for the Nineties," Institute for World Economics Working Paper, no. 1 (Budapest, 1991).
3. The Brezhnev Doctrine, announced by the Soviet leader after the 1968 invasion of Czechoslovakia, stated that once a country has been brought under the direct Soviet alliance system, it will not be permitted to leave that alliance.
4. David Lipton and Jeffrey Sachs, "Creating a Market Economy in Eastern Europe: The Case of Poland" (Paper for the Brookings Panel on Economic Activity, Washington, D.C., April 5–6, 1990).
5. Wlodzimierz Brus, "The Political Economy of Reform in Poland," in P. Marer and W. Siwinski, eds., *Creditworthiness and Reform in Poland* (Bloomington: Indiana University Press, 1988), p. 78.
6. Wlodzimierz Siwinski, "Why Poland Lost Its Creditworthiness," in Marer and Siwinski, *Creditworthiness and Reform*, pp. 25–31.
7. Marer and Siwinski, *Creditworthiness and Reform*.
8. Dariusz K. Rosati, "Institutional and Policy Framework for Foreign Economic Relations in Poland," in United Nations Economic Commission for Europe, *Reforms in Foreign Economic Relations of Eastern Europe and the Soviet Union* (New York, 1991).
9. Gordon Skilling, "Czechoslovakia Between East and West," in W. E. Griffith, ed., *Central and Eastern Europe: The Opening Curtain* (Boulder, Colo.: Westview Press, 1989).
10. Institutional-legal factors contributed also. In 1970 the government almost inadvertently passed a law, proposed earlier as part of the reform package, providing for a substantial degree of independence of the central monetary authorities, making the monobank co-responsible for central planning. In a traditional centrally planned economy the planning office

prepares the plan, the finance ministry is in charge of the budget, and the monobank is subordinated to the ministry and must finance all activities approved by the planning office and any deficit in the state budget; by contrast, the new law made the monobank formally independent of the ministry of finance. That, in turn, gave the bank an opportunity to pursue a monetary policy that was not fully accommodating. (Václav Klaus, former staff member of the central bank of Czechoslovakia, personal communication.)

11. Vladimír Dlouhy, "Inflation in the Czechoslovak Economy," *Europaeische Rundschau* (Summer 1989), vol. 24, no. 3, p. 11.
12. David S. Mason, *Revolutions in East-Central Europe: The Rise and Fall of Communism and the Cold War* (Boulder, Colo.: Westview Press, 1992), pp. 63–64.
13. Ibid, p. 81.
14. Paul Marer and Salvatore Zecchini, eds., *The Transition to a Market Economy*, 2 vols. (Paris: Organization for Economic Cooperation and Development, 1991).
15. Rychard Rapacki and Susan J. Linz, "Privatization in Transition Economies: Case Study of Poland," Paper for the Southern Conference on Slavic Studies (Jacksonville, Fla.: March 26–28, 1991).
16. Jurgen Muller, "Mergers in East Germany," Centre for International Studies Working Paper, University of Toronto (Toronto, 1991).
17. Horst Brezinski, "Privatisation in East Germany," *Nomisma*, no. 1 (1992), pp. 28–47.
18. Ibid, p. 32.
19. Birgit Breuel, "A Social Market Economy Cannot Be Introduced Overnight," *European Affairs* (January 1992), p. 12.
20. Michael Montias, "The Romanian Economy: A Survey of Current Problems," in Commission of the European Economies, *European Economy*, special edition no. 2 (Brussels, 1991).
21. Ivan Angelov, "Bulgaria's Economy and Reform During 1992–1993" (unpublished, 1992).

3

Economic Reform in the USSR and Its Successor States

Robert W. Campbell

A would-be guide offering an interpretive tour through the great dismal swamp of Soviet economic reform is hard put to find a tussock stable enough to serve as a platform from which to start his spiel. Trying to describe the features of the reform on the basis of the excitements of recent history does not satisfy, given the way each choice and act of the last six years has seemed to get undone or overshadowed by the next. An interpretive stance has to go well beyond economics to consider politics, military affairs, and the dynamics of empires, but one's fellow specialists in those fields seem unable to offer much in the way of firm interpretations or perspectives. A predictive approach seems positively foolhardy, given the multiplicative contingencies one can foresee, the lack of models, and the differences from the closest analogue, Eastern Europe. And with the dissolution of the Union, our swamp has turned into fifteen distinct ecological habitats. But this is so dramatic a landscape, holding such portentous possibilities, that we can hardly call off the tour. I will start with an explanation of what the transformation of the old USSR means, then describe the efforts up to the time of the coup and the dissolution of the empire, and conclude by offering some reflections on prospects.

Introduction

The classic Soviet system combined territorial integrity over an imperial economic space with a highly centralized administrative approach to directing economic life within that space. It is help-

99

ful to think of the Soviet system as a single corporation that administered the whole economy, with the added complication that this entity fused economic control with totalitarian political power. Along with the function of economic administration, USSR Inc. also exercised the functions and coercive power of the state. In the Soviet case, moreover, "state" meant the state as empire rather than the state as an expression of nationhood. Figure 1 attempts to capture this dual function by labeling USSR Inc. the "state production establishment," or SPE.

All issues of economic allocation and decision making got settled within that framework, usually in a highly centralized fashion. It is important to remember that among these decisions were some of great territorial (and hence intra-imperial) significance, such as location of production and interregional commodity flows; interregional flows of savings and investment; and manipulation of the distribution of income, in part by income transfers, including interregional income transfers.

The interlocking directorate of party and state elites that exercised a monopoly of political, ownership, and management rights within the SPE were *not* able to settle *all* economic variables by direct administrative command. First, they had to deal with the outside world, on price terms the competitive conditions of the world market dictated. Second, they found it expedient to conduct much of the SPE's economic transactions with the population (or households), through market interactions, specifically via a consumer goods market and a labor market. That was a special kind of market relationship, however, in which the SPE was monopolist on the one hand and monopsonist on the other, exercising tremendous market power. This characteristic permitted the system to turn the terms of trade with households sharply in its own favor and to extract a heavy tribute to be used for investment, military expenditures, research and development (R&D), and other leadership-chosen goals. As regards the polity, households were simply excluded from meaningful participation, and politics in the classic Soviet Union was more or less identical with party politics and bureaucratic politics. In ethnic terms, the power structure of the SPE was dominated by Russians, even on the local level. The standard practice in the party,

FIGURE 1.   SECTORS OF THE SOVIET ECONOMY:
A PERFECT-ADMINISTRATION INTERPRETATION

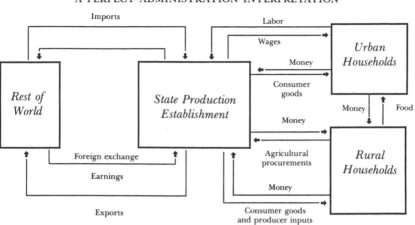

for example, was to name a native as the figurehead first secretary of an ethnic jurisdiction, while a Russian as second secretary constituted the real source of power. The well-known "we/they" division in this "uncivic" society thus had multiple connotations—population/*nomenklatura*, household/SPE monopoly, local official/central official, local manager/corporate headquarters, minority nationality/Russian.

In its traditional state functions the SPE was not accountable to the population; in its role of economic management it acted essentially as patrimonial owner. In such a system the traditional distinction between public and private affairs familiar in civic societies was almost nonexistent. For instance, there was no public finance—the state budget was essentially an element in the internal accounts of the corporation. The banking system functioned more as a corporate comptroller's office than as an institution with "public-sector" responsibilities. Both the Ministry of Finance and the State Bank, moreover, were passive executors rather than makers of corporate policy. Such instruments as monetary policy, fiscal policy, an exchange rate, and tariff policy were irrelevant. Control over the behavior of firms in the economy was exercised in a mode of micromanagement from headquarters, rather than in the civic-society mode of public policy establishing a parametric environment of rules of the game, tax policy, and so forth, applicable to all, within which autonomous firms could make their own decisions.

The relationship of the SPE to the outer world was highly autarkic. The Soviet Union carried on a significant amount of foreign trade, and trade grew especially rapidly from the mid-sixties, but the foreign trade of the Soviet Union was always less than would be normal for a country of its size. The most important consequence was that the system's economic decision-making institutions powerfully buffered it from any influences from the world economy that might have measured Soviet outcomes against world standards, impinged on internal economic decisions, or offered a corrective to the economic choices made by the management of the corporation.

Reform means dismantling these fundamental features of the system, which defined the essence of the economic/political/social order that we call the Soviet-type system. The SPE's management of the economy must be transferred to the impersonal mechanism of market signals and market forces. The SPE needs to withdraw from its monopsonist/monopolist relation to subject households in both politics and economics in favor of a civic relationship to its citizens. The diktat of an imperial center imposed on minority nationalities in both political and economic terms must give way to more local autonomy, and perhaps to national/territorial sovereignties. The fiscal system (including the tariff system) and the banking system need to be transformed into active instruments of commercial and public policy. The economy needs to be integrated into the world economy, and this change will have to take place under conditions where the world economy is becoming a truly integrated global economic system, in which corporate players frequently must have a global reach to function effectively.

The transition from Soviet socialism thus involves three crucial partitionings: the political/economic one, discussed above; a top/bottom split of the SPE into a public sector and a private sector; and a territorial division.

In terms of production the division of the economy into a public and a private sector means dividing control between a sphere of marketized-privatized producers and a sphere of public regulatory policy. In terms of finance it means a division between financial markets that serve private finance and the fiscal institutions associated with public policy. The banking system must be split into a sphere of commercial banks operating on the general principles of the market economy and a central bank carrying out public policy goals by influencing the interest rate and the money supply.

One corollary of the usurpation of the rights of citizens by the communist leadership was a profound distortion in the allocation of resources among final uses. The leaders opted for huge military expenditures, and a vast military-industrial sector that served leadership paranoia and megalomania rather than citizen-generated demands. They also diverted an extraordinary share of the nation's output into investment. That was partly a function of misguided strategy, but more fundamentally it reflected a decision imposed from above to sacrifice current consumption in favor of growth and more output in the future. The split chosen by the bosses was far out of line with what the populace would voluntarily have saved for investment in the future. When these imposed choices about investment and national security come under public scrutiny, the inherited structure of capacities and activities in the economy is revealed as badly distorted, calling for painful adjustment in the short run. Similar distortions of economic structure induced by autarky parallel this structural problem.

As for the territorial partition, strong centrifugal forces are leading to devolution of control over the imperial space of the old USSR to new sovereign republics, and the new institutions succeeding the old SPE are being created on a republican, rather than on an all-Union, basis. The formerly unified economy seems destined to be split into regional economies separated from each other by the economic instruments of state sovereignty—tariffs, controls on population movement, different currencies issued by separate national banks. Formulation and execution of public-sector functions—financing defense, use of fiscal and monetary policy for stabilization and income redistribution—will differ among territories.

The range in the possible degree of local control over the new economic institutions is very broad. Alternatives include a federal form, with allocation of powers governed by a constitutional process and differing degrees of devolution from the federal to the local or intermediate level; a more confederal or treaty form of association—such as the commonwealth arrangement established at the end of 1991—with rights and responsibilities much more subject to negotiation and renegotiation than in a federal structure; and full sovereignty and economic independence for constituent areas. It is now virtually inevitable that the old USSR will become independent countries based on the old republics, but the same central/local problem is nested within each, as is already obvious within Russia. Tatarstan is as avid for complete economic independence from Russia as the Russian Soviet Federated Socialist Republic (RSFSR) was from the USSR.

The partitioning into public and private spheres is complicated enough. In carrying out that aspect of reform, the reformers face issues common to all countries making the transition from socialism—sequencing, dislocation, coherence, equity, and so on. The additional dimension of territorial untangling in the Soviet case injects all sorts of new shocks, passions, and disputes into the process.

Heated arguments and power struggles surround whose income is being transferred to whom (each national group contends that it has been exploited by the others); the proper structure for a monetary authority (various republics are trying to regulate the money supply and the interest rate independently of the Union bank); the allocation of fiscal responsibilities and rights among different levels, including within the new sovereign states (each is trying to capture budget revenues and shift budget expenditures to another level; all of the republics have begun to run deficits, which they have expected their local central banks to finance); and control of interregional resource flows (most local units are instituting beggar-thy-neighbor policies that keep food and other supplies at home, with the predictable result of a cascading decline in output). The fact of interdependency is poorly understood—every subunit thinks it will be able to control its own economic destiny if it is independent, ignoring the instruments by which others will still influence the outcome.

These partitionings may also be thought of as a process of autonomization or empowerment. Decisions that were once the province of the imperial center as *principal*, to be implemented by its *agents*, are now in the hands of autonomous *actors*. But this is not a fully controlled reallocation of power, and the evolution of reform is very much a matter of who moves most skillfully to pick up the pieces that fall in the street. The old *nomenklatura* may outmaneuver the working class in translating former position into property rights, or in capturing political power in its new legislative form. Groupings around production monopoly structures within the old system may survive to forestall the competitive-market outcomes that the transition is supposed to achieve. It seems especially difficult to predict who will gain control over powers and choices up for grabs as a result of deimperialization.

Having laid out the agenda for reform, and the setting in which it is to be taken up, we can now turn to the question of how the triple untangling is going.

Perestroika under Gorbachev

As suggested, we have to keep our eye on at least three main threads in this process—economic reform, political reform, and regional separatism or localism. We will start by reviewing progress on economic reform alone, without the complications that dissolution of the Union has introduced. A good part of the history of *perestroika* occurred in an all-Union setting. Mikhail Gorbachev proceeded in such a framework for six years and fought consistently against breakup of the empire. The legacy and lessons of this period carry over to the new actors, who must still face the same problems of political and economic reform within their more restricted geographic perspective. We will also put off for a bit discussion of the political context. Reform of the political structure took place only some way into the process. In the early stages the Communist Party controlled the degree and pace of change. After election of the Congress of People's Deputies and the new Supreme Soviet in 1989, reform had to face a different set of political conditions. Most reform measures then originated as laws passed by the USSR Supreme Soviet, and their shaping and implementation were increasingly subject to popular pressures.

The Agenda for Economic Reform

A kind of standard agenda for economic reform can be summarized under the following six headings:

(1) Marketization—making enterprises autonomous by dismantling the power structures of the SPE (firing the bureaucrats and dismantling the party) and moving from administered pricing to market pricing

(2) Translating enterprise autonomy into entrepreneurial and marketlike behavior by privatizing property rights or improving enterprise governance

(3) Defining and institutionalizing public-sector functions and establishing the legal and fiscal basis for effective operation of the public sector

(4) Reforming the financial system—creating new financial markets, channeling savings and new credit to investors, making governments compete with the private sector for loanable funds, and generating a structure of meaningful interest rates to guide and motivate these decisions

(5) Opening the economy to the external world

(6) Creating a system of social protection against the costs the transition imposed on the population

Until resolute action is taken in all these areas, there is no coherent new system, and any improvements in economic performance are unlikely. Worse, as Soviet experience has shown, partial efforts just disrupt the old system without creating a new one, turning *perestroika* into *katastroika* (a Russian pun on catastrophe).

Work on this agenda started later in the Soviet Union than in the East European socialist countries, and the Soviet leaders temporized consistently in facing up to the imperatives of reform. Most of Gorbachev's early efforts were in the venerable tradition of "administrative tinkering"—trying to reorient strategic choices, tweak policy, and improve administration, within an essentially unchanged administrative approach. Nearly all the measures of the first couple of years—the antialcohol campaign, the *gospriemka* experiment at improving quality by a new administrative body, personnel weed-outs, a shift in investment priorities—were of this kind. On each of the main agenda items above the reformers ran through a catalog of typical halfhearted reforms familiar from the earlier history of Eastern Europe. They barely touched the "four whales"[1] on which the administrative approach rests—subordination of enterprises to a bureaucratic ministerial system; cyclic target setting and evaluation; central plans for output and allocation of inputs; and administered pricing.

On increasing enterprise autonomy, the most significant milestone was a packet of measures enacted in 1987. The centerpiece was the Law on the State Enterprise, but it was accompanied by new decrees on the organs forming the environment of the enterprise—the Gosplan, the ministries, and Goskomstat.[2] The central elements in the new status for the enterprise were *samofinansirovanie*, or self-financing; the *goszakaz*, or state order; and some choice as to how enterprise gross revenue would be allocated between materials cost, wages, several kinds of special-purpose funds, and payments to the state budget. The idea of the state order was that the central planning apparatus would pass down orders for amounts of output to be delivered for state needs, rather than full-scale output plans, and that these orders would cover less than the enterprise's whole output. For output included in the state order the central planners would still operate the usual balancing system, providing inputs to producing enterprises from the output other firms produced under state orders. Enterprises could sell any output produced above the state order on their own, but such production was not supported by centrally allocated inputs. The share of state orders was intended to diminish with time. The idea in effect was to cut the economy into a planned sector and a partially marketized

sector, with the dividing line running through individual enterprises, as well as through the economy as a whole. A moment's
thought will suggest that the economy cannot easily be torn apart
this way. The planners had no way of figuring out what outputs
they had to "order" to assure availability of inputs for enterprises
to which they were assigning state orders. So the tendency was to
keep on planning everything, and indeed the planners often
assigned state orders exceeding the old plan targets.

The change in enterprise finances in effect introduced a
parametric revenue-sharing *formula* by which income, after payment for inputs purchased from other firms, was divided according to fixed percentages among wages, a fund for
investment, an incentive fund (which would be used in part for
wages), and the state budget. By fixing the share of the state's
take, this system was intended to make workers see their income
as more closely dependent on individual work effort, and to give
the enterprise its own sources for financing investment, which
would eliminate the need for access to the state budget. But the
new income formula was a poorly designed instrument, and
ultimately it diverted income away from taxes and from investment into wages, providing one of the conditions for the growth
of a budget deficit and a cash overhang in the hands of
households.

Though in the first phase of *perestroika* the major effort
concerned the *state* enterprise, the door was concurrently
opened a crack for the emergence of nonstate economic activity.
The first step was permitting "individual labor activity" (such as
driving taxis), but the 1986 law on such activity fairly quickly
began to be used as the vehicle for cooperatives as well. A much
more elaborate law, permitting co-ops "of a new kind" to produce a variety of services and products, took effect in 1988.[3] The
new law was fairly liberal in its provisions, though far from
consistent in encouraging the co-ops. Local officials often made
it difficult to obtain a license; no access to inputs through standard channels was envisaged; co-ops had to pay much higher
prices than state enterprises. Despite discriminatory conditions,
however, the legitimation of co-ops was a significant break-

through in the opportunity for private enterprise, and the response was a rapid growth in numbers, employment, and output in the co-op sector. But the co-ops were subsequently hit with still more discouragements. When medical co-ops began to take business away from the arrogant and inefficient state health system, the state prohibited co-ops from operating in that area. Though taxes were originally set low, rates were sharply raised in the summer of 1990. Local authorities often interfered with co-op initiative, as in a famous case in 1989 in the Krasnodar region. The region is a big producer of fruits and vegetables, and a large share of the harvest typically rots in the field or is fed to animals. Co-ops from northern regions, traditionally short of food, and especially of fruits and vegetables, contracted to buy up this surplus produce for sale in the northern regions. But the Krasnodar party organization, opposed to any kind of private activity, intervened to prevent these deals, going so far as setting up roadblocks, jailing these entrepreneurs, and confiscating their trucks and produce.

In this climate of hostility the co-op sector was able to survive and grow primarily by developing symbiotic relations with state enterprises, whose officials often used them as a channel for escaping central controls and for private gain. Along with exploitation by the Mafia, this got them a bad name, and limited their ability to add to consumer goods output.

Closely allied to co-ops were some small-scale experiments with leasing productive facilities to workers. When the state leased an enterprise, someone had to assume the responsibility of lessee, and this was typically the employees of the enterprise organized as a cooperative. In agriculture the legitimation of leasing, together with a much more direct permission in a new land law passed in 1990, offered farmers the possibility of exiting from the collective farm, taking land with them.[4] Those who left the co-op were not given outright ownership of the land, but were granted lifetime tenure with the right of passing the land on to their heirs. Some privatization of housing has also occurred. Finally, during 1987 and 1988 conditions were gradually made easier for forming joint ventures with foreign firms, as another form of essentially private activity outside the state sector.[5]

These were all useful innovations, but were too grudging to permit the emergence of a significant private sector, and the continued dominance of the state sector stunted and distorted the efforts of what entrepreneurial actors did emerge. Many took advantage of the decline in control to engage in illegal, exploitive, unproductive schemes. The most famous of these was the ANT cooperative, which by an audacious pattern of suborning officials in the state sector was able to receive huge payments—as a middleman in R&D contracts; on the promise of supplying highly valued foreign goods, such as computers; and by negotiating special tax exemptions for itself. It finally ran into difficulties when it brokered the sale of Soviet T-72 tanks and MIG-23 engines to a foreign customer. Needless to say, it could manage all this only under an umbrella of connivance and protection by bribed state officials.

The share of activity privatized under all these measures remained almost imperceptible. Quantitatively the only important change was growth of the co-ops, which in 1989 had 4.9 million employees (compared with a state labor force of about 120 million persons), and whose sales of 40 billion rubles contributed perhaps as much as 2 percent of total national income. Numerous joint ventures were chartered, but they were typically small, most never became active, and their total investment and production was almost invisible.[6]

Only a halfhearted effort at price reform was made. The policymakers resolutely refused to make the crucial change from administered to market-determined prices. The Law on the State Enterprise envisaged a "reform" of industrial wholesale prices (to take effect January 1, 1990), and of construction prices and agricultural procurement prices (to take effect January 1, 1991). Prices would be raised significantly to eliminate losses, and to create the conditions for self-financing. These reforms, which both changed the structure of wholesale prices somewhat and raised their general level by a factor of two, got carried out a year late, in January 1991. The Law on the State Enterprise also envisaged introduction of "contract prices," to be negotiated between buyer and seller for a fairly broad range of items. This, together with an innovation authorized later—goods auctions— became a loophole through which enterprises were able to raise prices above the frozen administered prices.

But nothing was done about reforming the highly distorted retail prices of consumer goods. Many food products were priced far below cost, and in 1989 the state spent almost 90 billion rubles—in an economy where gross national product (GNP) was less than 800 billion rubles—to subsidize food prices. The 1987 complex of reform measures spoke of raising food prices at some later date, and in 1990 Prime Minister Nikolai Ryzhkov's government floated a proposal to raise food prices significantly. But it got cold feet in the face of public reaction and backed off. Only in April 1991 did the government at last raise consumer goods prices appreciably, roughly doubling them.

The government made a few gestures toward opening the economy to the world market. Beginning in 1986 various measures began to undercut the foreign trade ministry's monopoly on foreign trade by giving a select set of enterprises and ministries the right to trade on their own. In April 1988 this right was extended to all enterprises. Exporting enterprises were also allowed to keep some of the foreign currency proceeds from exports. But given the huge disparity between the domestic and world-price structures, profit-driven choices would have been disruptive. For any good whose world market price was very high in relation to its ruble price, the attractiveness of export would have undercut supply to domestic customers. To prevent such short-run disruption, the government kept most exports under state orders, and introduced highly differentiated exchange rates to insulate domestic enterprises from world-market-price signals. Unification of the exchange rates and devaluation of the ruble by 70 percent finally came in November 1990. A separate rate for tourist transactions was retained, but this rate was drastically devalued in early 1991. Moscow instituted an experiment in a parallel auction market for hard currency in 1990, but transactions in it were minuscule compared with the traditional distribution of foreign exchange by the central planners.

The process of breaking up the monobank into a two-tier bank system began as part of the 1987 package. A decree of the Central Committee and Council of Ministers directed that the Gosbank's function as banker to enterprises be hived off to several commercial banks, leaving the Gosbank to function as a central bank. At first the five new "specialized banks" were to deal with separate sectors, and enterprises were tied to whatever office had served them before.[7] The lower level of this two-tier system was augmented by newly formed independent "commercial banks." The co-op movement spawned its own banks, and ministries sponsored creation of others to help in financing their investment needs under the new *samofinansirovanie* regime. This independent bank sector grew rapidly, though repeating the co-op experience, it found itself in a battle with the remnants of the old state bank system. At the end of 1990 the private commercial banks were still small relative to the remnants of the old Gosbank system, as measured by credit extended to enterprises (30 billion rubles for the new versus over 300 billion for the old) and deposits of households and enterprises (26 billion rubles versus 570 billion). A new law on banks and on central banking that the USSR passed, and the republics emulated, at the end of 1990 reinforced this reconstitution of the banking system. This law envisaged the reconstitution of the interim specialized banks into units more like the emerging commercial banks. It also envisaged the reformulation of the Gosbank into an all-Union central bank and separate republican national banks. Before the new system actually got established in any stable form, however, it got tangled up in the republic-Union split.

New initiatives in fiscal policy were less an effort at a rational tax system than a desperate effort to raise money. Under the Law on the State Enterprise, state enterprises were to pay some fixed share of their profits to the budget, divided according to a set formula between the all-Union and the republican budgets. Co-ops and joint ventures were each subjected to their own special tax regime. There was a tax on personal incomes, but highly differentiated by type of income—from cooperatives, from work in state enterprises, and from other sources. A proposal, later withdrawn, called for taxing co-op income at a 90 percent rate, with mixed revenue and political motives. In December 1990 the reformers introduced a penalty tax on wage payment increases to try to control the growth of money incomes of the population.[8] As the budget situation became desperate, they introduced a 5 percent sales tax in 1991. All these tax measures were designed largely by the Ministry of Finance, in an effort to raise income for the state budget, with little influence from any reform ideas about the kind of fiscal system appropriate to a market economy. So the evolving tax system continued to violate most of the "canons" laid down by world experience in public finance—it was not predictable, did not treat similarly placed firms equally, and was difficult to administer.

On the other side of the budget ledger, inconsistent application of the principle that enterprises were to be self-financed, failure to curb the demands of the military establishment, and growing responsiveness to populist pressures as politics became more democratic meant rapid growth of budget expenditures. So continuous and accelerating growth brought the budget deficit from 18 billion rubles in 1985 to 90 billion in 1988. By the end of 1989 the budget deficit had cumulated to 320 billion rubles since the beginning of *perestroika*. This deficit was "monetized" by the easy path of giving Treasury IOUs to the Gosbank, with a corresponding increase in the money supply. The state attempted at last in 1990 to replace direct borrowing from the Gosbank by selling bonds to enterprises and the public. But this effort was generally unsuccessful—the interest rate was too low to offset the suspicions of the population, and individuals preferred to hold their assets in cash or in deposits in the savings banks.

There was so little in the way of social protection or antitrust policy that it is not worth mentioning.

Considering the reform effort as a whole through early 1989, one would have to characterize it as a ragbag of measures incoherent in their totality, reflecting weak understanding of what had to be done and an unwillingness to tackle major issues head-on. And the reformers did too little too late in using such central control as they still had to achieve the most important structural shifts—that is, reducing defense and investment as claimants on total output. Even the halfhearted measures they did enact were partially vitiated because of opposition and foot-dragging on the part of the bureaucrats who were supposed to carry them out. Enterprises found that whatever the law might say they had authority to do, the real boss was still their minister. Private entrepreneurs found that whatever the law said, the bureaucrats were still not willing to let them compete with state-sector actors on a "level playing field."

Political Developments/The Shatalin Plan and Its Rejection

It became clear to Gorbachev and his reformist allies that they could not "radicalize" reform without tackling its political dimensions. Progress on economic reform depended on curbing the power of the party, creating a government more responsive to popular wishes, and moving to undercut the bureaucratic power of the military establishment and its ally, the defense-industrial sector. Gorbachev's efforts to reduce the weight and influence of the military and the military-industrial sector had been rather covert in the first several years,[9] but the Mathias Rust affair provided an opportunity to move against the military, which had previously been exempt from the pressures of *perestroika*. A party plenum in October 1988 that reorganized the party's central apparat undercut its power to interfere in economic affairs. And the new Congress of People's Deputies elected in 1989 created for the first time a legislative body that could offer some degree of popular control.

Toward the end of 1989 the push for economic reform was renewed in the new setting. The State Commission on Economic Reform was set up in July 1989 and was soon issuing proposals for reform. In 1989 Leonid Abalkin, the head of the commission, presented a more or less coherent program to a large body of officials and industrial managers, but their reaction was extremely negative. The second session of the Congress of People's Deputies, in December 1989, directed Ryzhkov to work out a government program, and he presented the main lines of a reform proposal to the Supreme Soviet in May 1990. Unfortunately, that program included a proposal to raise consumer goods prices, an idea that engendered so much opposition the government had to back down, leaving its reform program dead in the water. While the government was stalemated, several other initiatives were moving forward. The economist E. G. Yasin proposed a "400-days program." Abel Aganbegian, one of Gorbachev's economic advisers, was simultaneously working on an alternative program. At the beginning of summer 1990 Boris Yeltsin and Gorbachev agreed to launch a new effort at designing a reform plan under a joint working group led by the radical reform economist Stanislav Shatalin; the group developed the "500-days program," which it sent to the government at the end of that summer.

With the proclamation of the Shatalin plan it looked as if economic reform might start in earnest. The 500-days program was the first serious attempt to put forward a comprehensive set of measures covering the whole agenda. It was a serious and professional effort, distinguished by an effort to quantify what might happen to some major economic magnitudes, such as employment and the price level, though the group received far less than full cooperation from the government in getting the data required for its calculations. Very importantly, the program contained a timetable. The Shatalin program was far from a perfect blueprint, and an especially serious problem was the political premises on which it was built. It was intentionally elaborated in cooperation with representatives from the republics to gain their support. At that point separatist feeling had already progressed so far that not trying to co-opt the republics in the design of a reform would have been unrealistic. But acceding to demands for republic autonomy would put the central government at the mercy of the republics in fiscal affairs, posing a clear threat to the Union. That was no doubt one reason the program was ultimately unacceptable to Gorbachev. Though Gorbachev first endorsed it and recommended it to the Supreme Soviet, he then backed off and asked Aganbegian to meld it and the old government plan into a compromise version to become the official reform plan. Compared with the 500-days plan, this official plan was vague on action, omitting timetables and removing much of the concreteness that made the Shatalin proposal an action plan.

Rejection of the Shatalin plan was a crucial turning point, at which Gorbachev veered sharply to the right. He dumped Ryzhkov and the old government, appointing a new prime minister—Valentin Pavlov—who formed a government in which the hand of conservatives was greatly strengthened. Gorbachev received approval from the Supreme Soviet to accelerate reform by taking initiative through presidential decrees. The new government put up a brave pretense that it would really go ahead with reform; indeed, it issued numerous decrees, passed laws, formed a property agency to carry out privatization, raised consumer goods prices in April 1991, and so on. But in effect, the rightward turn at the end of summer 1990 marked the end of focused and sustained push for reform. The period from October 1990 until the coup at the end of August 1991 was wasted in a slow shuffle of pretense, reaction, incompetence, and misguided policies. The year marked a slide into economic chaos, as all the trends mentioned above accelerated and deepened. The central disaster was the failure of the supposed understanding reached at the end of 1990 concerning the split of tax revenue between the all-Union and the republican budgets. In the first half of 1991 the republics were to hand over to the Union budget 42 billion rubles, but actually paid only 11 billion. Though a deficit of 27 billion rubles was planned, this revenue failure, along with increases in various expenditures to offset price rises, was pushing the deficit in the 1991 central government budget toward 200 billion rubles when the farce ended at the end of November 1991.[10] These deficits, paralleled by similar deficits in the republican budgets, were covered by printing money, and the monetary overhang ballooned. The only effort to deal with the overhang, already serious enough, was Pavlov's thoroughly stupid currency conversion, in spring 1991, which resulted in virtually no decrease in the amount of money outstanding, but caused tremendous dissatisfaction and loss of confidence. Output fell in 1991 in all sectors.[11] In a situation where prices were controlled in varying degrees, the rapid growth in the money supply meant repressed inflation, disappearance of goods from normal channels, and disparities between black-market and official prices. When the government could no longer hold the line on prices, open inflation took off. Excess demand inevitably spilled over into the foreign balance. Falling output hit the USSR's major export (oil),[12] the government greatly increased foreign borrowing, and it acquired a foreign debt burden whose interest rates and repayments it could not handle with its hard currency earnings. To cope with the problem, the USSR had to deplete its gold reserves. Investment fell, and though many of the abandoned projects were no loss, in some sectors—most importantly, the energy sector—the investment crunch planted the seeds of further decline in output. Since energy is the most important commodity the Soviet economy can export for hard currency, the sharp decline in output led to a loss of exports and worsening of the balance-of-payments crunch.

Agriculture was a special disappointment. Many outside observers thought on the basis of Chinese experience that this would be an easy sector to work on. It is less entangled with the rest of the economy than most industrial sectors are, so can be reformed independently. The land is there, and if the farmers can be induced to plant the seed, feed the pigs, tend and dig the potatoes, the output response can be fairly quick. The sector cannot operate without fuel and spare parts for its machinery, but interference with some of the other industrial inputs—fertilizer, electricity, and so forth—is less disruptive. So the expectation is that if agriculture is cut loose to operate without bureaucratic interference, and in response to price incentives, it will respond quickly. One cannot say that the Soviet government set out vigorously to reform agriculture, but the response to what measures it did take was surprisingly weak. One of the unexpected outcomes was the virtual lack of a response to a special program of hard currency payments for extra output beyond the levels procured earlier. The government offered collective farms hard currency for output increases on the rationale that rather than buying extra agricultural goods abroad, it might get them cheaper by offering hard currency to the USSR's own collective farmers. Agriculture illustrates perfectly the stultifying effect of remnants of the old system. Getting land out of the collective, acquiring inputs and selling the product outside collective farm channels, and surviving the envy and enmity of former associates and officials are indeed daunting tasks for the would-be private farmer. It is very difficult for independent producers to bypass the transport, marketing, storage, and processing systems that get agricultural output to its customers, if the latter remain in the control of the old bureaucracies. And there is a very high threshold of distrust to be surmounted, impossible to overcome by mere promises, requiring a long period of stable policy.

In summing up the precoup period, there are a few positive developments to report. The existence of an entrepreneurial spirit was clear. The cooperative movement elicited an impressive rush of capitalist energy until it was crippled by the reaction of the old system. Some construction co-ops the author visited in the Komi SSR differed from their state counterparts as night from day. Entrepreneurial figures and organizations like Sviatoslav Fedorov and his Eye Microsurgery MNTK or the Scientific Instruments firm Nauchnye Pribory, now autonomous from the Academy of Sciences, operate quite differently from the old state organizations.[13] This vigor is equally evident in the burgeoning commodity exchanges, the new commercial banks, and a whole new science services sector that grew up to meet needs the clay-footed state organizations could not handle, as in computer applications. A major defect of the reform effort so far is that the government seems to have done little to try to explain to the population the rationale for moving to a market economy, and what the process would involve. Acceptance and understanding of market ideas among the general public is still not widespread, but we need not worry about a leavening of entrepreneurial types to take advantage of market opportunities when they appear.

Territorial Separatism
While Gorbachev moved rightward, political developments were enhancing local power, increasing its challenge to the center.

Legitimate or semilegitimate governments came into being at lower levels with mandates, sometimes ambiguous, to move forward on economic reform. These new forces had a strong separatist or localist tinge, sometimes ethnic in origin, but not always. Good patriotic Russian citizens in the Far East, in Sakhalin, in the Komi SSR, wanted to be free of central control that held them back from reforming the economy.

The attitude and actions of these governments with respect to economic reform were mixed. In the Baltic nations autonomy and accountable government were intimately tied with serious reform intentions. Boris Yeltsin's election as chairman of the Supreme Soviet of the RSFSR posed a challenge to Gorbachev that was partly personal but also decidedly proreform. Yeltsin won on a platform of berating the foot-draggers in the Kremlin, and promising action on reform to improve economic performance. His acquisition of the RSFSR power base created a locus from which the economic reformers could challenge central obstructionism. The RSFSR parliament was less progressive than Yeltsin, but its legislative acts were probably on the whole a considerable step forward, as in the laws it passed on land, property, privatization, banking, entrepreneurship, and entrepreneurial activity.[14] Tatarstan declined to hold an election for RSFSR president, but did hold one for a Tatarstan president, whose program has been both separatist and progressive in economic terms. In other areas an increase in regional autonomy sometimes left the forces of reaction and foot-dragging undiminished, or even strengthened. This was especially true in Central Asia—the Uzbek government, for example, is really a holdover communist government. Conservatives have often survived by catering to the more extreme nationalist forces, sometimes by retreading themselves as economic reformers.

These separatist tendencies and disputes interfered both with the continued functioning of the economy and with concentrating on economic reform. Contradictory legislation at the level of the republic often undercut the laws that the center passed. This was especially important in financial matters. The RSFSR simply annulled for operation on its territory some of the tax provisions worked out at the center. There was a "bank war" as laws and directives from new republican central banks overrode the USSR Gosbank's directives. Republican structures began to simply assume autonomy and ignore controls from Moscow. For example, the RSFSR Ministry of Communications declared that it would act on its own on such questions as whether to finance a proposed satellite switching system, join Intelsat, and form joint ventures with foreign firms.

Localist inclinations exacerbated supply crises as republics and regions tried to solve shortages by keeping local supplies for use at home. For consumer goods this meant actions like restricting sales in Moscow to residents.[15] In the producer goods domain local authorities increasingly intervened to prevent local firms from supplying outsiders. That stimulated a reversion to barter, as warring jurisdictions engaged in bargaining to get something in return for any goods going out of their region. A typical example was a Krasnoyarsk steel producer that could not get refractories from its old suppliers in Lithuania. The director gathered information on all shipments from the region to Lithuania and pressured the Krasnoyarsk government to tell the Lithuanians that if the refractories were not supplied, all shipments from Krasnoyarsk would be cut off.[16]

But this war of laws and contest over authority is the kind of conflict in which the rules are unclear, and neither side could prevail unequivocally. If the localist efforts of cities, oblasts, and republics undercut the ability of the old system to keep production going, the continuing power of the center kept local bodies from moving much ahead of the central foot-draggers on reform. On a visit to Komi SSR in winter 1990, the author found impressive local initiative, readiness to move ahead with privatization, and opening to the world economy, but the ministries and other authorities in Moscow blocked all its proposals.[17]

The Coup and Its Aftermath

The coup in August 1991 brought to a decisive end the sorry spectacle of rightist reaction. It failed as a last-ditch effort by the *nomenklatura* to stop the dissolution of the Union, to protect the privileged position of the military-industrial sector, and to hold together an all-Union government that could continue in the old centralist tradition. Its failure ended any effort to keep the Baltic states in the Union, and created the conditions that would ultimately lead to the secession of the rest, and to the disintegration of the Union. It destroyed the party as an organized national institution. The setback to conservatives was especially true at the all-Union level, where the government fell; all the ministries were decapitated; and a process of conversion of state firms to joint stock companies, corporations, concerns, and associations accelerated. At lower levels the defeat of the old elites was less thorough, and differed across jurisdictions, and many of the old *nomenklatura* stayed in position, equivocating on their relation to the coup, and doing some fancy footwork to take advantage of the new forms.

In short, the coup created conditions under which reform could be tackled on the republic level. During the remaining part of 1991 much of that republican initiative was spent in efforts to finish off dissolution of the Union and transfer sovereign power to the republics. But in addition to diverting attention from reform, it actively helped create the final fiscal crisis. Contributions from the republics to the Union budget virtually ceased after the coup, leaving the all-Union budget dependent on the printing press as the sole source of finance.

Reform Prospects after the Coup

As regards economic reform, the central event since the second coup is that Russia under the leadership of Yeltsin has moved vigorously toward radical reform. If until the fall of the all-Union government reform had been a joke—a "big nothing," in contrast to Poland's "big bang," as one commentator put it—the situation is now drastic enough that radical reform can no longer be put off. The real game, to be played for keeps, has begun. As Yeltsin said in his speech on October 28, 1991, to the RSFSR Congress of People's Deputies, "The period of progress by small steps is over. The minefield hampering reforms has been cleared. A large-scale reformist breakthrough is needed." He appointed a new cabinet of strongly determined reformers who have freed prices to be set by supply and demand, announced plans for large-scale privatization, and let the currency become de facto semiconvertible. Yeltsin's mandate for radical reform was no doubt extended without a full appreciation of what is implied, and could be revoked. After the first several months of the program his popularity fell sharply, and he has at times wavered on standing foursquare behind the reform program in its original form. But as of fall 1992 his government was still unevenly pursuing radical reform, analogous to the Polish model of "shock therapy," and Yeltsin's actions were forcing the other republics to move ahead as well.

The shape and speed of reform will increasingly diverge among the republics. The basic agenda for the transition to a market economy is more or less standard, and the reform programs of all the republics start off with a core of common features, since the various republics' laws on property, privatization, land, banks, taxation, and social protection largely grow out of laws originally enacted at the Union level.[18] In the early stages each has found its course conditioned by the constraints of an untangling process that is not yet complete. The most important of these is the commitment, at the start, to a common currency area. But there are also lingering elements of jointness in the form of external debts and obligations, responsibility for the internal national debt, and incomplete separation of the armed forces. Yet the untangling process is proceeding apace. If the first coup opened the way to dismantling much of the central structure, the second coup made it possible to get rid of most of the rest.[19] The republics are each creating their own governmental and economic policy structures. Most had already set up some kind of military organization, and most had a ministry of planning and forecasting. Numerous functions were already organized on Union-republic basis—for example, education, health, telecommunications—so organizational bodies were already in place to oversee or operate these branches. The republican central banks are behaving increasingly autonomously, and that process will be complete for individual republics when they shift to their own currency.

As the republics begin to turn national borders into economic frontiers, they will more and more be able to follow independent courses, making their own choices on issues of price policy, conversion of state property, monetary policy, and controlling interrepublic flows of goods and resources. It would be impossible to attempt here a point-by-point analysis and comparison of fifteen sets of legislation, fifteen declarative programs, and fifteen choreographies of the reform ballet. That is all the more so since, as of fall 1992, most of the programs were only beginning to be put into effect, and are almost certain to be modified significantly in execution.

In this process the RSFSR will naturally dominate our interest, because it is the largest of the republics, and because it has assumed the role of locomotive in accelerating the pace of reform, to some degree forcing others to follow suit. So let us take it as the most salient case for assessing how reform is going. We can then discuss separately the interdependence/untangling problem, speculate as to differential longer-term prospects for individual republics, and offer some reflections on how the Soviet case differs from the East European one.

The Yeltsin Reform Program

Yeltsin's intentions, first laid out in a speech in October 1991, are for something close to shock therapy, even if that speech left the details vague.[20] Yeltsin was elected president, but has chosen to be his own prime minister, putting his prestige behind the reform. He reconstituted his government, filling it with ministers generally young and committed to radical reform.[21] The most important step has been to abandon price control. Under the label of "liberalization" nearly all prices—retail prices on consumer goods, wholesale prices for producer goods, procurement prices for agriculture—were decontrolled, to be determined by supply and demand. The exceptions were a short list of producer goods (most importantly, energy products, transport services, and communications) and a more extensive list of consumer goods,[22] for which increases are to be limited (in most cases) to a threefold-to-fivefold increase.[23] This price liberalization contains twin dangers, like most hybrid approaches. Freeing most prices opens the possibility of rapid inflation if monetary expansion continues and no strong supply response ensues. But maintaining caps on important categories of goods means production and allocation controls and substantial subsidies will have to continue and perhaps be extended. A second stage of price liberalization, later in 1992, reduced controls further, notably on many energy commodities.

The process of autonomizing enterprises and privatizing ownership was already started in the RSFSR, raising all the standard choices and disputes we know from experience elsewhere. The first step is "corporatization." The reformers are setting up new investment funds to take title to the divested property and to exercise social stewardship as property is transferred to private owners. These funds will also have the longer-run task of making a market in shares. On the social justice issue the plan is to transfer gratis to citizens some ownership claims against state property. According to the law passed in the RSFSR in 1991, each person was to receive 5,000 rubles spendable only for acquiring property being privatized. But this provision was suspended for 1992, to be replaced by a giveaway of 25 percent (in some cases only 10 percent) of a privatized enterprise to its current employees. The pace of privatization is being accelerated over earlier plans. Evgenii Saburov, the economic policy leader in Yeltsin's original RSFSR cabinet, had announced an intention to sell off 200 medium-size and small enterprises. Yeltsin stated that within three months, the state could sell off 50 percent of all medium-size and small enterprises—that is, about 10,000 enterprises. But guidelines for activity in 1992, promulgated in early January 1991, shifted tactics, setting as the target *obligatory* privatization of *all* enterprises in trade, public dining, services, and construction; all enterprises servicing agriculture, food processing, and textiles; and all loss-making enterprises. The reformers hope they can sell assets valued at 92 billion rubles, basically by auction. The focus on these sectors indicates sensible priorities, but privatizing the core of the state sector will take longer and be more complicated. As in all the old centrally planned economies, production in the RSFSR is highly concentrated in very large and unwieldy enterprises, many of which are monopolies in their line of production. Devising plans to turn them into privately owned corporations compatible with the competitive and entrepreneurial goals of marketization raises much more complicated issues. The way the law was originally set up, it is likely that a strong bias will favor the old *nomenklatura*, which in any case has already stolen a march on the reformers in getting control over some key large enterprises. The reformers are aware of the problem, and the privatization law stipulates a review of all property that has gone through "spontaneous privatization," renationalizing it where some privileged insider dealing seems to have occurred. But carrying out that task seems beyond their administrative capacities, as indeed has been the case in other countries' reform experience.[24]

The other, probably more important component of privatization is the creation of conditions for the emergence of new firms. The legislative base for that has been put in place in the form of a law on small enterprises and the RSFSR Law on Entrepreneurship, which went beyond the all-Union legislation; but this area seems to be receiving little emphasis in the current drive.

We do not know enough yet to judge whether the government has a workable stabilization plan. The RSFSR took over the old USSR Ministry of Finance and the Gosbank, which controls the printing of money and the supply of bank notes. In the hybrid system operating in 1992, each republic had its own national bank, but as long as a common currency area using the ruble survives, paper money is the "high-powered money" constituting the reserve base, and the Gosbank can stop the growth of the money supply by not printing more rubles. But it can do that only if it is not called on to finance the RSFSR budget deficit.[25] The RSFSR started out without a budget for 1992, substituting a first-quarter total for planned outlays nearly balanced on the basis of very shaky projections of revenue. To satisfy the International Monetary Fund (IMF), the government has greatly cut all kinds of expenditures, especially military procurement,[26] R&D, investment, subsidies, and expenditures for social protection. In a memorandum to the IMF it has promised a still stronger austerity program for the rest of 1992, pledging to turn a deficit of 14 percent of GNP in the first quarter to one of 1 percent of GNP for the rest of the year.[27]

This goal was not, however, achieved. Success in keeping to planned expenditure levels depends on the rate of inflation and of unemployment.[28] There were strong pressures for expenditure increases both for subsidies and for compensation to offset the consumer goods price increase and to finance the safety net measures as unemployment rises. The revenue side is especially problematical. The RSFSR fiscal system is now based on four major taxes—an enterprise income tax (with high rates and some "excessive profits" features), a personal income tax (at a moderate rate of 10–12 percent with some progressivity), an excise tax on some consumer goods, and a value-added tax. The first two were more or less inherited from the preindependence period, but had emerged in RSFSR versions. The value-added tax is new, and central to the stabilization effort. It has a high rate—22 percent for certain kinds of activity, 28 percent on others—and was intended to yield half again as much as the other three taken together.[29] As to whether these revenue projections can ever be realistic, both we and the RSFSR Ministry of Finance still remain in the dark. The value-added tax was already at one point reduced or eliminated for certain categories of goods and institutions under political pressure, but then increased again. The earlier Soviet version of the "Balcerowicz razor," which heavily penalized wage increases, is no longer in place to serve as a wage stabilization policy (one of the announced principles of the Yeltsin reform is that there are to be no caps on earnings), but its reintroduction is being proposed.

On opening to world markets, the Gaidar team wants a quick shift to convertibility. The old system of centralizing 40 percent of all foreign exchange earned has continued in effect, but the government is using some of it to intervene in an emergent free market to make the ruble appreciate, a maneuver that has been only partially successful. Real convertibility, however, with all the goodies that are supposed to go with it, can come only with the emergence of a robust market economy, and I take less seriously than others do the convertibility element of the program.

Overall, if the reform intentions are fulfilled, 1992 will see severe inflation, a sharp decline in output, and rapid growth in unemployment. So reforms must include some provision for "social protection." How that will work is unclear as yet, but experience suggests that the social protection package either will be inadequately financed to compensate for unemployment and inflation, increasing hardship, and the danger of a political backlash, or will be so expensive as to make stabilization that much less likely. In the summer of 1992 a sharp expansion of the money supply took place to provide liquidity to firms hard pressed by falling demand and rising costs. Thus in 1992 the projected stability was emphatically not achieved.

Interregional Interactions

A number of legacies left from the old Union structure, such as the military establishment, foreign treaty obligations (arms control) and economic obligations (debt liabilities), and membership in the institutions of the world community, are not easily divisible or sloughed off. We have seen a somewhat frightening demonstration of that proposition in the military case, discussion of which here would take us too far afield. In the economic domain some minimal coordination of the pace at which reform proceeds is essential. For example, if prices are freed at different times in different republics, while there is still a common currency, complicated demand spillovers between members with different degrees of price liberalization could occur. Whether the new commonwealth can accommodate the pressures of coordinating reform is a big question, the most likely answer being that it cannot. If the republics are really sovereign, and follow the logic of the position that they can reform only with full freedom to follow independent economic policies, they are likely to use the instruments that go along with economic sovereignty in a way that will be very disruptive and engender conflict. The earlier era left a terrible legacy of suspicion. Each republic and region has the idea that the others were exploiting it. In announcing his reform program, Yeltsin asserted that the RSFSR subsidized the other republics to the extent of 30 billion rubles per year, and that this subsidy would have to be eliminated in the reconstructed relations of the RSFSR with the other republics. Other republics make similar counterclaims, but all of them are suspect. This legacy of suspicion is bound to lead to efforts to use the levers of economic policy in a way to improve each republic's relative position. Once the republic authorities get the degree of control sovereign states have over these new instruments—such as restricting goods flows across republic borders, controlling population flows and residence, regulating how firms or banks chartered elsewhere can operate in their territory, and so on—they are certain to begin to try to engage in the kinds of beggar-thy-neighbor approaches that lead to collapse through a process of mutual retaliation.

The principle of a common currency area agreed to at the establishment of the commonwealth is being abandoned. Ukrainians have been committed to a separate currency for some time. The Commonwealth agreement supposedly committed the three participants to continue using the ruble, but President Leonid Kravchuk of Ukraine indicated immediately following that agreement that Ukraine's plans to introduce its own currency were unchanged. The Baltic states were already on that course, and nearly all republics have now announced such plans. Estonia has replaced the ruble with its own currency—the crown. The Russians fear that the existing hoards of money will be used to rob them. That could be a real problem, to the extent that the other republics issue new currency or proxy currencies in the form of coupons, as Belarus and Ukraine have already done, without a corresponding withdrawal of rubles. To avert such an outcome, the RSFSR seriously contemplated replacement of old rubles with a new overprinted RSFSR version. It may well be that breakdown into separate currency areas is a better outcome than the alternative of trying to restrict interrepublic goods flows by administrative controls. The foreign exchange mechanism for settling accounts will no doubt be clumsy, but surely less of an obstacle to trade than administered barter exchanges.[30]

Another interdependence difficult to untangle is found in environmental problems, many of which cut across the new republican borders. It is interesting that in the original signing of the Commonwealth agreement, the three presidents declared that Chernobyl is a legacy of the whole nation, and that the Ukrainians should not be left to deal with it alone. One wonders how long that spirit of assistance will hold up.

While some of the old center/local suspicion and struggle will be converted into international conflict among the new sovereign states, some will remain as a center/local conflict within national formations. The RSFSR, for instance, contains many territories now organized as ethnic subunits that want economic sovereignty. Other regions, not ethnically differentiated, also want more autonomy. Examples are the special regimes Moscow, St. Petersburg, and Kaliningrad oblast want; the desire of the Far East and Sakhalin to reorient themselves to the Pacific Rim; and the independence that Tatarstan has claimed for itself. The independence urge cannot well be satisfied in these cases by separation, but will have to be met by some kind of "fiscal federalism." The goal of fiscal federalism is to divide public-sector functions (provision of public goods, income redistribution, and economic stabilization or stimulation via fiscal policy) among different levels of government according to a principle of accommodating differential tastes and income levels, while avoiding external spillovers. For instance, some jurisdiction might feel it could afford an above-average level of public amenity in a function like education or provision of public health, and would burden itself with taxes that exceed the national average to do so. Or it might conclude it would want a more liberal privatization program, or one with different income and wealth distribution characteristics than the rest of the nation. The problem of spillovers is that the smaller the jurisdiction, the more difficult it is to impose a distinctive regime, or to depart from the standard taxing and spending norms, since the objects of taxation and beneficiaries of favorable treatment are mobile. A tax levied in Voronezh on private business firms will drive them to other jurisdictions to the extent they are mobile. It would be much harder for a firm to evade a similar tax levied by the Russian government. This is far too big an area to dig into extensively here; the main point is that the search for fiscal federalism is "a continuation of the separatist war by other means," visible especially in Russia, but elsewhere as well. More-over, it is often fired by the same ethnic passions as led to the disintegration of the empire into independent republics.

One problem in economic reform is balancing public- and private-sector functions, and differences in the treatment of this issue will have consequences for regional outcomes. One inter-esting case is possible differential potentials for technical pro-gress. In the public/private split mentioned in the introduction, R&D needs differentiated treatment. The commercial motives of firms operating according to the profit criterion in the market economy should support and guide the applied end, but public support should still go to basic science and to training. As 1991 came to a close, the prospects of support for the old Soviet R&D establishment looked bad. The center, now Russia, is determined to cut funding of science, especially since the whole enterprise was so topheavy with military work (maybe 50 percent of all R&D was military). As public support falls and institutes lose budget support, many need to find customers in the private sector. But commercial firms do not yet have the vision or the understand-ing that will make them support enough R&D. Everywhere in the former Soviet Union, these will be hard times for scientists, and there will be a large brain drain.

The opportunity for particular republics or regions to gather this abundant resource for investment in the future is great. Some of them think they could become analogues of Silicon Valley. Officials in Kaliningrad oblast, which had a lot of military R&D activity, would like to convert it to civilian use, and to create a grand "technopark." Armenia is an example of a republic that has a strong R&D base, and might aspire to some-thing similar. But such hopes are probably illusory. The smaller the jurisdiction, the less likely it will benefit in proportion to its spending on R&D, because of the public-good character of R&D. A recent visit to Estonia suggests to me a possible way out. The Estonian reformers know their R&D effort is hypertrophied, and that they cannot support it on the old scale in their new circumstances. So they invited the Swedish Academy of Sciences to come in and evaluate where their strengths are, with an eye to pruning and specializing accordingly.

Differences from Eastern Europe

The reader will note numerous differences between the USSR case as described in this essay and that of Eastern Europe, covered in the chapters by Paul Marer and Richard Portes. I have already commented on some of these in passing, but it will be useful to conclude with a few that merit special emphasis.

First, size makes a difference. The economy of the old Soviet Union was much bigger than any of the East European economies, and in most important aggregates it surpassed them taken together. Hence, many of the reform-generated magnitudes policymakers have to cope with are larger. The number of people unemployed, the scale of foreign investment needed, whether World Bank loans for infrastructure or private oil company investment to modernize exploration and drilling technology, the number who lose their jobs as a result of the trade shocks, the size of the possible "brain drain" or general emigration—all are frighteningly bigger. These magnitudes are important in assessing the ability of the outside world to speed the reform and ease its trauma, and are relevant to how fast the domestic reformers ought to proceed.

A useful comparison is with the East German transition, which represents the ultimate form of shock therapy. That country was exposed overnight to the standards of the outside world, revealing that much of its capital was worthless, that most of its output could not meet the test of market competition with the West, and that it lacked the worker habits and managerial skills to compete or to respond effectively to the shock. A safety net was available in this case in the form of West German resources— unemployment compensation, investment to modernize factories, managerial expertise to restructure and restart old firms, and an established legal and institutional infrastructure that could be adopted immediately. That infrastructure included a valuable policy tradition of sober monetary and fiscal policy. In terms of general economic weight, as measured by GNP, the West German source was nine times as big as the East German sink. But even so, the costs of transition are turning out to be a huge resource drain, and assimilation to the standards of the West German economy a more drawn-out process than most thought it was going to be. The needs of individual East European countries are of the same general magnitude, but these countries are unlikely to find a similar outside source. The relevant magnitudes in the reform of the Soviet Union make this kind of transfer from the outside unthinkable. To take only one small component of the total resource need, modernizing the East German telephone system has already cost $37 billion. Against that standard, one wonders how much impact the $20–$30 billion per year considered the upper limit of feasibility for Western aid to the Soviet successor states could possibly have.

One corollary of this view is that there may be a case for slowing the structural adjustments of the former Soviet Union's transition. It may make sense to insulate the reforming economies of the old USSR from world market pressures to some degree, since the West cannot offer them a comparable adjustment cushion. It will be better for the Russians to continue producing vehicles (trucks, autos, commercial jetliners, tractors) that do not meet world standards for quality, emissions control, or fuel economy than to equip Aeroflot with Airbus aircraft, buy Komatsu bulldozers, close domestic producers down, put workers on the dole, or sell off the auto and aircraft factories to foreigners for their scrap value. The same case might be made *mutatis mutandis* for shoes, television sets, chemicals, and many other goods.

Size considerations, moreover, certainly contribute to the rationale for imperial dissolution, and mean that it will bring stronger gains and smaller disadvantages than similar breakups in smaller countries, like Czechoslovakia. Reform can probably occur more effectively with some regional variation. Even as independent open economies, the reformed former Soviet economies will no doubt benefit from preferential ties with other blocs, and in contrast to East European gravitation toward the European Community, the reaction of the Soviet successor states is likely to be more complex. Ukraine, Belarus, and the Baltic countries may follow the East European lead, but the Central

Asian republics may find that they will benefit by retaining close ties to Russia. Alternatively, efforts are already afoot to integrate the "southern" republics into some kind of trade bloc around a Black Sea focus, or a bloc focused on Turkey.

Second, the former Soviet republics have a distinctive difficulty in the scale of their military conversion problem. Military expenditures represented a much greater share of GNP in the Soviet Union than in any of the other socialist economies (12–14 percent versus 4–6 percent). The number of workers who will be displaced in the military-industrial sector is correspondingly large, and they are concentrated in ways that will make them a powerful political force. The Soviet military-oriented R&D establishment was both much larger and more sophisticated than its counterparts in Eastern Europe, posing tricky problems of proliferation as it disintegrates. The issue of conversion is too big a subject to deal with in a short paper, but a few points are clear.[31] First, in a conscript army much of the manpower can be absorbed—it will just drift back to the collective farm. This is less true for the officers and more technical types—the older ones can be pensioned off, the younger ones are perfect candidates for some kind of GI bill, and it is strange that this analogy with U.S. experience is scarcely ever mentioned. World experience tells us that conversion of defense plants is inherently difficult and only occasionally successful. Cutting procurement is one of the big structural shocks mentioned above, akin to exposure to world market standards. Nevertheless, there seems little rationale for cushioning the shock of reducing military production. Shoe factories should be kept in operation because shoes are relevant to the output pie it is important to maximize; armaments are not. Russian energy policymakers want to limit imports of equipment by foreign investors in oil production on the ground that most of the equipment needed could be supplied domestically by converting military plants. That kind of indirect protection may make sense, but overall, the slimmer the crutch offered to the enterprises of the military-industrial complex, the more likely they are to make an effort to convert. Effort alone is not enough, of course, as suggested by the interesting case of an

R&D organization serving arms production that developed and sought to sell emissions-control technologies to Russian internal combustion engine manufacturers. It mounted a dog and pony show with experts and prototypes, and toured the country trying to interest clients, but got a very cold response. Russian firms would much prefer to deal with established leading firms in the West. Reading the Soviet press, one can compile a voluminous case book documenting efforts at conversion, varying from ingenious and promising to harebrained and feckless. But it is very difficult to form any general quantitative assessment as to what is feasible and likely on the spectrum between successful conversion and deadweight loss from abandoning these skills and capacities.

Conversion has an interesting connection to the imperial untangling problem. The Soviet defense industry was integrated on a national basis. Under separatism, the problem of shrinking the total is compounded with moving toward coherent national industrial structures. The last step of the Union government was to try to break up the defense-industrial ministries along territorial lines. Minobshchemash (the "spacecraft and payload ministry") was split up into Ukrainian, Russian, and Kazakh corporations. Much the same happened with other defense-industrial ministries. But the resulting territorial collections have no coherence. The Ukrainian defense minister noted that Ukraine produced warheads, but no individual arms. Kazakh officials claim that since Baikonur is on Kazakh territory, they should control it. But Baikonur is not just a launch facility whose services can be sold in a simple market interaction. It carries on a great deal of other activity, highly integrated with plants elsewhere in the former Soviet Union. As the republics try to recreate military-industrial complexes within their own borders to serve new national security goals, they will lose the gains that can come from arms commonality trade and specialization, as important in military industry as in any kind of production.

Finally, the question often comes up about possible differences between the Soviet successor states and the East European countries regarding public willingness to accept the declines in consumption and the rise in inequality that come with the transition, its degree of political sophistication and commitment to modern political processes and democratic values, versus susceptibility to demagogic and antidemocratic messages. This whole section seems to be about "questions too big to answer," and this is certainly one. But so far, the Russians have shown remarkable ability to detect and reject demagogic and antidemocratic values.

Prospects for Reform, Recovery, and Resumption of Growth

After all these pages the reader has some right to ask for an answer to the big question: Is reform going to work at all? Will the pioneer case, Russia, soon achieve a turnaround in inflation, recession, unemployment, productivity, and international solvency? Will the currently resolute reformers be able to stay the course? If Gaidar's shock therapy does not work, will the reformers be so pigheaded that the reform ends in revolution? Or will popular reaction be so great that the reform gets aborted, and the economy reverts to stagnation? Looking across the breadth of the old USSR, will the rest of the fifteen new nations succeed in mounting and sustaining effective reform programs? There is a kind of three-variable problem here, in which a successful outcome depends on what we might characterize as the three R's—reform, recovery from the disruption of transition, and resumption of growth to continue the historical effort to catch up with the modern nations of the world. We cannot solve this equation for all fifteen cases, but a brief characterization of differences among the republics on these dimensions may be useful.

We have focused on Russia because it is by far the most weighty of the successor states. But it is also the republic that has gone furthest in terms of a determined reform program. Except for the Baltic countries, all the others have been less radical and resolute in putting in place and executing reform. In Russia it seems inevitable that some backsliding à la Poland will occur as the pain of the adjustment mounts. I am willing to venture an optimistic forecast of consistent forward movement, but I temper that with a prediction that recovery and resumption of growth will take not a year or two but more like a decade.

Supposing the others follow on delayed timetables, will they eventually come through in the same way? Even though we cannot discuss each case separately, it is instructive to suggest that the economic prospects for the different republics will vary significantly. Separation, independent efforts at reform, and differentiation of economic policy will have important consequences for potential growth. Economic transformation will in general create winners and losers, and one dimension of that distinction will be among republics and regions. Even under the old system, despite efforts to even out income levels within the USSR, there was great unevenness in development. Today, the regional and republic leaderships think that by becoming sovereign, they will be able to control their own economic fate and grow rapidly. But I think they differ significantly in their ability to take advantage of independence.

First, the separation of republics creates a "trade shock" as the imposition of national frontiers and clumsy international trade mechanisms sever traditional trade links.[32] The smaller the republic, the greater this cost will be. A given absolute drop in some trade flow represents for the smaller partner a bigger share of the total supply or demand, and hence a bigger disruption.

Moreover, under the old system there were hefty net surpluses and deficits in the current accounts of republics with the rest of the USSR, which can be interpreted as the "real" expression of income transfers (subsidies) or investment flows. As mentioned earlier, it is difficult to evaluate the claims regarding who was subsidizing whom, but most observers agree that the amounts of these net resource transfers were considerable. The direction of the flow is almost exclusively from the RSFSR to the other republics. Valued at world market prices, these outflows are considerably larger than they appeared in the old planned economy price system. Whereas between market economies this investment would be recorded as a debt of the recipient, this was not the case here. As the Union breaks up, there are demands to get any current account imbalances acknowledged, to reach some agreement as to whether they can be continued, and, if so, to get them formalized as claims on capital account, or as agreed-to subsidies. If a region with current-account surpluses—for example, Russia—is not willing to support net exports by lending or transfers, there will have to be balance on current account, and there will be an income reduction in the recipient republic, reducing its potential either for consumption or for growth-inducing investment. Whether the surplus republic will gain what the others lose depends on whether it is able to realize the former exports either in some domestic use or as exports elsewhere.

On both these counts all the republics other than Russia are likely to pay a differentially burdensome price for separation.

Many of the newly independent republics have not yet gone through the demographic transition—for example, those of Central Asia, Armenia, and Azerbaijan. Kazakhstan is intermediate on this score. These states have high birthrates, and though their young populations give them low crude death rates, their high infant mortality makes them vulnerable to a population explosion, one of the standard obstacles to a development takeoff.

The prospects for growth are improved if a country has a rich endowment, are hurt if it does not. With the exception of the Baltic republics, the new republics are comparatively poor in material wealth. The productive fixed capital per member of the work force is lower than the old all-Union average in Armenia, Azerbaijan, Georgia, Moldova and Tajikistan, Kirghiztan, and Uzbekistan in Central Asia; Turkmenistan and Kazakhstan look better because of their stocks of expensive extractive industry capital. Ukraine is appreciably less well-off than Russia by this indicator. The poor republics are also poor in total capital per member of the population. The Baltics are advantaged in both measures, but not much above the RSFSR.

Cultural variables are important in the development formula, for both entrepreneurial activity and labor discipline. The general level of education is important, as is the availability of scientific and technical manpower to undergird technical progress. In terms of the share of the population with higher education, the poor republics are not so bad off, except for Moldova. In the more specific measure of scientific workers per 1,000 persons employed, the pattern is the usual one, with all Central Asia,

Georgia, Azerbaijan, and Moldova low (Armenia matches Russia). Most of the southern tier is not heavily industrialized or urbanized, and on the whole that is probably a bad sign for future development. Taking Russia as the norm, only Estonia has a lower ratio of agricultural to nonagricultural labor force. Ukraine and Belarus (and of course the southern periphery) are much more agricultural than the RSFSR. Russia is the most urbanized of all. Of the others, only Latvia and Estonia are in the same ballpark, except for Armenia, which is anomalously high. Ukraine and Belarus lag a couple of percentage points behind here, too. Kazakhstan is again a mixture, and the most rural areas turn out to be the rest of Central Asia, Azerbaijan, and Moldova.

In summing up, we might remember that there is no reason that economic activity should be uniformly distributed throughout the world. Furthermore, resource endowments, cultural habits, capacities for the wise making and execution of policy, geographic distance, and transport costs may make some regions of the former Soviet Union development backwaters rather than poles of growth. The likely candidates for this pessimistic forecast are the republics of Central Asia, Azerbaijan, Georgia, Moldova, and possibly Kazakhstan. Ukraine surely has exaggerated hopes for its economic prospects under independence. References to its rich agricultural resources and its industry ought to be evaluated in the light of the fact that in the world as a whole, agricultural prices are low relative to industrial prices, and that much of Ukrainian industry resembles what is characterized in the United States as rust-belt industry. The Baltic nations start the recovery and reindustrialization task under better conditions, though their small size means that the trade shock phenomena will hit them especially hard in the short run. Wide divergence in achieving reform, recovery, and resumption of growth seems inevitable.

Notes

1. Soviet discussions of reform frequently invoke cosmologies in which the world rests on the backs of varying numbers of whales.

2. The whole set of decrees may be found in the collection *O korennoi perestroike upravleniia ekonomikoi*, M, 1987.
3. For a full-length treatment of the emergence, flowering, and faltering of the co-ops, see Anthony Jones and William Moskoff, *Ko-ops: The Rebirth of Entrepreneurship in the Soviet Union* (Bloomington: Indiana University Press, 1991).
4. The law on leasing of land was adopted in November 1989. The law on land took longer—a draft law was published in December 1989, and the law was approved in February 1990. The land law was first adopted as a USSR law, and separate laws were also passed at the republican level, not always consistent with the USSR version.
5. Leonard Geron, in *Soviet Foreign Policy Under Perestroika* (New York: Council on Foreign Relations, 1990), writes: "The most worrying issues for western businessmen involved in joint ventures are taxation, currency [convertibility], participation share, labor questions, quality control, supplies, areas of economic activity, and instability in rules" (p. 45). Though government actions could not solve all of these, a decree of December 1988 greatly liberalized the rules, giving tax concessions, allowing majority ownership by the foreign partner, and so on.
6. By 1990 total sales of joint ventures were about 4 billion rubles. (*Ekonomika i zhizn'*, no. 48, 1991, p. 7.)
7. The new banks were the Agroprombank, the Promstroibank, Zhilsotsbank, Vneshekonombank, and Sberbank.
8. The detailed instruction for this tax was published in *Ekonomika i zhizn'*, no. 5, 1991, p. 17.
9. Some speeches warning that he planned to curb the resource drain of military programs, and alter the influence of the defense-industrial ministries, were never published—for example, a speech in Minsk to the military brass in 1985 and a speech on the machinery industry in 1986. See Robert Campbell, "Resource Stringency and Civil-Military Resource Allocation," in T. Colton and T. Gustafson, eds., *Soldiers and the Soviet State* (Princeton: Princeton University Press, 1990), p. 148.
10. The end came when the RSFSR delegation in the Supreme Soviet refused to authorize further financing of the all-Union government by printing money, and RSFSR essentially took over the Ministry of Finance.
11. The Goskomstat review of 1991 put the drop in GNP at 17 percent, and the drop in consumption at 15 percent. (*Ekonomika i zhizn'*, no. 6, 1992.)
12. Oil output fell from 570 million tons in 1990 to 515 million tons in 1991; exports of oil and refined products fell from 160 million tons to 94 million tons.
13. Anyone who visits Fedorov's firm, as did the author, must come away exhilarated by the extraordinary drive and vision of this man.
14. Up to the time of the coup, however, these intentions were not really being translated into action. Perhaps the best judgment regarding what was happening in the RSFSR was the resignation of Boris Fedorov, the young economist who had been appointed minister of finance in the Yeltsin government. He concluded that there was not going to be any reform and he should exit rather than try to work from within.

15. Traveling around the USSR in the summer of 1990, the author found the following feuilleton in the Kostroma paper:

> Remember the old riddle—"what is long, and green, and smells like sausage?" Answer: "the train from Moscow." Supplies have been short in Kostroma for a long time, but an expedition to Moscow could get you some sausage. Now, like snow on the head, it is decreed that to buy in Moscow stores one must prove Moscow residence. The train from Moscow no longer smells like sausage—the only smell now is from the dirty socks of those who have spent the day tramping around Moscow trying to find a store that will sell them something.

16. *Rabochaia tribuna*, Oct. 25, 1991.

17. The Syktyvkar city government, for example, had thought seriously about the core group of enterprises crucial to its future growth; had inventoried their readiness for privatization, including worker attitudes; and had made proposals to the relevant ministries in Moscow for investing local resources in them and assuming control. But all its proposals were rejected.

18. Even in the process of adopting republic versions of the all-Union laws there was a great deal of divergence. For example, in Kazakhstan, the sharing formula is to give individuals an amount equal to the average price for housing space up to the amount of the "sanitary norm." It is clear that the reformers do not intend to endow citizens on a scale to enable them to buy the assets of state firms. And as reform continues, there is more differentiation. In Lithuania privatization was proceeding rapidly in 1992 under a process that sells off assets with very little effort to determine their real value. The other Baltic states are proceeding more conservatively.

19. During December 1991 many ministries and other Union administrative bodies simply closed their doors, and 36,000 people employed there were put on the street.

20. *Izvestiia*, Oct. 28, 1991.

21. The government structure is presented in *Pravitel'stvennyi vestnik*, no. 47, 1991, p. 8; short biographies of the appointees are available in *Izvestiia*, Nov. 22, 1991. Several alternative teams have been considered (*Izvestiia*, Nov. 5, 1991), among which the most radical was chosen. Yegor Gaidar is the first deputy prime minister, and his portfolio contains the economic reform and management mission. Originally he was minister of finance and economics, as well as deputy prime minister, but later relinquished the ministerial post to one of his deputies.

22. The controlled-price goods are bread, milk and a few milk products, vegetable oil, sugar, and salt (but not meat); energy products; rent; transport; and communications.

23. The set of decrees detailing the price liberalization may be found in the New Year issue of *Ekonomika i zhizn'*. (It is not numbered, but must be 1992, no. 1.)

24. An illustrative case is the Kamaz truck factory, which was turned into a joint stock company while Union authority still existed. Some stock was reserved for workers, some was sold to other enterprises, much was retained by the state, and some was sold to foreigners. The intricacies of the deal remain unclear, but there seems to be a strong feeling that the control went to insiders. The Tatar authorities will have a hard time trying to

reverse that fait accompli to shift ownership of those assets back to the local population of workers, and managers.

25. The RSFSR central bank will not finance the budget deficits of the other republics or expand the monetary base of the republican bank systems. But this will not stop inflation in the republics. For example, Ukraine and Belarus have responded to the shortage of cash with the inflationary tactic of issuing ersatz money in the form of coupons.

26. In taking over responsibility for financing much of the old Union apparatus, the RSFSR has the expensive legacy of financing the armed forces. The more of the armed forces Yeltsin keeps, the more difficult it will be to stabilize budget expenditure and stop monetary growth. Paying, housing, and feeding armed forces personnel is not the problem—these costs account for no more than about 15 percent of the total; the big ticket items of procurement, operations and maintenance, and R&D account for the lion's share.

27. The text of the memorandum is available in *Ekonomika i zhizn'*, no. 10, 1992.

28. The provisions of the original law on unemployment compensation worked generally as follows (*Pravitel'stvennyi vestnik*, no. 49, 1991, p. 2): Those who lose jobs are entitled to payments for about six months, on a sliding scale, and with a specified minimum. Payments would be 75 percent of the old salary for the first three months, 60 percent for the next three, then 45 percent, with the total not to exceed twelve months. So for a person who had earned about 300 rubles, after being out of work for six months, the cost would be 1,215 rubles; for a million persons thrown out of work the cost would total 1.215 billion rubles. These calculations need to be radically revised, of course, as wages rise sharply under the price liberalization of the reform. In March 1991 the government made these provisions more austere.

29. Some data for an early budget projection are given in *Moskovskie Novosti, Business*, no. 1, 1991, p. 3.

30. In all these bargaining situations it is possible to go in the other direction, as in the postwar effort to remove trade barriers through reciprocal concessions, or the antiarms race that the United States and USSR have conducted since the mid-eighties. The successor republics may be wise enough to see the folly of beggar-thy-neighbor policies, and to back off in the same way the former Council for Mutual Economic Assistance (CMEA) partners have realized that they only hurt themselves when they tried to cut off trade with each other when CMEA collapsed. But in the climate as it now exists, I am not optimistic. The interrepublic process seems more likely to go in the degenerative direction.

31. For a fuller discussion of conversion as an aspect of the transformation, see Julian Cooper, *The Soviet Defence Industry: Conversion and Economic Reform* (New York: Council on Foreign Relations, 1991).

32. Territorially integrated systems like railroads, pipelines, airlines, and telecommunications pose special problems. How will a call from Moscow to Kiev work after the breakup? There is no reason the republic governments could not have treaties to handle these interactions just as other nations have treaties for mutual landing rights for airlines and agreements over mutual connection of telecommunications systems. But we know that these

approaches often do not work very well. State monopoly airlines in Europe insist on high transatlantic cartel fares as price for agreeing to participate—they control landing rights, and negotiate them through treaties. International telecommunications gives rise to similar problems—for example, a big conflict currently surrounds the question of whether the United States is getting cheated on revenue from international calls.

4

Western Financial Assistance and Russia's Reforms

Jeffrey Sachs

Russia's postcommunist future balances precariously on the knife-edge. On one side lie democratization, market reform, and an end to the downward economic spiral of recent years. On the other side lie hyperinflation and, in its wake, growing political and social instability. A movement in either direction during the first years of Russia's new democracy—toward growing stability or instability—is likely to gain momentum and determine Russia's destiny for decades to come. Western financial assistance, closely linked to economic reforms in Russia, can play a critical role in pushing the process toward stabilization and democratic rule.

Every country in Eastern Europe and the former Soviet Union must grapple with the disastrous conditions left by decades of communist economic mismanagement, including a mind-boggling misallocation of resources, which systematically favored heavy industry at the expense of consumer goods and services; the wanton despoiling of the environment; the isolation of the economy from global advances in technology; and, of course, the destruction of the basic institutions of markets and private property. This legacy holds hostage the new and fragile democratic institutions of the region. In the face of deep economic crisis, the postcommunist governments are generally unpopular, and are under considerable pressure to meet the rising aspirations of a newly free citizenry. At the same time they are confronted with an economic collapse and a range of technical and institutional problems unrivaled in their complexity.

The case for foreign assistance arises in this cauldron of

economic and political tensions. Throughout history international financial support has enabled reformist governments, and their reform programs, to surmount the twin challenges of deep institutional change and day-to-day political survival. The foreign assistance by itself does not make a significant contribution to economic growth or to average living standards. Rather, the real contribution of foreign assistance is to help cushion the burdens of reform, especially for vulnerable groups, and to give hope to the population that the reforms will pay off in the medium term. Only the reforms themselves, and the hard work of the population, rather than the foreign assistance, can do the real work of economic change.

While these points are relevant for every country in the region, I will focus my attention on the case of Russia. Not only is Russia's economic situation particularly urgent and complex, but Russia's success or failure in reforms will have a pivotal impact on the rest of the region. Also, aid for Russia has naturally generated more political controversy than has aid to other countries of the region, since support for Russia will entail especially large financial outlays by the West.

Following dramatic reform steps of President Boris Yeltsin's government at the start of 1992, the Bush administration joined the other Group of 7 (G-7) nations on April 1 in supporting a 1992 aid package for Russia of $24 billion. This announcement followed months of public debate in which the administration itself, joined by many commentators, had opposed a large-scale effort, or at least had questioned its timeliness. One key point in the aid package should be stressed. Almost all of the aid, perhaps $22 billion of the $24 billion, is in the form of loans (or debt rescheduling) rather than grants (or debt cancellation). Assuming that Russia repays the loans, the financial burden of the West, in present value terms, is nearly zero. The reliance on loans rather than grants—on debt rescheduling rather than debt cancellation—is a sound, if not generous, choice.[1]

Though the Russian reform measures, and the G-7 announcement, have led to a considerable shift of public support in favor of a large-scale assistance program for Russia, vigorous opposition remains. In my view, the opposition to financial assistance rests largely on several misconceptions. The first is that foreign assistance can play no useful role, since the free-market reforms are doomed to fail in any event. Many political analysts have judged that the empty shelves and explosive inflation are nearly irremediable, and will require decades of structural changes to overcome. Aid, therefore, looks like a useless and costly expedient. This view is losing force in the face of Russia's progress in overcoming the hyperinflationary conditions inherited from the past.

A second error, committed by supply-siders, is that free-market reforms are bound to succeed in Russia if done right, so there is no case for foreign assistance. This position simply flies in the face of logic and experience. For reasons presented below, the early stages of reform inevitably generate great uncertainties as well as keen opposition among "losers" in the reform process. Therefore, throughout history, radical reforms have needed a boost of foreign financial assistance to help them sustain their policies long enough for the large benefits of reform to become widely apparent.

A third mistake is to overlook the knife-edge character of Russia's situation, that early developments can have a decisive effect on the success or failure of the reforms. Certain observers have argued, for example, that since reforms will be a long, drawn-out process, haste in providing aid will lead to a waste of money with little result. This view neglects the urgency of financial support to assist in stabilization, which itself is a prerequisite to success of other reforms.

A fourth mistake is to believe that financial assistance is an endless burden that the West can ill afford. Henry Kissinger has remarked that since Germany is spending around $100 billion per year for the 16 million citizens of the former German Democratic Republic, the cost of aiding Russia would be around $1 trillion per year for its population of 160 million. But this calculation betrays a misunderstanding of the goals of financial aid (not to mention the fact that German transfers are mostly in the form of grants, rather than loans). Germany is rebuilding the former East Germany, and is aiming at a convergence of living standards within a generation. The West has no similar responsibility or capacity to rebuild Russia. Aid would support the successful introduction of market reforms and democracy, not the rapid convergence of Russia's living standards with those of Western Europe.

A fifth, related mistake is the charge that Russia received substantial assistance in 1990 and 1991, and wasted it, so there is no case for further help. This argument, also made by Kissinger, is both factually and logically off base. As the appendix shows in detail, the charge that Russia received large amounts of aid in 1990 and 1991 is based on a simple misreading of the facts. More generally, it is plain that the communist regime poorly used financial flows. The case for aid now relies on the fact that the assistance will accompany, and be conditional upon, the radical economic reforms currently under way.

To move beyond these errors, this essay shall examine the role of financial assistance more closely. Subsequent sections discuss in general terms the political vulnerabilities of economic reform programs of the sort under way in Eastern Europe and the former Soviet Union; analyze the role of financial assistance, both conceptually and historically, in helping governments to implement reforms; examine Russia's financial needs in detail, and outline the Western aid package of $24 billion for 1992; examine financial assistance in the medium term, and outline the special role the G-7 can usefully play in the next few years; and summarize the main conclusions.

The Political Vulnerability of Economic Reform Measures

The utter political precariousness of economic reforms is, at first blush, a paradox. Why should something "so good" feel "so bad"? If Russia must desperately turn toward a market economy to escape from decades of communist economic mismanagement, why do reform measures generate so much controversy? Part of the answer, of course, involves a valid technical debate over specific measures. Various analysts have differing ideas about the means to a common set of ends. The answer is much deeper than this, though, since virtually every major economic reform program, not only Russia's, is bitterly attacked, and highly vulnerable, at the outset. And this virulent criticism is always present, even in cases where the economic reforms turn out to be splendidly successful, where the technical judgments of the reformers are powerfully vindicated by the eventual economic results.

The Backdrop of Falling Living Standards

Certainly one factor at play is that fundamental economic reforms typically begin at a time of sharply falling living standards. The old political and economic regime is crumbling and cannot sustain living standards of the recent past, much less immediate improvements. With or without reforms, economic conditions were bound to deteriorate in Russia. In these circumstances the first year of economic reform will *coincide* with a sharp drop of living standards that is already under way, and that cannot be immediately stopped. It will be utterly natural to blame the economic reforms themselves for the further deterioration in living standards that will occur in the near term.

Consider Russia's current macroeconomic situation. During the final years of communist rule, the regime temporarily propped up national consumption by allowing the capital stock to run down at a steep rate. Moscow slashed public infrastructure investment; postponed vital industrial investments, causing sharp declines in production in the oil fields, the main single source of export earnings; sold off gold bullion to maintain imports; and accumulated a huge stock of foreign debt. By 1991 these temporary expedients had reached an end, since foreign exchange and gold reserves were essentially depleted, while oil production plummeted to levels that cut to the core of export earnings. International bankers called in loans, rather than extending new ones.

When Yeltsin's government took power in November 1991, its leaders knew that even the sharply depressed living standards of that year could not be sustained, given the devastating underlying trends. The government knew that oil production, for example, was likely to fall from 460 million metric tons in 1991 to around 400 million metric tons in 1992, a decline that just about equals the total level of 1991 exports. Desperately needed imports were being curtailed, to the point that 1991 imports in Russia were down by around 45 percent from the previous year. Inventory stocks of imported raw materials and spare parts were being rapidly depleted.

In these circumstances many Russians are bound to blame the economic reformers for the sharp drop in living standards in 1992. Even though the consumer markets were devoid of goods at the end of 1991, it was the end of price controls at the start of 1992 that much of the Russian public blamed for the fall in living standards. Similarly, even though the black-market value of the ruble had *already* reached more than 100 rubles per dollar by the end of 1991, some viewed the large depreciation of the official exchange rate at the start of 1992 (from the artificial level of 1.8 rubles per dollar to 110 per dollar) as another cost of the reform.

Underestimating the Gains from Reforms

A second, and probably the most important, reason why most reform efforts are politically precarious is the vast underestimation of the potential benefits of the reforms to the society. Most Russians, and most Western pundits, fail to appreciate the enormous gains in living standards that are likely to occur in Russia if market reforms are maintained for several years. The virulent attacks on the economic reforms in Russia are mostly not rational, in the sense of being based on a knowledgeable view of the plausible economic consequences of the sustained application of the reforms. Rather, the attacks result from panic, economic ignorance, and self-serving obfuscation by political actors (for example, former communists, and members of the military-industrial complex) who know they will be losers in the reform process.

History shows again and again that the long-term gains tend to be vastly underestimated at the start of radical economic reforms, especially given underlying macroeconomic instability, so reforms remain extremely vulnerable to political challenge. The case of history's most famous economic reform, the postwar reconstruction of Germany, is illustrative. Finance Minister Ludwig Erhard, the father of the postwar German economic miracle, recalled the utterly bleak prospects that were widely held in Germany at the start of the reforms:

> It was calculated that for every German there would be one plate every fifty years; a pair of shoes every twelve years; a suit every fifty years; and that only every third German would have a chance of being buried in his own coffin. . . . Few realized that if people were allowed once more to become aware of the value and worth of freedom, dynamic forces would be released.[2]

Nor was Erhard's proposed solution—a capitalistic economy with social welfare protection, which he dubbed the "social market economy"—universally admired. On the contrary. Many pundits today, ignorant of postwar history, fail to appreciate just how precarious Erhard's market-based reforms were at the end of the 1940s and the early 1950s.[3]

In fact, Germany was deeply divided between capitalism, promoted by Konrad Adenauer and Erhard, and a "third way," promoted by the socialist leader Kurt Schumacher.[4] More generally, in the view of Adenauer the German people were in a state of "mental instability" following the traumatic events of the first half of the century.[5] Democracy itself, as well as a market economy, was far from assured. Adenauer, and the program of market-based reform, won the chancellorship by a single vote in September 1949.

The mood in 1950, two years after the start of the reforms, should be recalled, since it underscores the shortsightedness with which most observers judged the reform efforts. Unemployment had risen in the first wave of stabilization, reaching 12 percent of the labor force in the first quarter of the year. Erhard was under attack not only by internal critics, but even by U.S. advisers, who urged more planning and monetary expansion.[6] He later recalled:

> It was a time when opinion seemed resigned to the ruin of West Germany. . . . Opposition at home joined with international criticism. . . . With prices rising day by day, and the foreign trade balance becoming ever more unfavorable, to speak of such things was only possible through a deep conviction that the market economy was right. It still took months before the change became apparent, but this turn towards salvation was, as a result, all the more positive and lasting.[7]

As we shall see, Marshall Plan support provided the margin of difference for the continuation of Erhard's program. "By 1953 [five years after the start of reforms] recovery was clearly visible and assured the virtually uncontested dominance of Erhard's economic ideas in practice until the mid-1960s."[8]

The pessimism in Germany at the start of the reforms is characteristic of the public mood in most deep economic crises. The costs of reform are extravagantly overstated, and the long-term gains understated. Similarly, pessimistic assessments emerged in Japan in the late 1940s, at the start of the greatest boom in world history;[9] in Korea at the end of the 1950s; in Chile in the late 1970s; and in Mexico in the late 1980s. In each case the steady application of reforms dispelled the pessimism, but only after a period of several years.

In a 1991 comprehensive study of economic liberalization attempts in the developing world, the World Bank analyzed the political sustainability of such reforms.[10] In a large number of countries, reform efforts were abandoned after a year or two. In cases where reforms were sustained for five years, however, they tended to be sustained indefinitely thereafter. The most plausible interpretation of this finding, consistent with the cases just described, is that it takes several years for the benefits of reforms to become clear and politically self-sustaining. Before that occurs, reforms are highly vulnerable to political challenge.

The huge skepticism inside and outside Russia that has greeted the introduction of Yeltsin's reforms is not surprising in the light of the repeated experience elsewhere, but it is particularly naive when judged with careful economic analysis. If ever there was a country where reforms could be expected to improve the quality of daily life within years, it is postcommunist Russia. Some 75 years of communism left Russia with a per capita income level of a middle-income developing country (around $2,000 per capita). The economy has been so cut off from the rest of the world that it exports almost no nonmilitary manufactured goods, despite having an enormous base of heavy industry and perhaps one-fifth of the world's engineers. The overmilitarization of the economy has meant a prolonged and systematic deprivation of consumer goods, as well as a chronic and deep neglect of the service sector. The raging monetary instability has led to intensive hoarding, shortages, and billions of man-hours lost to queuing for basic needs.

All of this adds up to the possibility of making huge gains in real living standards over the next decade, coming from a re-establishment of macroeconomic balance; a substantial demilitarization of the economy; an opening of the economy, and society, to the rest of the world, to support a rapid increase in manufacturing exports; and the growth of the service sector. No doubt these developments will generate anxieties in parts of the society, political clashes over the distribution of costs and benefits, and real economic losers in declining economic sectors. But the enormous potential gains should also be clearly evident, assuming that the market reforms are given time to take hold.

The Uncertainty of Winners and Losers

Another reason that reforms are vulnerable is that they inevitably create uncertainty that can cause strong political opposition, even when a majority of the population will benefit strongly from the reforms, and *even knows it*. The point is that while the public knows that the reforms will help, individuals are generally not sure that they will benefit personally from the reforms. A heavily contrived numerical example helps to make the key point.[11]

Suppose that 49 percent of Russia's labor are skilled workers, and 51 percent are unskilled workers. Suppose further that *all* of the skilled workers will benefit from the reforms, and they know it. Meanwhile, only 40 percent of the unskilled workers will be better off, while 60 percent will suffer a fall in living standards as a result of the economic measures. Furthermore, individual unskilled workers do not know whether they will be "winners" or "losers." They know only that *on average* they will lose, since there will be 60 losers for every 40 winners.[12]

In all, 70.6 percent of the population (the skilled workers, plus 40 percent of the unskilled workers) will benefit from the reforms, while 29.4 percent will lose.[13] The winners outnumber the losers by more than two to one. But now look at the politics, assuming that each worker votes his narrow self-interest. In a majority vote the reforms will go down to defeat. All of the unskilled workers will oppose the reforms, since *on average* they will be losers; all of the skilled workers will vote for the reforms. A straight up-or-down vote on the reforms will fail by 51 percent to 49 percent, even though potential gainers outnumber losers by 69 percent to 31 percent.[14]

In theory, part of the way to sustain the political support for the reforms would be for the winners to compensate the losers— that is, "bribe" them to support the reforms through added social benefits. But this solution works very imperfectly, especially in the absence of international financial support to help pay the costs of targeted compensation. Since *all* social groups will claim in the political arena that *they* are the victims of the reforms, and since all are indeed likely to suffer declines in living standards in the short run because of underlying trends carried over from the past, it is naive to assume that a domestic political consensus can be reached on an income redistribution program.[15] This is even more true when public administration is in a shambles, and political authority has collapsed, so that actual administration of any sophisticated compensation scheme is beyond reach. Moreover, income transfer programs (such as subsidies for loss-making sectors) can have high efficiency costs that can strongly undermine the overall gains of the reforms for all groups.

The Challenge of Vested Interests

The discussion so far has focused on the attitudes of the broad public. As Russia continues to democratize, the fabled "median voter" of political science will indeed gain in prominence, so the attitudes of the general Russian public will be of prime importance. But in all democracies well-organized vested interests can assert their claims against the broad mass of the society; the median voter, who stands to gain or lose a small amount from a particular decision, frequently loses out to the well-organized lobbying group for which the decision is of fundamental importance.

In Russia the most powerful vested interests are found in the heavy industrial sectors—and particularly the military-related industries—that stand to be cut back sharply by market-oriented reforms. The state managers and bureaucrats attached to these industries were the most powerful agents of the communist system. They remain strongly organized, particularly in the structures (especially the People's Congress) that are holdovers from the period before the communist demise. This group constitutes the strongest force arguing for continued subsidization of production, cheap credits, continued state ownership, and a plethora of other actions designed to insulate the military-industrial complex from market forces.

To judge what is at stake here, it is useful to observe the remarkable overgrowth of heavy industry in Russia, at the expense of the other sectors of the economy. With an aggregate gross national product (GNP) of around $580 billion in 1988, Russia produced 163 million tons of steel; the United States, with a GNP of $5 trillion, produced 90 million tons. Thus, the steel intensity of the Russian economy (metric tons per dollar of GNP) was more than 10 times that of the United States. The result, of course, was virtual starvation of other sectors of the economy, particularly services (including trade, transport, finance, and personal services). One statistic is telling. In the United States in 1988 there were 61 retail outlets per 10,000 population; in Russia, only 20 per 10,000. Plenty of tanks, few shops.

These gross distortions of the Russian economy have several implications. First, powerful industrial interests are likely to undertake sustained and concerted defensive actions as restructuring goes forward. Second, foreign assistance might be useful in bridging the political and economic battlefield: by helping to finance social protections for the "losers" in the restructuring process and by helping to finance worthwhile projects in converting the industrial sector to civilian uses. Third, and not to be forgotten, large efficiency gains—rises in real living standards—are likely to occur as the economy reallocates resources away from heavy industry to other sectors.

Financial Inflows to Support Economic Reforms

Given the enormous political difficulties of carrying out a program of economic stabilization and reform in virtually every country in deep crisis, international financial assistance has almost always been a crucial factor in political and economic success. Throughout the century international financial support has played a particularly critical role at the onset of macroeconomic stabilization. In general, that aid has entailed an inflow of funds from official creditors (governments and international financial institutions) to support the convertibility and stability of the exchange rate; emergency loans to finance basic imports; financing for longer-term investments; and some sort of standstill or refinancing of an existing stock of foreign debt.

No doubt, many financial aid packages have failed to sustain reform programs—aid is not enough, if the reforms are poorly designed, or if the domestic political and economic circumstances are too turbulent to permit the implementation of reforms. On the other hand, almost no successful reform programs, and even fewer (if any) undertaken by democratic governments, have been able to function without sustained international support. Simply put, financial assistance has almost always been *necessary*, but not sufficient, for the success of economic reforms.

In the case of Russia, the merits and demerits of foreign assistance are being argued from first principles, typically without an adequate appreciation of the historical record. Ideas like a currency stabilization fund for Russia have been objects of vigorous attack, without recognition that such proposals simply draw upon the "usual" mechanisms of macroeconomic stabilization throughout this century. Consider, as just one early example, the stabilization of the Austrian economy after the post–World War I fall of the Hapsburg empire, a circumstance in important ways similar to Russia's situation today. Following the collapse of the Hapsburg empire and the creation of Austria as a successor state, the overwhelmed Austrian economy slipped into hyperinflation in 1921. The new government inherited a huge and expensive bureaucracy from the old empire; enormous social demands; soldiers from all over the empire returning to Vienna after the war; a breakdown of trade relations with the other new successor states of Czechoslovakia, Hungary, and Poland; a heavy reparations burden; and a collapse or dismemberment of the old administrative structures. Even the young Schumpeter, as Austrian finance minister in 1919, had no success in trying to stanch the monetary hemorrhaging, especially in the light of the unbending demands of the Allied victors for war reparations. (As John Kenneth Galbraith has quipped, Schumpeter went from being a failed finance minister to a great academic economist, thus reversing the usual order of events.)

To a remarkable extent, Austria's monetary misfortunes were reversed when the League of Nations decided to offer stabilization support to the desperate government. The 1921 League of Nations Committee on Austria concluded that linking international financial support to strong conditions of internal monetary reform was necessary for Austria's recovery:[16]

> In its report submitted to the Supreme Council of the Allies on June 3, 1921, the Committee laid down the following two conditions as prerequisite to any restoration of Austrian finance:
> (1) The suspension, for a period of at least 20 years, of the liens on Austrian assets in respect of reparation and of relief credits; and
> (2) The adoption by Austria herself of the most stringent measures for the improvement of her internal financial situation.

The committee held that the League of Nations should organize a stabilization loan, on the condition that Austria agree to undertake internal stabilization measures and that the Allies agree to suspend debt and reparations servicing for a sustained period.

For several months the League of Nations did not act upon the committee recommendations. What is most remarkable is that when the League began to act in 1922 in support of the recommendations, Austria was able to achieve currency stabilization on the mere commitment of future financial assistance, *even before the arrival, or indeed completion of negotiation, of specific loans.* Confidence in the currency was restored on the basis of the mere expectation of an agreement between Austria and the League:

> The moment the Council of the League decided to take up in earnest the question of Austrian reconstruction, there was immediately a widespread conviction that the solution of the problem was at hand. This conviction communicated itself first of all to that delicately adjusted mechanism, the international exchange market. Nearly two weeks before Chancellor Seipel officially laid the Austrian question before the Council of the League, on August 25 [1922], the foreign exchange rate ceased to soar and began to

decline, the internal price level following suit three weeks later. The printing presses in Austria were still grinding out new currency; the various Ministries were still dispersing this new currency through the country by means of budget deficits. Yet the rate of exchange was slowly declining. The crisis was checked.[17]

Since it took a while to arrange the international financing, Austria received support through short-term international credits until the main loan could be arranged.

The whole episode has a wonderfully modern air about it. The League played the role of the International Monetary Fund (IMF). It set conditions for international financial support, helped to arrange the international financing, and called upon the creditor governments to grant debt service relief (in the same way that the IMF today should represent to the Paris Club of official creditors the need for Russia to secure a standstill on most debt financing for a few years). It based its assistance on macroeconomic conditionality.

In fact, these same mechanisms have come into play many times—with other countries in the 1920s, in the aftermath of World War II, and in the context of IMF-support packages in more recent decades. Indeed, foreign assistance has been so important for successful stabilization programs that it is hard to think of *any* major postwar stabilization in which substantial financial assistance was absent. Conservatives have been quick to point to success stories—such as Chile or Mexico—as counterexamples to the appeal for aid, without realizing that such countries depended on substantial financial assistance during critical periods of their reforms. Let us review, very briefly, the experience of several countries in the postwar period.

• *The Marshall Plan.* All of the large countries of Western Europe, and several of the smaller ones, benefited from Marshall Plan inflows at the time of price liberalization, currency stabilization, and demilitarization. In 1949 Marshall Plan funds accounted for about 6 percent of GNP in Austria and the Netherlands; 4 percent in Norway and Belgium; and 3 percent in Denmark, France, Italy, and Britain.[18] In a series of articles, Barry Eichengreen of the University of California at Berkeley and coauthors have shown that the Marshall Plan acted as a kind of high-conditionality structural adjustment loan. Its effects were powerful precisely because it nudged the political equilibrium toward liberal, market solutions, and away from left-wing calls for nationalization and protectionism.

• *Japan.* The postwar economic miracle in Japan began under the aegis of American occupation. Large-scale financial support was combined with the imposition of rigorous stabilization measures (particularly, the Dodge Plan in 1949), and political actions to suppress labor unrest.

• *Korea.* It is well known that Korea's decision to open its economy to international competition in the early 1960s came in response to U.S. plans to phase out large-scale financial assistance. Nonetheless, the U.S. assistance was critical in helping Korea to end the very high inflation of the 1950s, and to rebuild its basic infrastructure after the Korean War.

• *Indonesia.* The economic performance of Indonesia under the Suharto regime is one of the success stories of stabilization and reform in the developing world. Analysts often forget, however, that the start of those reforms depended on debt cancellation, and a large-scale mobilization of financial assistance through the Inter-Governmental Group for Indonesia, chaired by the Netherlands.

• *Turkey.* The stabilization and liberalization of the Turkish economy at the beginning of the 1980s was made possible by large-scale financial support and generous debt rescheduling by the countries of the Organization for Economic Cooperation and Development. The decision to assist Turkey was taken in part because of the North Atlantic Treaty Organization's urgent strategic interest in stabilizing Turkey at the time of the Iranian Revolution.

• *Chile.* While some analysts hold up Chile's economic reforms as a counterexample to the case for foreign assistance, the opposite is more nearly true. In the mid-1970s, when Chile began its reforms, it borrowed very heavily on international capital markets.[19] When the market lending dried up at the end of the 1970s, and Chile's reforms hit a hard stretch, Chile received very substantial financial assistance from the international financial institutions. Total official credits (IMF credits plus medium- and long-term loans from other official sources) rose from $1.2 billion in 1982 (5 percent of GNP) to $5.4 billion in 1987 (31 percent of GNP).[20]

• *Mexico*. Large-scale financial assistance was critical for Mexico's stabilization in the late 1980s, and has remained so for the resumption of economic growth in the early 1990s. By 1991 Mexico had become the second largest debtor of the World Bank (after India), with outstanding debts of $19.2 billion.[21] The United States has also extended several billion dollars of credits and credit guarantees through the Export-Import Bank (Eximbank) and the Commodity Credit Corporation, making Mexico the largest recipient of Eximbank loans. In 1989 the United States led the effort to cancel about 35 percent of Mexico's commercial bank indebtedness.

• *Israel*. Israel's successful 1985 stabilization program relied in part on an extraordinary grant of $1.5 billion from the United States, equal to approximately 7 percent of GNP. (A comparable grant for Russia would be about $20 billion, assuming a GNP of $300 billion.)

• *Hungary*. One of the reasons Hungary has avoided a more severe financial collapse in recent years is that it has received considerable balance-of-payments support. In 1991, according to IMF estimates, Hungary received around $2.0 billion in official capital, not counting private flows backed by official export credit agency guarantees. Given a GNP of approximately $33.3 billion, the official financing, excluding credit guarantees, equals about 6 percent of GNP.

Mechanisms of Foreign Financial Assistance

Analytically, it is useful to distinguish among four types of emergency international assistance that have usually formed a package of aid in the context of stabilization: humanitarian aid, balance-of-payments support (other than humanitarian), stabilization fund, and debt relief. Humanitarian aid includes financial grants and credits for imports of food and medicine, as well as in-kind donations. Balance-of-payments support is grants and loans designed to finance imports. A stabilization fund is a grant or credit designed to increase the foreign exchange reserves of the central bank, to expand the capacity of the central bank to defend currency convertibility at a stable exchange rate. Debt relief can range from rescheduling (postponement) of interest and principal to actual cancellation of debt.

Note the difference between balance-of-payments support and a stabilization fund, at least as these terms are now used in current policy discussions. Balance-of-payments funds are granted with the intention that they will in fact be used to augment the country's imports in a given period. A stabilization fund, on the other hand, is designed to augment foreign exchange reserves, and not to be used for imports unless *unexpected, adverse* developments force the central bank to intervene in the foreign exchange market to defend the currency.

As the case of Austria showed, the promise of international financial assistance can have a galvanizing effect on a country's economic prospects, even before any aid is delivered. First, the commitment of funds sends a strong signal to an often confused and demoralized population that the government's economic policies are "on the right track," and even worthy of international financial support. The importance of this kind of "signaling" should not be underestimated, although it might seem unimportant. The Russian people simply have no way to assess whether their new government is competent and professional, or made up of "kids in yellow pants," as Vice President Aleksandr Rutskoi colorfully and damagingly put it at the beginning of the reform program. They trust Yeltsin, at least grudgingly these days, but they feel even more confident when they see that the IMF and the Western governments are willing to back up their praise with real money.[22]

The second effect, of course, is to provide a cushion on living standards during the initial dislocation of change. It is eminently sensible, and responsible, for a government to mobilize loans during the toughest period of economic adjustment if it is confident that the reforms will lead to higher living standards. The borrowing simply enables consumption smoothing, to ease the current pain by raising consumption now, at a modest cost of slightly lower consumption when the loans are serviced at some point in the more prosperous future.

Similarly, the borrowing also helps to cushion the decline in production, by providing vitally needed imports used in the production process during the period between the onset of reforms and the expected growth of exports. As outlined below, Russia's exports have collapsed in recent years, both because of crisis in energy production and because of a general, and intense, antiexport bias of the old system. As a result of the sharp fall in exports, there has been a collapse of imports, which is a critical factor in the current collapse of production. Under the new trade regime being established as part of the reforms, exports will rise sharply; but until that happens, the case for foreign loans to help maintain adequate levels of imports is strong.

The political consequences of this cushion are no doubt as important as the economic ones. The financial assistance allows the government to target funds to key political groups (the poor, displaced workers, the army, heavily affected enterprises in the military-industrial complex) to bolster the reform alliance. In the earlier illustration of skilled and unskilled workers, it was clear that reforms would fail the electoral test, since unskilled workers would fail to back them. If foreign assistance can provide a cushion for even a small cohort of unskilled workers (just 2 percent of the labor force in the original example), a majority of the population can be mobilized to support the reforms. That vantage point helps us to understand why a little money can go a long way. (Since Russia's economic crisis is most acutely a *fiscal* crisis, the government lacks the means to provide these resources out of its own revenues.)

Another major effect of stabilization support, particularly important in understanding the merits of a stabilization fund, is that support ends a sense of panic that, by itself, can kill a reform program. The knowledge that a stabilization fund exists, for example, can stop a speculative run on the currency that can undermine an otherwise defensible exchange rate. In effect, the speculative attack becomes a self-fulfilling prophecy: the public runs to the central bank to convert domestic currency to foreign currency on the expectation that the domestic currency will be devalued, while the central bank is forced to devalue precisely because of the run. A large stock of foreign reserves enormously reduces the risk of this kind of panicked behavior, in the same way that federal deposit insurance in the United States has stopped bank runs on insured banks, even when funds from the Federal Deposit Insurance Corporation are not actually used. Food aid similarly can forestall speculative hoarding by farmers, and thus make a liberalization of food prices far safer politically and economically.

Poland's stabilization fund, which Western nations established in 1990, is a clear example of how stabilization support can play a decisive role in a reform program. When the Solidarity-led government of Prime Minister Tadeusz Mazowiecki took power from the communists in August, it inherited an explosive inflation, running at 2,000 percent per annum in the second half of the year. Shortages were intense, and getting worse, because of extensive government-set price controls. The black-market foreign exchange rate, around 10,000 zlotys per dollar, was four times the official exchange rate of 2,500 zlotys per dollar. The currency was treated with contempt; stability and convertibility seemed, to almost all observers, to be years away.

The Polish government decided to embark on a tough stabilization program, combined with a rapid liberalization of the economy and an extensive privatization process. The economic team recognized that successful stabilization would require ending price controls, closing the budget deficit, tightening central bank credits, and stabilizing the market value of the currency. The economic team also attached particular importance to a quick move to current-account convertibility of the currency, as a way to open the economy to international trade, and thereby to instill competition in the highly oligopolistic industrial sector.

The stabilization fund no doubt played an essential role in the move to convertibility, at three key junctures: first, in convincing parts of the economic team that the rapid move to convertibility was in fact feasible; second, in permitting the economic team to convince a skeptical Parliament to back the stabilization approach; and third, in calming the public upon the onset of full convertibility.[23]

As is well known, the stabilization fund worked magnificently. Confidence in the currency was enhanced, and the new exchange rate was maintained without the need of the Central Bank of Poland to draw on the $1 billion fund. The Polish experience makes a mockery of recent claims that a Russian stabilization fund should be established only when overall macroeconomic stability has already been achieved. Such a view is backward. As the Polish case shows, a stabilization fund (linked to the start of an IMF standby, as in Poland) should help to achieve stability, rather than arrive precisely when such a fund is no longer needed.

Designing a Financial Assistance Package for Russia

It is not possible to measure a country's precise financial assistance needs, as foreign assistance must serve several economic and political ends. It must help to stop a collapse of living standards; it must help the government to provide a meaningful cushion for vulnerable groups in the population; it must provide resources to begin restructuring; it must provide foreign reserves to forestall a panic in the population. In the case of Russia, analyzing the country's dire balance-of-payments situation in 1991 is a way to make some estimates about the amount of aid that should be extended. Financial assistance is needed, first and foremost, to help put a brake on the downward spiral of living standards and industrial production.

Russia began its radical economic reforms amid an acute balance-of-payments crisis. As shown in Table 1, export earnings have fallen sharply since 1990, particularly in the hydrocarbon (oil and gas) sector, but in other sectors as well. At the same time, as of early 1991, most creditors stopped extending new loans to Russia and, on the contrary, began withdrawing credit lines as rapidly as possible. The combination of falling exports and heavy debt servicing resulted in a collapse of imports and a depletion of foreign exchange reserves. Imports fell from $81.6 billion in 1990 to only $44.3 billion in 1991, an astounding drop of 46 percent. By the beginning of 1992, foreign exchange reserves were essentially depleted, falling to a few hundred million dollars, or the equivalent of a few *hours* of imports.[24]

TABLE 1. RUSSIAN EXPORTS, 1990–1992 (BILLIONS OF U.S. DOLLARS)

Exports	1990	1991	1992*
TOTAL	80.9	56.8	49.4
Oil and gas	36.7	21.4	19.3
Other	44.2	35.4	30.1

Source: IMF balance-of-payments estimates, March 1992.

* Projected.

The fall of exports and the withdrawal of financial credits have led to an intense scarcity of foreign exchange in Russia, which has been reflected in the collapse of the real purchasing power of the ruble vis-à-vis foreign exchange. Consider, for example, an average worker's ability to purchase dollars (or dollar-priced items) using ruble wage earnings. The average industrial worker earned about 1,900 rubles per month in March 1992. Since dollars are so scarce and therefore so expensive, this wage translates into only $16 per month at the current cash-market exchange rate of 120 rubles per dollar.

According to extensive evidence at the enterprise level, as well as at the sectoral level, the cutback of imports is a major cause of the steep decline in industrial production and in living standards. In 1991 industries were subjected to sharp cutbacks in centralized allocations of imported inputs, including raw materials, intermediate goods, and spare parts; the result was a fall in gross domestic product (GDP) of about 11 percent compared with the 1990 level.

In 1992 the intense shortage of foreign exchange continued, but it is now hitting the enterprises through market mechanisms rather than through central allocations of foreign exchange. Specifically, enterprises cannot afford to purchase those inputs at the current free-market exchange rate, since they cannot pass the high costs of those inputs on to their domestic consumers, in view of $16 per month average wages. Similarly, enterprises cannot afford to purchase domestically produced tradable goods, such as metal ores, since the prices of such goods are determined by world market prices in the same way as prices of imported goods.

The individual enterprise is therefore caught in a jackknife between soaring input costs and falling purchasing power of customers. The result is a wave of plant closings, sharply rising unemployment, and sharply falling industrial production. While we should naturally expect a fall in industrial production as the result of tight credit policy and the withdrawal of government subsidies for industry, Russia's balance-of-payments squeeze poses the greatest risk of a grave collapse of production. Moreover, the balance-of-payments squeeze is intensifying as enterprises deplete their inventories of imported inputs. In 1991 imports fell far more sharply than output. In 1992, the output decline caught up with 1991's collapse of imports. According to widespread reports, machinery is breaking down and factories are continuing to close for lack of imported spare parts.

The economic consequences of the balance-of-payments crisis are severe. First, unless the 1991 decline of industrial goods imports undergoes a partial reversal, the output shortfall in 1992 will exceed even the pessimistic estimate of a 20 percent GDP drop. Second, the import shortfall is also causing serious human distress, as the country lacks the normal financial means to import urgently needed foodstuffs and medicines. Imports of medicines fell by an estimated 47 percent between 1990 and 1991. Third, the lack of foreign exchange reserves at the Russian Central Bank threatens the anti-inflation efforts of the Yeltsin government. Since the government lacks foreign exchange reserves, it is unable to commit itself to defending a stable nominal exchange rate. But without a commitment to a stable exchange rate, it is difficult to prevent an ongoing wage–price–exchange rate spiral.

Some Political Implications of the Balance-of-Payments Crisis

The shortage of foreign exchange remains a major threat to the Yeltsin government and to the economic and political reforms more generally. In broad terms, the balance-of-payments crisis is a chief cause of the ongoing industrial collapse and the precipitous fall of living standards, both of which threaten the viability of the reforms. More specifically, the reactions of the Parliament, the politicians, and the bureaucracy to the foreign exchange crisis may seriously undermine the key measures of the reforms.

Because of the foreign exchange crisis, several types of political pressures threaten the reforms: pressure to restore the central rationing of foreign exchange may undermine the basic step toward liberalization of the economy; powerful separatist movements in regions that produce valuable raw materials (oil, diamonds) are fighting to keep control over their products; key ministries are under pressure to maintain or reimpose export controls and state orders between enterprises, to try to ensure that industrial enterprises can afford to buy the inputs of tradable goods that they need to keep operating; some regions are flirting with the introduction of their own currencies in view of the continuing weakness and instability of the ruble. Of course, while none of the possible steps—renewed rationing, separatism, export controls, and so on—would actually improve Russia's balance-of-payments situation, and would tend to reduce Russia's exports still further, pressures to introduce these steps are likely to intensify in the absence of significant Western financial assistance.

The Necessary Scale of Western Support

According to its standard practices, the IMF made an estimate of Russia's financial needs for the calendar year 1992, basing it on an assessment of Russia's balance-of-payments prospects for the year.[25] The IMF determined Russia's international financial needs in 1992 at $18.3 billion, of which $12.3 billion should be directed to supporting the payments for imports, and $6 billion should back a stabilization fund to support the ruble.

To make this determination, the IMF estimated the foreign exchange that Russia will need to pay for a minimally acceptable level of imports of goods and services. It then examined the level of Russian export earnings that are likely to be available to pay for the imports. Since the estimated import needs exceeded the anticipated export earnings, the IMF found a "financing gap," which must be filled by grants and loans from the West. In addition to direct import needs, the IMF estimated the level of foreign exchange reserves that the Central Bank of Russia should have in order to peg the foreign exchange rate of the ruble. On the basis of this assessment, it calculated a plausible size for an internationally backed ruble stabilization fund.

The IMF estimate of $18.3 billion should be regarded as an *absolutely minimum estimate* of Russia's needs, rather than a generous estimate. Most importantly, the IMF assumed, and implicitly accepted, a real GNP decline of 20 percent for Russia in 1992, even though more financial support would mean a smaller decline (of course, we cannot precisely predict GNP for 1992, in any event, but more financial support would almost surely lead to a smaller GNP decline). As seen in Table 2, the IMF estimates assume that the import level in 1992 will remain more than $30 billion below the 1990 level. The estimates make no allowance for critical investment needs in sectors such as military conversion, energy, and agro-industry.[26] Russian government experts also found the IMF's projections of Russia's exports to be over-optimistic, a viewpoint that is supported by Russia's actual export performance during the first part of 1992.

As of July 1992, the IMF had dramatically lowered its forecast of 1992 exports from $49 billion to just $35 billion. As a result, it has also dramatically scaled back its estimates for the level of imports that Russia will be able to finance in 1992, from $50 billion to $37 billion. Part of the discrepancy of the March projections and the July projections may result from a rise in unreported trade in 1992, leading to an underestimate of actual export earnings and import flows. Part, however, almost surely

TABLE 2.   RUSSIAN IMPORTS, 1990–1992 (BILLIONS OF U.S. DOLLARS)

Imports	*1990*	*1991*	*1992**
TOTAL	81.6	44.7	50.0
Food and medicine	14.0	12.1	14.9
Other	67.6	32.6	35.1

* IMF estimates as of March 1992, judged to be the minimum level of imports necessary to limit the 1992 decline in GDP to 20 percent.

results from the excessive optimism of the earlier export projection, as the Russian experts had warned.

On April 1, soon after the IMF determination of Russia's needs at $18.3 billion, the G-7 announced a program of $24 billion of support for Russia. The link between the IMF estimate and the G-7 program remains somewhat vague. The best interpretation is that the G-7 governments recognized that the IMF estimates were too low—as is the case—and that Russia should receive more generous assistance in the critical first year of the reforms.[27]

Sources of Western Financial Support

The $24 billion in financial support offered by the G-7 is to be provided in roughly the following forms: stabilization fund, provided out of IMF resources ($6 billion); balance-of-payments support loans, through the IMF, World Bank, and the European Bank for Reconstruction and Development (EBRD) ($4.5 billion); rescheduling of interest falling due on medium- and long-term foreign debt ($2.5 billion); and grants, loans, and export credits to support imports, provided on a bilateral (government-to-government) basis ($11 billion).

A few technical explanations are necessary to understand the package. First, the IMF is to provide the stabilization fund, out of special resources that ten industrial countries and Saudi Arabia provided to the IMF during the 1970s, under an arrangement known as the General Agreement to Borrow (GAB). The eleven countries must approve specific uses of the GAB, as they did at the end of April 1992 for a ruble stabilization fund. Second, the $24 billion was to be provided during the calendar year 1992. Third, the $2.5 billion of interest relief will involve rescheduling of Russia's debts to official creditors in the Paris Club, plus relief on interest payments to Russia's bank creditors in the so-called London Club (in addition to the relief on interest payments, there will also be a rescheduling of principal payments of several billion dollars, a sum not included in the $24 billion package). Fourth, the $11 billion of bilateral support includes an amalgam of humanitarian assistance (food and medicine grants), short-term financing of imports, and long-term financing of investment projects by export credit agencies in the industrial countries.

Notice that from the Western governments' point of view, the package is attractive in that it will involve very little by way of explicit budget outlays. Almost all of the sums involved are mobilized through international financial institutions (IFIs), debt relief, or off-budget entities in the donor countries, such as the export credit agencies. The United States is a good case in point. Within the G-7 package, the United States will have an indirect stake of roughly 20 percent of the total in the $6 billion stabilization fund, and the $4.5 billion in contributions of the IFIs, but according to the U.S. administration, no direct budgetary appropriations for these funds is necessary. The U.S. share of the $2.5 of estimated debt relief is also negligible and off-budget.

As for its share of the remaining $11 billion in government-to-government support, the United States will provide roughly $620 million in direct budgetary assistance and another $2.5 billion in various kinds of credit guarantees from Eximbank, the Commodity Credit Corporation, and other agencies. In all credit guarantee programs, the bulk of the loans are off-budget. Under the accounting procedures of the 1990 Credit Control Act, however, a modest proportion of every loan must be appropriated to account for the expected loss on the loan due to the possibility of default.

Linking Aid and Reform

Critics of financial aid to Russia are correct to stress that assistance without reforms will surely be wasted. Financial flows will be well used only if they help to support the radical economic reforms needed to overcome the economic crisis and to put Russia solidly on the path to becoming a normal market economy. The reformers themselves are explicit on this point. Konstantin Kagalovsky, the Russian government's minister plenipotentiary for IFIs, testified to the Banking Committee of the U.S. House of Representatives that the Russian government not only acknowledges the logic of mutually negotiated conditionality on international loans, but welcomes such conditionality as an effective vehicle for maintaining a proper direction and pace to the reforms.[28]

The core conditionality should revolve around the Russian government's borrowing from the IMF. A $1 billion loan was negotiated for the period from August to December, 1992. A follow-up one-year loan for 1993, of about $4 billion, was negotiated during the fall of 1992. Each loan agreement with the IMF must outline the overall strategy with respect to the budget, credit control, exchange rate system, trade liberalization, and pricing policy. In essence, the loan agreements describe the government's stabilization and liberalization strategy, and set quantitative targets for macroeconomic policy in support of those goals. In a one-year program, the IMF reviews these targets each quarter, on a range of variables such as interest rates, exchange rates, credit targets, budget deficits, foreign exchange reserves, and the like. Serious deviations of the actual policies from the policy targets lead to a suspension of lending.

This kind of conditionality can be potent in keeping the overall reform program on track, assuming that the targets are set meaningfully and are backed up with sufficient (conditional) financial assistance. Poland's reforms in 1991 and 1992 provide a useful illustration of the workings of conditionality. The Polish government began to deviate from fiscal targets in 1991, in part because of the adverse revenue consequences of the collapse of Council for Mutual Economic Assistance (CMEA) trade, and in part because of political pressures to raise social spending. After a highly populistic parliamentary election at the end of 1991, a new government took power, committed to significant increases of public spending, in amounts that threatened Poland's fragile stabilization. The IMF declared its readiness to suspend further loans to Poland in the event that the budget deficit was allowed to explode. In large measure as a result of this warning, the new government changed course, and reached agreement with the IMF on credible budgetary targets.

IMF conditionality on monetary policy is also key to overcoming one frequently voiced fear about the aid package: the risk that the aid will simply be recycled in the form of capital flight. The most potent cause of capital flight in any country is the combination of a fixed exchange rate and an overly expansionary monetary policy. The central bank issues too much domestic currency, which households and firms then convert into foreign exchange and take out of the country. Administrative controls cannot stanch the flow; only high domestic interest rates and tight credit can keep money at home.

Capital flight from Russia certainly is a serious risk, and has been substantial in the past year or two, which is not surprising in view of the reckless monetary policies up until the start of 1992. Various estimates put unrecorded, offshore deposits of Russian enterprises at between $5 billion and $14 billion, though the upper estimates are probably exaggerated. In any event, as extensive experience with Latin American stabilization programs has demonstrated, the only way to stop the flow is through a significant tightening of monetary policy. The only way to achieve a reversal of the previous outflow is to stabilize the macroeconomic conditions at home for a sustained period.

IMF conditionality, however important, will not be enough. Since IMF conditions deal with macroeconomic variables, they tend to ignore other crucial aspects of reform, most importantly the pace of privatization. Since Russia's reforms cannot work if privatization is long delayed, the international community should give special attention to adding rapid privatization as a core condition of large-scale finance. The World Bank is the natural interlocutor for this aspect of conditionality. Moreover, as described in the next section, the G-7 itself should play a role in Western assistance and conditionality in the medium run.

Financial Assistance in the Medium Term

The nature of financial aid to Russia should evolve over time, as the reform program itself is evolving. In the first year of the reform, most attention is necessarily going to macroeconomic stabilization and trade liberalization. In this phase the aid should be directed mainly to general balance-of-payments support (financing of imports) and to currency convertibility, via a stabilization fund and a buildup of central bank reserves. In later years, as reform efforts shift to privatization and structural adjustment,

the aid should be directed increasingly toward specific investment projects and support for the emerging private sector.

One can sketch a plausible evolution of financial assistance,
on the key assumption that underlying political conditions in
Russia remain supportive of economic reforms. Official financing should be greatest in the first two to three years, on the order
of $15–25 billion per year (counting all official sources, multi-
lateral and bilateral), then should taper off significantly. After
five years of radical reforms, private capital inflows should certainly begin to exceed official inflows, with the latter falling
below $10 billion per year, and perhaps well below that level.

For 1992 most of the financial support is targeted at humanitarian assistance (food and medicine), currency stabilization and
foreign reserve accumulation, and the financing of basic imports
(via loans from the export credit agencies). Conditionality is
linked to progress on macroeconomic stabilization, trade and
price liberalization, and the onset of privatization. A few billion
dollars (perhaps $2–$3 billion) will be linked to specific investment projects in the energy and agro-industrial sectors, via
World Bank and EBRD projects. A similar amount from export
credit agencies will help to finance specific investment projects at
the enterprise level.

Already by 1993, and certainly for the years 1994–1997, the
aid should shift from general balance-of-payments support to
specific project financing, including infrastructure investment
and private-sector investment. The World Bank should help to
mobilize funds for significant restructuring of key sectors of the
economy, including military conversion, financial services, and
communications and transport. These World Bank sectoral
loans should involve a mix of policy conditionality, infrastructure
investment (needed to support private economic activity in the
sector), and direct financing (equity and debt) for private-sector
projects. World Bank funds should be combined with cofinanc-
ing from the export credit agencies and private investors. In
order to support privatization in these sectors, the World Bank
should maintain a standard that loans to individual Russian
enterprises should be conditional on those enterprises either

being private, or being corporatized and on the way to being privatized.[29]

At the same time, the EBRD should focus its energies on supporting the rapid development of the private sector. One promising model is the U.S. enterprise funds that have been established for Czechoslovakia, Hungary, and Poland. These funds, capitalized by a budgetary appropriation, and managed by private U.S. firms, spur private-sector activity in the three Central European countries by making loans and taking direct equity positions in local, private start-up firms. In addition, the enterprise funds work with relevant governmental structures to help develop an adequate legal environment for the growth of the private sector. The EBRD could establish similar operations in Russia and the other former Soviet Union republics.

It should be well understood that official assistance will be insufficient, by itself, to play a major role in "rebuilding" the Russian economy. The primary resources for rebuilding will be indigenous savings, over the course of decades. But even within the limited domain of foreign capital, it will be private inflows rather than official assistance that will have the greater role in the long term. Private capital, mainly in the form of foreign direct investment, will bring with it not only resources, but critically needed technology, management skills, links to Western markets, and so forth. Having noted this, however, we must be realistic about the timetable for significant foreign capital flows.

While some large-scale investments are likely to begin in particular sectors (mainly oil and gas development), foreign investment in manufacturing is likely to start at modest levels and build up gradually for half a decade or more. Before investors commit large amounts of money, they will want to learn about the local market, have sustained evidence of macroeconomic stability, see a stable and sensible tax and legal environment, and be convinced of the overall staying power of the reforms. Those who believe that Russia can attract large private foreign inflows in the short term should look closely at the cautionary lessons of Mexico and Chile. These two successful reformers in Latin America started out their reforms in a far better state than Russia's, but nonetheless had to pursue stabilization and liberalization policies for several years before foreign investors were prepared to invest significant amounts of money.

An Institutional Framework for the Medium Term: The G-7 Role

In the first year of reform, Russia's links with the IMF and the World Bank will provide the basic framework for conditional financial assistance. As the reform issues move beyond immediate stabilization and liberalization, however, those institutions alone will be unable to manage the range of issues that will arise between Russia and the West in the course of reforms. Almost every aspect of structural adjustment—whether in energy, military conversion, international trade, financial-sector reform, or environmental policies—involves a complex linkage of private-sector initiatives, public policy changes, and infrastructure investment, which will require the active involvement of Western governments together with the Russian government. The process of reintegrating Russia in the world system will require a broader framework of cooperation. The G-7 is the natural locus of that cooperation.

Perhaps an analogy is helpful here. In the case of the Central European countries, the European Community (EC) is the natural counterpart in the medium term for problems of structural reform. The Central European countries want to join the EC, and so are designing their reform policies with the goal of eventual membership very much in mind. The association agreements reached between the EC and Czechoslovakia, Hungary, and Poland in 1991 provide the broad framework through which the process of harmonization and eventual EC membership will take place.

Similarly, Russia aims to become a normal member of the world economic community. But Russia's size and potential economic strength make it a natural candidate to become a leading member of the G-7 (thereby making it the G-8), rather than a member of the EC. Just as the association agreements with the EC will be crucial guideposts for Central Europe in the next few years, a structured relationship between Russia and the G-7 could provide an overall framework for cooperation, leading eventually to Russia's normal participation as a member of the group.

The G-7 should make clear its intention to support Russia's reforms with financial assistance over a period of several years, as well as its intention to help coordinate the overall Western effort. The G-7 should invite Russia to attend G-7 ministerial meetings on a fairly regular basis, in order to maintain a high-level political and economic dialogue on the progress of the Russian reforms and the Western support for them. Moreover, it should become standard for the Russian president to attend part of each summit meeting. One responsibility of the G-7 chairmanship, which rotates annually (to the country hosting that year's summit), should be coordinating the G-7 efforts vis-à-vis Russia.

Each year the G-7 and Russia should agree on a few specific areas to which all will devote special attention. These should be areas that require reform actions in Russia, as well as financial assistance and political support from the West. Obvious candidates for high-level G-7 interactions with Russia include energy (where the links to the European energy grid are crucial); military conversion (which intersects with security issues, trade restrictions, and so on); and trade liberalization (which requires high-level political decisions in both Russia and the West).

Conclusions

Historical experience, and the logic of current events, underscores the urgency of Western support for Russia's economic reforms. After spending trillions of dollars in the arms race, the West should now set aside some tens of billions of dollars to help Russia stabilize its economy and nascent democracy. Russia's economic challenges are unprecedented. It must stop an incipient hyperinflation inherited from the past, and it must bring about a fundamental changeover to a working market system. Even reforms of much less ambition have required sustained international help for their success.

The G-7 package of $24 billion for 1992 was a realistic start, but the funds were not provided in a timely way. The package was based broadly on an IMF assessment of Russia's urgent foreign exchange needs, and attempted to address those needs through a mix of humanitarian aid, debt rescheduling, balance-of-payments support loans from the international financial institutions, and a stabilization fund for the ruble. In later years the aid will shift from this emphasis on stabilization support to financing for infrastructure investment and private-sector development.

The financial assistance will succeed in its purpose only if it is closely linked to Russia's economic reform program. IMF and World Bank conditionality will be key, especially in the early years. To deepen the links of assistance and reform, however, it will be useful to move beyond the international financial institutions, and assign the G-7 a special role in coordinating the Western support for Russia's reforms. The end goal of this G-7 role should be Russia's acceptance as a normal member of an expanded G-8.

Appendix to Chapter 4:

A Note on G-7 Assistance Extended to the Soviet Union

In the recent past the Soviet Union received substantial assistance, mostly in the form of credits and guarantees from export credit agencies, particularly Hermes (Federal Republic of Germany). Nonetheless, considerable and understandable confusion surrounds the actual extent of assistance, and in public debate, opponents of assistance to Russia have tended to magnify the flows that have already gone to the former Soviet Union.[30] By 1990 and 1991, inflows of credits and grants barely exceeded outflows of debt servicing (amortization and interest payments).

According to preliminary and partial data collected by the EC during 1990 and 1991, the Soviet Union received *commitments* of assistance of $52.6 billion—$2.3 billion in grants, $7.6 billion in untied loans, and $42.7 billion in tied loans.[31] In addition, Germany extended approximately $11 billion in assistance for the withdrawal of Soviet troops from the former East Germany. About two-thirds of these commitments ($28.1 billion) were actually disbursed. Only $1.7 billion of the disbursements came in the form of grants; the rest came as credits (of which $7.6 billion were untied, and $18.8 billion were tied). Russia's share of the overall disbursements was roughly 6 percent (approximately the share of the Russian economy in the Soviet Union), or about $17 billion over 1990 and 1991. Germany provided about half of the total disbursements ($14.6 billion). A large part of the German contribution involved credits to East German industrial firms to continue to ship goods to the Soviet Union after the breakdown of the CMEA and the unification of Germany.

The IMF has made independent estimates of the capital flows to the Soviet Union and Russia for these two years; the IMF figures are slightly lower than the EC estimates (see Table A1). There is, as yet, no careful accounting of the differences in the estimates of the two sources.[32]

TABLE A1.   EC AND IMF ESTIMATES OF FINANCIAL FLOWS TO THE
SOVIET UNION AND RUSSIA, 1990–1991
(BILLIONS OF U.S. DOLLARS)

	EC	*IMF*
Total flows		
Soviet Union	28.1	26.0
Russia	16.9*	15.6
Grants		
Soviet Union	1.7	2.6
Russia	1.0*	1.2

* The EC does not make a separate estimate for Russia. These figures are simply the result of multiplying the estimates for the entire Soviet Union by 0.61 (the share of the Russian economy in the Soviet Union).

TABLE A2.   RESOURCE TRANSFERS TO RUSSIA, 1990–1991
(BILLIONS OF U.S. DOLLARS)

Measure	*1990*	*1991*	*Total*
Gross flows	6.6	9.0	15.6
Credits	6.6	7.8	14.4
Grants	0.0	1.2	1.2
Amortization	4.9	5.0	9.9
Interest payments	2.9	2.7	5.6
Net flows	1.7	4.0	5.7
(gross flows minus amortization)			
Net resource transfer	−1.2	1.3	0.1
(net flows minus interest payments)			

Source: IMF estimates of balance of payments, March 1992.

The *net flows* to the Soviet Union and Russia were substantially less than the gross flows, because of substantial amortizations during this period. For the Soviet Union as a whole, the IMF records total amortizations of $16.3 billion for 1990 and 1991, with Russia's share amounting to $9.9 billion. Thus, according to IMF data, net flows for 1990 and 1991 were $9.7 billion for the Soviet Union and $5.7 billion for Russia. Subtracting the interest payments on the foreign debt shows that *net resource transfers* to the Soviet Union and to Russia from foreign creditors were *de minimis*: $0.6 billion and $0.1 billion, respectively. The calculations for Russia are shown in Table A2.

Notes

1. Russia should be able to absorb several tens of billions of dollars of increased international debt in the next few years, as long as most of that borrowing is directed toward profitable purposes in the context of overall reforms. The current Russian debt is about $40 billion, which is 61 percent of the total Soviet debt of about $65 billion. While the debt is posing enormous short-term liquidity problems, it represents a long-term manageable burden in an economy of around $300 billion, with excellent prospects for significant export growth. The implied ratio of debt to gross domestic product is around 15 percent, far below Poland's ratio of around 70 percent at the start of its reform program in 1990. (Technically, Russia could find itself responsible for more than $40 billion of the outstanding debt, if some of the other republics default on their debt obligations.)
2. *Transition: the newsletter about reforming economies*, published by The World Bank, vol. 2, no. 10, Nov. 1991, p. 10.
3. The point here is not that Russian conditions today mirror those of Germany in 1948, but that reformers then, as today, had to overcome a deep cloud of unwarranted pessimism. It is common today to say that Germany's conditions were self-evidently more favorable than Russia's, given the previous experience of a market economy. This may be right, but it is surely exaggerated, and was not much believed at the time. After all, a failed Weimar democracy followed by twelve years of Nazi dictatorship is hardly a self-evident basis for democratic capitalist institutions.
4. See Thomas Alan Schwartz, *America's Germany* (Cambridge, Mass.: Harvard University Press, 1991), p. 55.
5. Ibid., p. 78.
6. Ibid., p. 91: "Many Americans in Germany, including McCloy, while sympathizing with Ludwig Erhard's vision of a German economy with more competition, an export orientation, and less government tutelage, considered some forms of planning and control essential in a modern economy, especially when that economy relied on American assistance. Within Adenauer's government, Erhard and the members of the smaller

coalition parties resisted the American demands, arguing that expansionary credit measures would cause inflation and damage the value of the currency."

7. Cited in Dennis L. Bark and David R. Gress, *A History of West Germany, Volume 1: From Shadow to Substance, 1945–1963*, (Oxford: Basil Blackwell, 1989), p. 267.

8. Ibid., p. 271. Bark and Gress go on to state: "The basic operating principles of those ideas were: (1) a conservative fiscal policy rather than artificial stimulation of demand in the interest of full employment; (2) the greatest possible liberalization of export and domestic trade instead of economic planning; and (3) a rejection of short-term relief in favor of long-term reconstruction of the basic means of industrial production. The fact that the German mark was healthy and the government was committed to currency stability, provided the indispensable assurance—*Kalkulierbarkeit*—that German industry could depend without question on the stability of the currency, and therefore, unlike the period from 1945 to 1949, could pursue long-term planning and set long-term economic goals."

9. See Theodore Cohen, *Remaking Japan* (New York: Free Press, 1987), esp. ch. 23.

10. D. Papageorgiou, M. Michaely, and A. M. Choksi, eds., *Liberalizing Foreign Trade* (7 volumes) (Oxford: World Bank, Basil Blackwell, 1991). Volume 7 summarizes the results of the complete study.

11. This illustration is based on to the interesting article by R. Fernandez and D. Rodrik, "Resistance to Reform: Status Quo Bias in the Presence of Individual Specific Uncertainty," *American Economic Review*, 1991, p. 1146.

12. Since the reform is like a lottery for the unskilled workers, also assume that the relative magnitudes of the potential gains and losses among the unskilled workers are such that it is not worth it for an unskilled worker to take the risk of winning or losing. For example, if the lucky workers gain $1,000 per year, while the unlucky ones lose $1,000 per year, then a risk-neutral worker will oppose the reforms, since on average he would stand to lose $200 per year $(0.6 \times -\$1,000) + (0.4 \times \$1,000)$.

13. These proportions are calculated as follows: The winners include 51 percent of the labor force (skilled workers), plus 40 percent of 49 percent of the labor force (lucky unskilled workers)—or $0.51 + (0.4 \times 0.49)$, which is 70.6 percent. The proportion of losers is thus 29.4 percent.

14. The intriguing point here is that public support for favorable reforms can prove fickle in the face of high uncertainties. The example itself is obviously an incomplete picture of "democracy Russian-style," which still operates with a semi-democratic parliament elected under the old regime. The real forces opposing reform are not mainly the workers themselves, but the organized interests of state managers and bureaucrats in the industrial ministries, which together constitute a powerful "industrial lobby." That industry lobby has found important allies in the Parliament, which is heavily over-represented by hardliners. Nonetheless, the ability of the industrial lobby to hold sway in the Parliament and executive branch certainly depends, at least to some extent, on the social pressures emanating from the industrial workers and the broader society. Thus, the kinds of

calculations illustrated in this section find their counterpart in Russia's political struggles.

15. Politicians may support a "social safety net" for the poorest parts of the society, but a safety net for the poor is quite different from an income compensation scheme in which the winners of the reform compensate the losers (who may well be at income levels above the safety-net threshold).

16. Leo Pasvolsky, *Economic Nationalism of the Danubian States* (New York: Macmillan, 1928), for the Brookings Institution, p. 120.

17. Ibid., p. 116.

18. B. Eichengreen and M. Uzan, "The Marshall Plan: Economic Effects and Implications for Eastern Europe and the Soviet Union," *Economic Policy*, No. 14, 1992.

19. This was not a demonstration of the international market's sensitive appraisal and support for the regime's policies, since the borrowing took place at a time when virtually all countries—Argentina, Brazil, Bulgaria, Nigeria, and Poland—as well as Chile could borrow very heavily.

20. Data are from the *World Debt Tables, 1990–91* (Washington, D.C.: World Bank, 1991). The dollar value of GNP fell from $22.6 billion in 1982 to 17.4 billion in 1987.

21. World Bank, *Annual Report, 1991* (Washington, D.C.: World Bank), p. 183.

22. The sense of confidence IMF support gives has been very important throughout Eastern Europe since 1989, and will be important in Russia, as well, at the outset of reforms. The people have few touchstones of reliable authority on which to make judgments about the wisdom of the government's actions. Of course, the legitimizing effect of IMF support tends to wane over time among people spending many years traversing an economic crisis under IMF supervision. In Latin America the news of an IMF agreement is often greeted with trepidation of further austerity measures rather than renewed confidence.

23. I personally witnessed a dramatic confirmation of the galvanizing role of the stabilization fund. In late December 1989, a call came to Warsaw from the IMF saying that the stabilization fund might not be in place after all by January 1, 1990, because some of the donor countries had not yet signed on. When Deputy Prime Minister Leszek Balcerowicz reported on the phone call to some other key economic officials meeting at the Finance Ministry, a storm erupted and a key official stalked out of the meeting, declaring that the whole idea of convertibility was grossly premature and should be put off at least half a year. After an urgent phone call to Washington, and some further clarifications, the fund was put back on track, and the economic team restored the consensus to move forward.

24. The normal prudential guideline is that countries should maintain at least three months' worth of imports in the form of foreign exchange reserves.

25. The estimates were made as of February 1992.

26. This last point is made clear in the IMF March 1992 discussion of the financing gap, where the IMF says that Russia's capacity to "absorb imports" may "turn out to be larger than expected. . . . this may occur for example in energy or agriculture, where new investment projects are now being examined by the World Bank." In this case, the IMF advises that additional financing "would be beneficial." Most of that additional financ-

ing should then come from the export credit agencies of the G-7 countries, including Eximbank, and from the new European Bank for Reconstruction and Development (EBRD).

27. Subsequent to the G-7 announcement, the IMF has argued (somewhat implausibly) that when precise accounting is made of the G-7 aid offer, the ostensible differences between the IMF estimate and the G-7 program are in fact eliminated. As of 1992, the discrepancies had not yet been cleared away.

28. Testimony to the Subcommittee on International Development, Finance, Trade, and Monetary Policy of the Committee on Banking, Finance, and Urban Affairs. April 1, 1992.

29. Corporatization (also termed "commercialization") refers to the conversion of a traditional state-owned enterprise into a joint-stock company subject to the commercial code. One key requirement of corporatization is that an independent supervisory board, rather than a branch ministry or a workers' council, provide the corporate governance.

30. It is sometimes alleged that the squandering of the previous aid indicates the uselessness of financial assistance at this time, but this argument fails for two reasons. First, the previous aid was not made conditional on, and in fact was not accompanied by, radical economic reforms such as those under way in Russia. There should be no doubt or disagreement that in an unreformed Russian economy, even vast assistance would have little positive impact on living standards or economic prospects. Second, the actual extent of assistance in 1990 and 1991 is greatly exaggerated, both because of confusion about commitments versus actual disbursements, and because of confusion about gross flows versus net resource transfers (gross flows minus debt servicing).

31. In fact, the data refer to all of 1990 and 1991 for Germany, but only September 1990 through December 1991 for the other donor countries. Since Germany extended the bulk of assistance in this period, and since the other donors extended little in grants and credits during January–August 1990, the data give fairly good coverage for all of 1990 and 1991.

32. Technically, the IMF estimates refer to total flows recorded in the balance of payments, including private capital sources and official sources, while the EC data refer to official flows only. It is therefore surprising that the IMF's estimates magnitudes are actually lower than the EC's, although the IMF category of resource flows is more inclusive.

Conclusion: Problems of Planning a Market Economy

Shafiqul Islam

This book is meant to be "The Economics of Transformation 101": a lucid primer for noneconomist students of postcommunist societies and informed members of the policy community who are bewildered by the confusing—and sometimes incomprehensible—debates among economists. In this concluding chapter, I intend to pursue a simple goal: to underscore the points on which economists agree and on which they—including the authors of this volume—do not, and explain why. I also hope to pose a few questions forcefully, answer a few others clearly, demonstrate that some catchphrases dominating the policy debate are more illusory than illuminating, and suggest that some of the building blocks of the conventional transition strategy—at least the way they are put together—subvert the strategy more than support it.

The Package and the Performance: From Consensus to Contention

As Michael Mandelbaum notes in the beginning—and as our four authors repeatedly demonstrate—Western economists (and their market-friendly Eastern colleagues) display an amazing amount of agreement on the major components of the overall transitional policy package. While these economists rarely list the components in exactly the same way (our four authors are no exception), they broadly agree that the vehicle to reach a private market economy should ride on four interlocking wheels:

- *Macroeconomic stabilization* to the extent necessary, and supported by incomes policy if necessary.[1] This entails tight budget and credit policy to reverse the course of rising inflation and reduce the widening external trade and payments deficits to sustainable levels.

- *Liberalization.* This involves freeing up prices, including interest rates; devaluing the currency to a realistic—perhaps supercompetitive—level, and then managing the exchange rate under some "flex-fix" regime (such as pegging with periodic large devaluations, or frequent minidevaluations, or managed float); making the currency convertible for the current account (that is, for international transactions of goods and services); integrating with the world economy by eliminating barriers to cross-border movements of goods, services, capital, technology, and ideas; and reforming other (for example, financial and labor) markets.

- *Privatization of the economy.* This requires development of a *new* private sector; reform of ownership and management of *existing* state enterprises (liquidation, restructuring, commercialization, and *privatization of existing enterprises*); and property rights reform of land and housing.

- *Development of a market-supporting institutional infrastructure.* This encompasses constitutional, legislative, legal, accounting, regulatory, fiscal, monetary, and social insurance reform.

The last three wheels can be grouped together under the overall label of "marketization."

Economists also broadly agree on a fifth point: in order to move fast and maintain the momentum, the vehicle should *initially be fueled*, not just lubricated, by massive foreign *governmental* assistance—moral, intellectual, technical, and financial. The official *financial* assistance may involve financing a currency stabilization fund, providing debt relief where necessary, cushioning the consumption drop, importing critical raw materials and industrial inputs, building physical and institutional infrastructure, creating a social safety net, and providing humanitarian aid (food, clothing, and medicine) where necessary.

One can therefore view adequate external assistance as the essential start-up fuel to ignite the engine, get the wheels moving, and build up the momentum to put the economy on the turnpike to capitalism. Thus, the consensus strategy for capitalist transformation may also be described as a structure resting on three primary pillars: *stabilization, marketization,* and *foreign aid.*

Economists further agree—though with more qualifications—on the essential features of the transitional performance of the Central and Eastern European (CEE) countries since 1990, and of the former Soviet Union since 1991. For example, almost all agree that output has dropped more sharply than anticipated throughout CEE, including in the group of three big postsocialist economies (CEE-3)—Poland, Hungary, and the Federation of the Czech and Slovak Republics (CSFR).[2] But given the faulty official data, they disagree on how deep the decline has been.[3] Views diverge even further on the magnitude of declines in per capita consumption, living standards, and economic welfare.[4]

The divergence becomes the widest when it comes to explaining the output and consumption drop. Experts lay varying degrees of blame on four factors: stabilization policy, accompanied by an excessive credit crunch, (the demand side); micro rigidity further compounded by policy instability and macro uncertainty (the supply side); the Soviet/Council on Mutual Economic Assistance (CMEA) trade shock (internal trade); and post-liberalization competition from Western imports (external trade).

For example, Richard Portes (in this volume) places most of the blame for the deep and persistent economic contraction on three factors: the CMEA trade shock, some aspects of the implementation of stabilization or liberalization policies (for example, excessive devaluation of currencies in Poland and the CSFR requiring macro policy much tighter than what would have been necessary otherwise), and the lack of reform of the supply side. Andrew Berg and Jeffrey Sachs agree, but only partly: they challenge that devaluation in Poland was excessive.[5] Paul Marer (in this volume) views import competition from the West resulting from trade liberalization as a major contributor to the "output" decline. By contrast, Berg and Sachs find little evidence to indict import competition. Much disagreement notwithstanding, here also economists seem to converge on one point: they generally agree that the trade shock—the collapse of the CMEA trade and payments arrangements; the loss of East Germany as a major trading partner; the temporary shrinkage of the Middle East market due to the Gulf crisis; the additional chaos in the payments mechanism due to the Soviet decision to trade with the former CMEA partners in hard currencies from January 1, 1990; the adverse terms-of-trade shift resulting from the Soviet move to world prices for energy exports; and the increasing center-republic conflicts and the loss of Kremlin authority culminating in the breakup of the Soviet Union—has been a major force behind the deep and protracted contraction of the CEE economies.[6]

While economists generally agree on components that should compose the core of the transformation strategy, the convergence breaks down on the sequencing, speed, and stress (relative intensity of implementation) of these components, as well as on whether and how sectoralism (i.e., industrial policy) should shape their implementation. For example, Portes argues that if macroeconomic stabilization is possible only at the expense of "unsustainable output falls," selective sectoral focus should take priority. He cites Russia in 1992 as a case in point, advocating giving "macroeconomic-independent" sectors such as agriculture and energy greater attention than a high-stake gamble on stabilization. Marer, as well as Berg and Sachs, would reject this proposition outright in the case of Russia, which is on the verge of a hyperinflationary meltdown. They would agree instead with Stanley Fischer and Alan Gelb that "for countries with severe internal or external imbalances, macroeconomic stabilization has to be the initial priority."[7] Berg and Sachs—but not Marer—would also disagree with the Portes proposition that financial restructuring and demonopolization should precede privatization of large enterprises.

One instructive start toward understanding the debate on sequencing, speed, stress, and sectoralism is to separate the semantics from the economics of such catchphrases as "shock therapy," "big bang," and "gradualism," a task I turn to next.

Shock Therapy, Big Bang, and Gradualism: Economics and Semantics

Economists (our authors again are no exceptions) often debate the issues of sequencing, speed, stress, and sectoralism with three catchphrases: shock therapy, big bang, and gradualism. Most, however, do not define them precisely, and the consequences are what one would expect: miscommunication and misunderstanding resulting in much unnecessary confusion and controversy.

The conventional practice is to use the terms "shock therapy" and "big bang" interchangeably, and contrast them with the alternative of "gradualism" (some call it a step-by-step or conservative approach).[8] The shock therapy/big-bang strategy typically implies a simultaneous and rapid deployment approach on all fronts. In terms of the four interlocking wheels described earlier—stabilization, liberalization, privatization, and institution-building—the big-bang approach means exactly what it says: get all four wheels moving together and quickly with minimum emphasis on sectoral selectivism (industrial policy). By contrast, gradualism usually connotes an approach involving a great deal of attention to appropriate sequencing of the various components and subcomponents of the overall policy package, as well as differentiation in speed and stress of these component reforms determined in light of sectoral considerations.

Three observations are relevant here. First, the quality of the policy debate would improve if observers avoid the catchphrase "shock therapy," and say exactly what they mean. Economists would be better off if they returned this technical term to where it belongs—the psychiatry departments of hospitals. The reason is that this metaphor involves a misleading analogy; and worse, it carries a false negative connotation. Psychiatrists apply electrical shocks as a last resort to treat patients suffering from certain types of severe depression and catatonic schizophrenia. Here the electrical shock *is* the therapy. In other words, the shock is the intended means to achieve an end—relieve the symptoms, if not cure the patient. By contrast, for a postcommand economy, the shock that flows from a simultaneous and speedy implementation of a transitional strategy is an unintended—though unavoidable—consequence. Unlike the objective in psychiatry, the purpose is not to administer the shock to treat the symptoms of the underlying disease, but to apply a curative therapy that unfortunately involves a shock. Put succinctly, in psychiatry the shock is the intended therapy, whereas in the economics of transition, the shock is the unintended consequence of the therapy.[9]

These seemingly fine points of distinction have serious political implications. It so happens that observers often take this metaphor literally, and fall into the intellectual trap of viewing the shock as the intended therapy while interpreting the alternative approach as a therapy without shock (the psychiatric analogy would be the painless drug therapy), and thus preferable. All the complex issues of sequencing, speed, stress, and sectoral activism are thus reduced to a choice between shock or no shock. Consequently, critics view economists who advocate "shock therapy" as mechanical (electrical?) technocrats with little compassion for the victims of their cruel treatment, and with little understanding of the political implications for the sustainability of economic reforms. It thus makes sense to simply banish the term "shock therapy" from the vocabulary of the economics of transition.

The second point is that while the phrase "big bang" does not suffer from the adverse moral and political fallout of "shock therapy," this term, imported from astrophysics and cosmology, means different things to different people. One economist's big bang may be another economist's gradualism ("little whimper"). While a "Big Bang with two Big B's" ought to imply a simultaneous and speedy implementation of the transition strategy on all four fronts, most big bangers often differentiate among the four component reforms in terms of sequencing, speed, and stress. For example, *The Economist*[10] defines gradualists as those who put priority on creating market institutions (legal, accounting, and regulating frameworks; autonomous commercial banks; capital markets; and so on) over privatization, and advocate a strong state role in ownership reform of large enterprises with a step-by-step approach. According to this definition, Marer is a gradualist even though he believes "a transition economy requires 'shock therapy' if it inherits a highly distorted structure of relative prices or a large macroeconomic disequilibrium."[11] *The Economist* would also label Fischer and Gelb—along with many World Bank economists—gradualists, since they suggest, "It seems doubtful that the private sector could handle restructuring of very large, weak industries, so the state will need to restructure or close them."[12]

Interestingly, it is *The Economist's* version of the gradualist model that many often criticize as a painful big bang involving simultaneous, forceful, and speedy implementation of stabilization and liberalization, but with little progress on privatization and institution building. Indeed, this is the Polish big bang that many love to hate. Clearly, *The Economist's* big bang entails not only speedy implementation of stabilization and liberalization, but also rapid privatization of small *and* large state-owned enterprises (SOEs). This is the Czechoslovakian big-bang model. In practice, however, the bang from the Czechoslovakian privatization program has not been exactly big.

The upshot is that the dichotomy between big bang and gradualism is artificial and misleading. In reality, we are dealing with a four-by-four matrix—where the real policy question for a transitional economy at hand is the design of a strategy involving the four issues of sequencing, speed, stress (strength of implementation), and sectoral dimensions of the four core component reforms. The big-bang/gradualism debate reduces these critical policy decisions into a false identification problem of separating a "soft big banger" from a "hard gradualist." But more importantly, it impedes free exchange of ideas and thoughts by squashing all the practical complexities of the transition strategy into two conceptual pigeonholes.

Finally, as Portes has indicated,[13] the paradox of the big-bang strategy is that in reality it *cannot* be implemented. After creating the Universe with a Big Bang, God appears to have designed the planet Earth such that some things simply take longer than others. There is no conceivable way privatization of large SOEs and structural market reforms can be implemented as rapidly as liberalization and stabilization. This inherent speed-gap means capitalism cannot be created with a big bang. Even in Germany, where the western German institutions were simply imposed on the eastern part of the country and the iron fist of the Treuhand has been pushing privatization with full force, the time gap could not prevent the big bang from remaining what it is—an abstraction. The lesson—from the post–Industrial Revolution history of today's advanced industrial nations, as well as from experiments with "test-tube capitalism" since 1989—is clear: In the real world, there is no such thing as capitalism with a big bang, but only gradualism of different shapes, sizes, and, of course, speed.

The Dynamics of Reforms

Economists who wish to escape the confining trap of the big-bang/gradualism debate tend to conduct their analysis in terms of "sequencing of reforms." Some go one step further and add the issue of speed.[14] But the dynamics of implementation of the transition strategy in fact involve five related, yet distinct, elements: *sequencing; stress* (intensity with which a policy is implemented); *speed* (the pace at which a policy is implemented); *sectoralism* (the extent to which the state interferes with market forces to promote "winners" and suppress "losers" at the level of sectors, industries, and enterprises); and *duration* (the time it takes to complete the implementation of various policy measures). Out of these five elements, three involve time in one way or another: sequencing, speed, and duration. The other two involve differentiation in force (stress) and focus (sectoralism).

Figure 1, which I have borrowed from Alan Gelb and Cheryl Gray (1991),[15] further illuminates this distinction. This figure represents a stylized phasing of various reform measures with the premise that the full transition in a prototype CEE/former Soviet Union economy will take ten years. I am using this chart for illustrative purposes; it is not a consensus blueprint, nor does

FIGURE 1. PHASING OF REFORM OVER A TEN-YEAR PERIOD

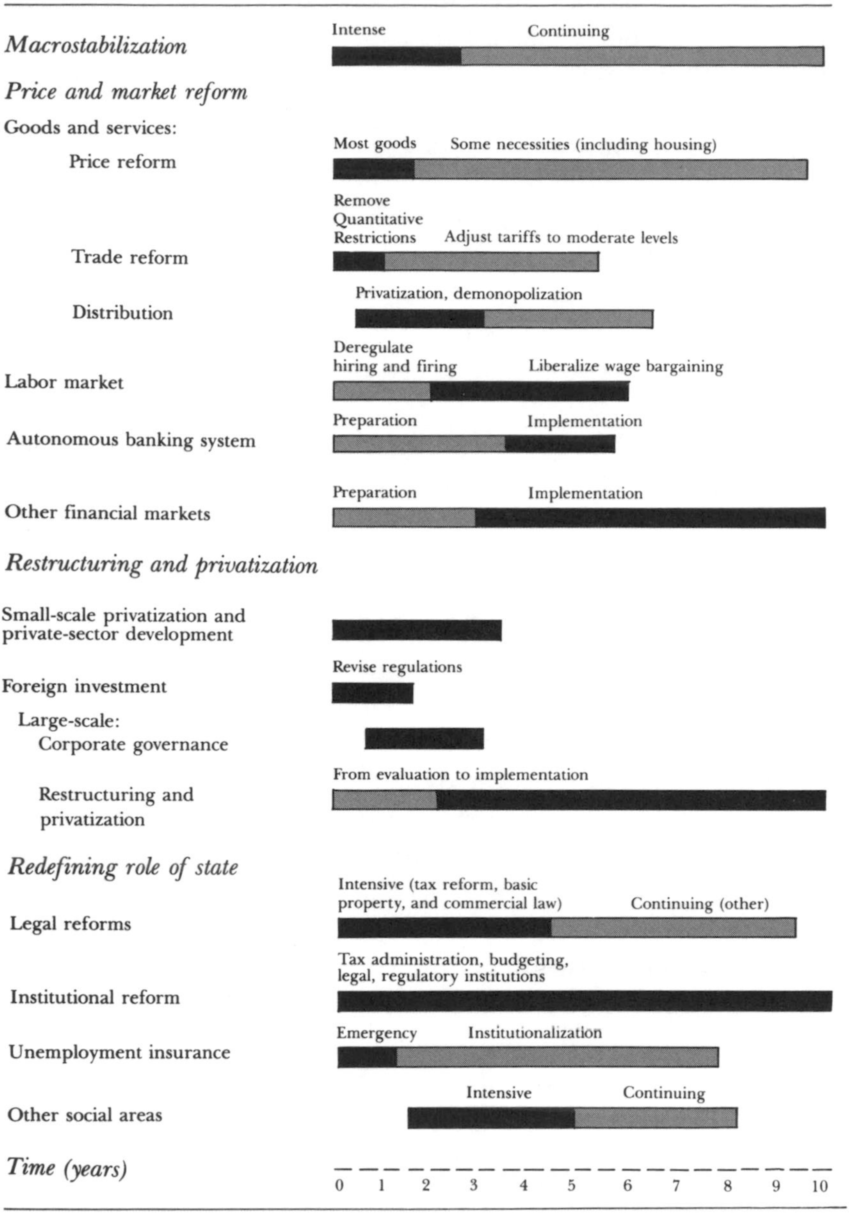

Macrostabilization
Intense
Continuing
Price and market reform
Goods and services:
Price reform
Most goods
Some necessities (including housing)
Trade reform
Remove Quantitative Restrictions
Adjust tariffs to moderate levels
Distribution
Privatization, demonopolization
Labor market
Deregulate hiring and firing
Liberalize wage bargaining
Autonomous banking system
Preparation
Implementation
Other financial markets
Preparation
Implementation
Restructuring and privatization
Small-scale privatization and private-sector development
Foreign investment
Revise regulations
Large-scale:
Corporate governance
Restructuring and privatization
From evaluation to implementation
Redefining role of state
Legal reforms
Intensive (tax reform, basic property, and commercial law)
Continuing (other)
Institutional reform
Tax administration, budgeting, legal, regulatory institutions
Unemployment insurance
Emergency
Institutionalization
Other social areas
Intensive
Continuing
Time (years)
0 1 2 3 4 5 6 7 8 9 10

Source: See reference 16.

it contain all elements of reforms that cause controversy. For example, exchange rate reform and currency convertibility are conspicuously absent from the diagram. Readers who do not wish to plow through the chart can get the main points from the text.

Four points deserve special emphasis. First, the authorities undertake the overall policy program with *most* reform measures beginning simultaneously, and a *few* sequentially. Because most measures are complementary, there is no linear sequence.[16] For example, out of the fifteen tasks Gelb and Gray identify, twelve begin simultaneously. Only three measures—privatization in the distribution system of goods and services, corporate governance of large-scale state enterprises, and "other social areas" (health, education, sick leave, maternity benefits, child care facilities, and so on)—begin after one year or even later. This representation may give the impression that sequencing hardly matters. But that impression is more apparent than real. In Gelb and Gray's formulation, sequencing plays a much greater role when two other practical distinctions are taken into account: the difference between preparation (shaded bars) and implementation (dark bars), and that between intensive (dark bars) and continuing (shaded bars) implementation. In terms of implementation—intensive or not—seven of the fifteen measures come later at various stages: the three mentioned earlier, plus liberalization of wage bargaining, creation of an autonomous banking system, reform of other financial markets, and restructuring and privatization of large SOEs.

Second, it is important to distinguish between the stress (the intensity) with which a policy can be pursued and the speed with which its implementation may proceed. A difficult and complex task, by definition, is one where you put in a lot of hard work and make little headway. Privatization (or restructuring or liquidation) of large SOEs—especially the fat and weak ones—is one area where a lot of stress would yield little speed. While Figure 1 does not explicitly distinguish between stress and speed, the distinction is discernible. The tasks that get top priority, require heavy stress (forceful application), and can be accomplished quickly are those that begin in year zero and end by the second or third year (short dark bars covering the first few years). Macro-stabilization and price reform are two good examples. The measures that also get top priority and require a lot of stress, yet move at a slow speed are those that need preparation or implementation from day one, but are completed only at the end of the decade (long dark bars extending to the tenth year). Examples are restructuring and privatization of large-scale enterprises, and institutional reform. Thus, it is the combined interaction of stress and speed that determine the duration of implementation.

Third, while initial economic conditions—the degree of macroeconomic imbalance and that of allocative controls and price distortions—and the nature of political transition should, and do, shape the overall thrust of the strategy, and with it the sequencing, stress, and speed of various measures, an element of choice still remains—especially when it comes to the details of implementing the policy package.[17] The Polish privatization policy could have been put together faster, whereas price and trade liberalization could have been more selective, and the zloty devaluation could have been smaller. The Hungarian reform program could have moved faster; and without Václav Klaus, the Czechoslovakian strategy would probably have been less "laissez-faire"-ish. East Germany's big bang had little to do with its initial economic conditions, and a lot to do with West German *political* imperatives. Even in Russia, the continuing battles on the transition strategy between the "Gaidar gang" and the "industrial lobby" demonstrate how complex is the process through which the political elite of a particular country choose (and abandon) particular transition strategy.

Finally, the figure cannot illustrate well how sectoral considerations can shape the implementation of the major categories of reforms, because its main purpose is to sketch the dynamics of design and implementation of the *main elements* (with little sectoral focus) of a prototype transformation strategy, not present a detailed sectoral analysis of restructuring and privatization of enterprises. Even then, the figure gives a flavor of what I mean by "sectoralism": prices of necessities and housing are decontrolled more gradually than those of other goods, privatization of the distribution system begins after that of small-scale enterprises, and so on. How sectoral considerations may influence the interlocking relationship among stabilization, liberalization, and privatization is the subject I turn to next.

The Internal Contradictions of the Transition Strategy: A Case for Conflict Management

As Figure 1 emphasizes, most economists agree that stabilization, liberalization, privatization, and institutional reforms are interlocking (complementary) wheels of the same vehicle, and therefore need to move together. At the same time, economists (including our authors) also agree that restructuring and privatization of *large-scale* enterprises (and some critical institutional reforms) in the economies of CEE and the former Soviet Union have been much too slow, and thus have delayed the transition and raised the level of misery by preventing price and trade liberalization from generating a positive supply-side response. The usual reaction to this "stabliberalization-privatization time gap" is to advocate an acceleration of privatization, if necessary, with "quick and dirty" methods.[18] The presumption is that intensified efforts at privatization will induce a quick birth of a substantially privatized *market* economy where strong and speedy "stabliberalization" measures will bear their intended fruits.

The problem with this prescription is that it ignores three aspects of the reality of the transitional economies: privatization of large enterprises takes a long time; a substantial portion of these enterprises are not viable at world prices; and the governments are not politically capable of liquidating them immediately.[19] First, as emphasized earlier, privatization of *large-scale monopolistic enterprises and conglomerates* is an inherently slow process (privatization of small or micro enterprises, especially in the trade and services sector—retail stores, for instance—is easy and quick, and has already taken place on a massive scale in CEE-3). Many roadblocks retard the pace of privatization of large SOEs, including the problem of asset valuation; the lack of domestic capital; the national security (and pride) considerations involving foreign ownership and control of the largest enterprises, concerns over social equity, settlement of claims by former owners (the restitution problem). The CEE-3 countries want to privatize about half of their state-owned assets by 1994, but they are unlikely to reach that goal. According to *The Economist* in late 1991, "At their current pace, they will be lucky to reach that goal in 30 years, never mind three. In practice, selling state-owned firms has proved time-consuming, frustrating, and expensive."[20] Even with a creative voucher system, one needs some degree of restructuring, demonopolization, and commercialization, and thus cannot accelerate privatization up to a speed high enough to significantly reduce, let alone eliminate, the time inconsistency problem.

For example, with all the enthusiasm for fast privatization it was not until June 1992 that the Czechoslovak government was able to complete the first round of "share sales" of the first wave of voucher privatization. That task took a year and a half since the launching of the stabilization/liberalization program, and required a lot of hard work by a lot of dedicated people. Further, in this round, only 1,500 out of a total of 11,000 projects were approved in the Czech Republic.[21] Only a big brother working "iron-fist-in-golden-glove" and round the clock—as is the case in eastern Germany—can accelerate privatization, and even that ultimate driving machine takes years. Put more succinctly, many "fast privatizers" seem to forget that left to market forces, only the *best* of the "good" large-scale enterprises (accounting for only a small portion of the economy's output) can be privatized. And the government already crippled by stubborn fiscal deficits ends up holding a big bag of the bad and ugly ones.

Second, by all accounts, a substantial proportion of the large SOEs do not appear to be viable at world prices. For example, according to Gordon Hughes and Paul Hare, the proportion of output with *negative* value added at world prices (the value of intermediate inputs alone—not wages and profits—exceeds that of outputs at world prices) in manufacturing may be as high as 35 percent for Hungary and Czechoslovakia, and almost 40 percent for Poland.[22] Even if these estimates overstate the presence of "the negative value-added enterprises," two other factors can make enterprises *inviable* at world prices (the present value of net cost of liquidation is lower than that of restructuring).

First, some loss-making enterprises may be adding positive value (a flow measure), but may have accumulated bad debts to an extent that their net worth is highly negative (a stock problem). These loans are typically liabilities to other domestic enterprises and banks. But some enterprises are also indebted to foreign official and private creditors, typically denominated in foreign currencies.[23] The debt problem, however, can be partially mitigated by state-owned banks' writing off bad loans for those enterprises that are otherwise deemed to be viable at world prices over the medium term. Another type of liability, however, cannot be written off: some enterprises are so burdened with the potential clean-up costs of past environmental damage (and eco-hostile technology) that it is cheaper to liquidate than restructure them. Second, and more important, for some loss-making enterprises, the resource requirements of restructuring (capital, managerial skills, the authorities' administrative capabilities, and so on) are so high, the enterprises may not be salvageable.

The upshot is that many *large-scale* enterprises, accounting for a significant proportion of the industrial sector, cannot be privatized at all: they are not amenable to restructuring and must be liquidated. Leaving aside the point that the act of privatization itself does not automatically improve corporate governance, efficiency, and productivity, the presumption that intense efforts at fast privatization will quickly produce a large privatized sector is simply not true. Given sweeping stabiliberalization measures, a more likely picture is a deepening and widening of financial distress in large state companies. Many recent developments corroborate these observations. For example, by September 1991, the Polish Ministry of Industry classified 700 out of 1,500 SOEs as having crossed the thresholds designed to trigger liquidation proceedings.[24] And in Hungary, according to the authorities, "hundreds" of the 2,000 state enterprises face imminent bankruptcy.[25]

Finally, for economic, political, and social reasons, the reformist governments are *not* able to liquidate the inviable enterprises immediately, or even within a year or two. The governments rightly fear that the public support for reforms cannot be sustained if massive liquidation and layoffs come in the wake of plunging outputs and cause intolerable social distress. The managers and the workers of the inviable enterprises faced with little prospect for alternative job opportunities also use all their political power to block the process of liquidation. The march toward marketization has already created gaping holes in the "socialist" social safety net, and the fiscally crippled governments with little help from abroad simply cannot prevent people from falling through if the proletariat are thrown off from their workplace onto the safety net in staggering numbers.

Signs of disillusion are already turning into reactionary resentment and cynical apathy. Polls show that the army and the police are the most trusted institutions in Poland—a country under martial law only nine years ago.[26] Additionally, the voter turnout plunged to a low of 43 percent in the October 1991 national election (which revealed the stunning fragmentation of national solidarity, with the strongest party getting less than 14 percent of the vote and 29 parties gaining parliamentary seats), from the euphoric high of 63 percent in the first semifree election, held only two and half years earlier. Further, in June 1992 Poland's fledgling democracy suffered another jolt when the Parliament voted no confidence in the prime minister, installing the fourth postcommunist government in three years.[27] In Hungary only a quarter of the voters participated in some parliamentary by-elections in 1991.[28]

Neither a well-designed bankruptcy law nor market mechanism can win against these formidable political and social forces. For example, in this environment a well-intended and often-repeated prescription turns out to be impractical. Western advisers advocate that the budget constraint of enterprises be *hardened:* the government should cut all subsidies, and banks should not lend to cover the losses of unprofitable companies. The policy can transform illiquid companies into insolvent ones. But one need not worry; since the government cannot liquidate most nonviable companies, it can implement this policy only *softly!*

The failure to harden the budget constraint of potentially nonviable companies also impedes another widely advocated step toward privatization—commercialization (or corporatization). Commercialization of an SOE involves three tasks:

clarification of ownership rights, typically by converting the enterprise into a joint-stock company; improvement of the corporate governance by appointing a board of directors consisting largely of outsiders; and hardening of the so-far-soft budget constraint. Since the last task cannot be accomplished even for many potentially viable companies, often all that can be achieved is "soft commercialization": the SOEs are converted into joint-stock companies with outside directors, but they still drain the treasury of their predominant owner—the state.

A program of massive liquidation and layoffs is also difficult to justify on pure economic grounds. In an already collapsing economy with no major new capitalist sphere of economic activity large and dynamic enough to cushion the "liquidation shock" and absorb the unemployed, sweeping shutdowns may only deepen the economic contraction, and thus cannot strengthen the credibility of reforms and inspire business confidence. And with eroding credibility and confidence, compounded by political and social unrest, threatening the viability of the government, one gets disillusioned domestic entrepreneurs desperate to take their capital out, not investors—local and foreign—flocking in with money to build markets.

These factors may explain why only a handful of loss-making enterprises have been shut down so far in CEE (again, eastern Germany is the exception for obvious reasons). Two examples from Poland illustrate how the inviability of enterprises has become the Achilles' heel of the reformist governments: After announcing a scheme for privatizing 400 large enterprises in June 1991, Poland withdrew 170 of them in October 1991 because the authorities later deemed them to be inviable, bringing down the proportion of industrial activity to be privatized from 25 percent to about 10 percent.[29] The second example speaks even louder. In July 1991 Polish Prime Minister Bielecki put the bankrupt Orsus Tractor factory in Warsaw back onto the life-support system, and fired his industry minister, along with a dozen other high officials, for pulling the plug and trying to let the market forces do their job. If market forces had gotten their way, not only would Europe's largest tractor producer have perished, putting its 22,000 employees out of work, but the shock wave would have also affected the work and liveli-hood of another 100,000 workers at 300 supplier factories.[30]

Sustaining unsustainable companies, however, creates an increasingly dangerous side effect: a rapid rise in enterprise debts as bankrupt state-owned banks and so-far-solvent SOEs provide liquidity to the candidates for liquidation. While severe undercapitalization (and net *negative* benefits of enforcing bank-ruptcy) may prevent these *state-owned* banks from foreclosing these "too-big-to-fail" enterprises, the real driving force behind this "liquidize, not liquidate" phenomenon seems to be the liq-uidation risk that the reformist state itself faces if it strictly enforces bankruptcy laws. The reluctance of the creditor banks *and* SOEs to foreclose the insolvent enterprises is likely to be greatly influenced by the fact that they are still *owned by the state*— they are not yet free to conduct economic calculations as *privately owned* entities.[31]

Whatever incentives may drive this apparently perverse (but broadly rational) behavior of creditor banks and enterprises, the adverse consequences of the growing enterprise debts are the same: they compound the enterprise nonviability problem by throwing up additional roadblocks to privatization; increase the difficulty in determining whether an enterprise should be re-structured or liquidated; aggravate the systemic risk that the failure of one debtor enterprise will start a chain of insolvencies, thus further reinforcing the government's (as well as the banks' and the creditor enterprises') reluctance to enforce foreclosures; and, of critical importance, *crowd away* scarce credit from profita-ble SOEs *and* new private companies to nonviable entities. Put succinctly, the vicious cycle of rising enterprise debts prevents the dynamics of market mechanism from working: it blocks the *exit* of inefficient and insolvent firms (as the state shies away from enforcing foreclosures), and it impedes *entry* of efficient and solvent firms (as bad credit drives out good credit).[32]

All this adds up to a central conundrum of the transition strategy: a "quick and dirty" approach to privatization in a post-command economy shocked by rapid and comprehensive liber-alization *and* strong and ongoing stabilization measures is likely to yield dirty, not quick results. With the privatization process inherently too slow, and the government incapable of engaging in massive liquidation of inviable companies, efforts to accelerate privatization do not correct the speed mismatch problem; instead, the sweeping stabliberalization programs succeed in forcing potentially viable enterprises into insolvency and putting the government into the fiscally and politically distressing position of holding a much bigger bag of bankrupt companies, thus undermining the whole reform program. By ignoring and aggravating the problem of nonviable enterprises, the fast privatization approach thus may help the reformist government become nonviable! The only way out of this conundrum seems to lie in standing the conventional wisdom on its head: correct the speed mismatch problem, not by speeding up privatization, but by selectively slowing down liberalization, and to some extent softening and redesigning stabilization.

Perverse Consequences of an Internally Inconsistent Strategy

Before I elaborate on how phased and selective liberalization and soft stabilization can be coordinated with inherently slow enterprise reform and privatization, it would be instructive to appreciate a paramount paradox that characterizes the transition problem: In order to sustain the economic credibility and political viability of the reform program, the four policy wheels must move in tandem; but they can do so only if the state actively *plans* and manages the coordination of the wheels with an appropriate mix of the four S's—sequencing, stress, speed, and sectoralism. More specifically, a strong and speedy stabliberalization program out of synch with the process of enterprise reform and privatization can actually create a vicious cycle of "destabilizing" stabilization *and* "depflationary" (a superstagflationary situation with depression accompanied by high or hyperinflation) liberalization. Together, they can accelerate the collapse of modernizing investment, retard the pace of privatization *and* development of a new private sector, provoke a perverse supply-side response, and ultimately derail the whole reform program.

More specifically, speed mismatch on a high-speed track can produce an internally inconsistent strategy, and—while the intensity and the nature of manifestations can vary greatly from one country to another—this inconsistency can provoke at least four types of policy-performance contradictions, seriously undermining the credibility and the sustainability of the reform process. First, strong stabilization in the short run can destabilize even a largely privatized market economy (typically, a developing country) suffering from high inflation and unsustainably wide external deficits. Sharp budget cuts (accomplished largely by shrinking the public *investment* budget) and tax hikes can immediately reduce the fiscal deficits, but accompanied by tight money and credit policies, they typically throw the economy into a recession. The economic contraction causes social expenditures to jump and revenues to plunge, and in no time the budget deficit returns. The authorities may axe the deficit again, but if that succeeds in driving the economy deeper into the recession, the deficit springs back again.

This vicious cycle on the output front can be accompanied by another cycle on the inflation front. Confronted with fiscal deficits that refuse to disappear and an economy that continues to collapse, the monetary authorities get caught between pressures to monetize the deficits and to battle the raging inflation. They end up doing both, and in the process lose credibility as they pursue the stop-go policies. Another typical component of the stabilization package also contributes to this depflationary process and makes the life of both the finance minister and the central bank governor difficult: a one-shot massive devaluation of the currency to improve the economy's price competitiveness and to narrow the external deficits. In the short run, the depreciation represents an adverse supply-side *and* demand-side shock, putting additional downward pressure on output while at the same time fueling inflation. The surge in inflation, of course, quickly offsets the gains in price competitiveness from the initial devaluation, and the currency is devalued again to correct the newly acquired overvaluation. Whether the postdevaluation exchange rate is fixed or managed with a crawling peg or some system of floating, the broad inflationary consequences are the same, except that the price dynamics could be different under different exchange rate regimes, as they may affect policy credibility differently.

So a stabilization package in the context of inherited inertial inflation and increasingly rigid inflationary expectations can create *a vicious cycle* of policy-performance gap: budget deficit cuts, tight money, and currency devaluation → falling output (and employment) and higher inflation → "recession-induced" fiscal deficits and "inflation-driven" loss of price competitiveness (currency revaluation) → additional budgetary tightening, partial monetization of the deficit, and further currency depreciation → deeper recession and higher inflation → widening budget deficit and currency overvaluation → new rounds of macroeconomic tightening and currency devaluation → deeper economic contraction and higher inflation → . . . ?

Furthermore, stabilization measures produce additional inflationary shocks in economies in transition. In a command economy, the main source of government revenues are the enterprise profits (surplus) that the government artificially generates by fixing prices of goods as well as labor (wages), and collecting them. During the transition, stabilization measures result in a collapsing economy with liberalized prices. The economic contraction turns the profits of the enterprises into losses and—with no tax reform in place—in effect destroys the government's tax base and swells the budget deficit. With no banking reform, the loss-making enterprises borrow from the banking system, essentially monetizing the losses even if the central bank acts prudently, which it often does not. To sum up, in a transitional economy with *increasingly rigid inflationary expectations*, stabilization measures running ahead of enterprise and other institutional (e.g., fiscal, financial) reforms can further destabilize the economy—add to economic contraction, investment slump, inflationary spiral, and external deficits—so that eventually, even stronger measures are necessary.

Lessons from the experience of the developing countries suggest that stabilization programs are likely to ultimately succeed when, among other things, the government (specifically, the head of state and his economic team) is strong, popular, committed, and credible; the lag of the economy's supply-side response (say, to a currency devaluation) is relatively short; the policy conditionality focuses on the broad goals, and not on narrow targets and ratios such as the budget deficit to GNP and monetary growth rates; and the programs are well funded and accompanied by measures to promote exports and other potential growth sectors.[33] In a typical postcommand economy, these conditions generally do not hold. In particular, the vicious cycle can be even more vicious in a partly privatized, nonmarket economy with greater rigidity of the monopolistic supply side.

There seems to be one exception, however, at least for the major CEE economies. Stabilization measures have succeeded in that they have contained the loss of foreign exchange reserves by controlling the balance of payments—the current account balance, as well as the capital account. The current accounts of the transitional countries have small financible deficits, and in some cases even small surpluses. This apparent success is largely the flip side of the economic depression: imports have plunged, and the collapsing *domestic demand* accompanied by supercompetitive exchange rates have, on average, boosted export earnings in hard currencies. With little stock of hard-currency capital in the hands of individuals and enterprises, and no currency convertibility for capital account transactions, capital flight has not become a major problem. In addition, foreign private capital inflows—especially in the form of direct investment—have added to the official reserves of Hungary and Czechoslovakia.

The second policy inconsistency arises from a comprehensive and rapid application of one component of liberalization measures—*price reform*—that typically accompanies the stabilization package. Price reform generally takes the form of an across-the-board lifting of price controls, except for some basic necessities and "special" goods and services (e.g., food, rents, utility charges, energy). Free prices get rid of the shortages and the queues, and they bring repressed inflation into the open—both desirable goals—but they also undermine one primary objective of the stabilization package by pouring gasoline on the inflationary fire. Thus the transitional strategy suffers from a peculiar paradox: stabilization measures meant to control inflation in fact contribute to it; at the same time, price liberalization provides additional powerful fuel. While a part of this paradox is unavoidable, a "selective gradualist" approach can avert many of these contradictory policies with costly results, a point I shall elaborate on shortly.

Yet another source of tension is one other liberalization measure—*trade reform*. Sweeping trade liberalization is a sword with the edge on the wrong side, usually swinging at the wrong enemy. Accompanied by the national currency largely convertible for international transactions of goods and services, trade liberalization is intended to import the world price structure into the economy, make enterprises efficient by introducing competition, and fight monopolies' inflationary price setting by exposing them to foreign competition. In practice, however, the enterprises face one of two types of consequences. If accompanied by large currency devaluation, trade liberalization may become a blunt sword against monopolistic price increases as the devalued currency—by increasing gaps between prices and costs—provides monopolistic enterprises solid protection: they can raise prices without facing world competition.[34] If unaccompanied by large devaluation or if continuing inflation erodes the initial devaluation-induced protection from world competition, an abrupt trade liberalization can begin to overkill by driving potentially viable enterprises (over the medium term) to insolvency.

So we have another paradox: trade liberalization may not succeed initially in importing the world price structure and in forcing the domestic monopolies to face world competition; but if and when they do succeed, they may compound the financial distress of the enterprise sector, forcing to insolvency companies that need temporary breathing time, thus aggravating the fiscal drain and the budget deficit that the government is trying so hard to contain.

Finally, stabilization and liberalization measures, if not applied gently, gradually, and selectively, can put a knife through the Achilles' heel of the reform program: the nonviability of state enterprises that are "too big to fail." Protracted and intensifying economic contraction caused by stabilization measures can deepen the pool of inviable enterprises by *aggravating* the financial distress of companies that would be insolvent even when half exposed to world prices, and widen it by *forcing* companies that were potentially viable at world prices to join "the club of the clearly insolvents." Also, cuts in direct government subsidies to enterprises to reduce the budget deficit (and correct price distortions) can increase the membership of the "Nonviable Unlimited." Thus, comprehensive and abrupt trade liberalization, even if the currency is not fully convertible for current-account transactions (full current-account convertibility means consumers and producers can freely buy and sell foreign exchange if they engage in cross-border transactions involving goods and services), can severely aggravate the enterprise insolvency problem.

Here the distinction between *static* and *dynamic* comparative advantage is critically relevant. For *the enterprises that cannot be salvaged* and are clear candidates for "bulldozer liquidation," an abrupt exposure to world prices does not make them "more nonviable" (which is like being a bit more pregnant). It only *undermines the stabilization program*, as the government, unable to liquidate the living dead, is forced to subsidize them, and thereby enlarge the budget deficit; *and* the banking system provides loans creating additional credit; *and* the suppliers sell them goods on credit, aggravating the problem of the runaway enterprise debts.

For *the enterprises that appear viable at world prices* but need temporary protection and subsidies as they modernize and restructure, an abrupt and sweeping liberalization package can spell the difference between life and death. These enterprises are not competitive today at world prices (they do not have *static* comparative advantage), but they could be competitive tomorrow at world prices if given a chance to slowly adapt, learn, and improve (they have *dynamic* comparative advantage). While it is often difficult to clearly identify these "gray enterprises," it is also true that this is what entrepreneurs and businesses do every day in the advanced capitalist economies. On balance, often they are right, but sometimes they are wrong. Indeed, one primary rationale for profits is nothing but compensation for the risk of failure. Sector-blind liberalization measures can kill off these risky companies.

Sweeping and speedy stabliberalization measures can have three other important adverse effects. They can discourage the formation of a private sector and threaten the survival of the start-ups. They can do so by depressing demand and output; by causing disruptive volatility of the relative price structure; and by aggravating financial distress of the illiquid and insolvent SOEs that cannot be liquidated, and thus by forcing the state banking system to divert scarce credit away from the credit-worthy embryos of capitalism.

The rapid growth of the small-enterprise–dominated private sector in Poland does not invalidate this argument. Poland's private sector was already large before the launching of the January 1990 reform program. The initial enthusiasm accompanied by the ease in importing needed inputs due to trade liberalization, the early success in controlling inflation, and the expectations that the collapse in demand and output will be reversed soon—perhaps within a year—led to a dramatic rise in start-ups in 1990, especially in retail trade and construction, and to a lesser extent in light manufacturing. With continuing economic contraction, a resurgence of inflation, and the increasing social distress and political instability, the growth of the start-ups slowed down considerably in 1991, and many of the new businesses have already failed or remain suspended.[35] While the data for late 1991 and for 1992 are not available, the increasing economic chaos and political fragmentation (caused largely by the widening gap between stabliberalization and privatization/institutionalization) may have further undermined "the Polish private-sector miracle."

On top of slashing public investment (some projects critical to private-sector development, such as developing physical and social infrastructure—telecommunication, highways, bridges, ports, as well as education, vocational training and retraining, and health care—and others wasteful—building a new weapons system or renovating a clearly nonviable enterprise), orthodox stabliberalization measures can also discourage private-sector investment. With shifting rules of the game, a plunging economy with no light at the end of the tunnel, volatile inflation and relative prices (often accompanied by a currency collapsing at an unpredictable pace), and political fragmentation in a fragile democracy, private entrepreneurs and enterprises—domestic and foreign—have little incentive to take a long-term view and invest. As mentioned earlier, stabilization policies can vastly aggravate these bewildering uncertainties and instabilities, and inhibit much-needed productive investment.

Finally, by contributing to the failure to control high, unstable, and rising inflation, mechanical stabliberalization policies can delay the prospect for the domestic currency's becoming *fully* convertible for current-account transactions, let alone for capital-account transactions. The Czechoslovakian success in controlling inflation does not invalidate the argument that orthodox stabliberalization measures complicate the task of putting a permanent lid on inflation. Czechoslovakia is the only transitional economy with no historical memory of inflation. Also, there was little inflation (and macroeconomic imbalance) when the stabliberalization program was launched on January 1, 1991. With budgetary and monetary tightening policy accompanied by a strict incomes policy (tax-based wage policy leading to a sharp drop in real wages) to counteract the jump in inflation from price liberalization and currency devaluation, and *no initial inertial inflation and inherited inflationary expectations*, the CSFR government was able to prevent the one-shot price increases from turning into a persistent and rising inflationary spiral.

But the CSFR success story on the inflation front is not over yet. Privatization-driven liquidations and restructuring will likely reinforce the declining output, employment, and enterprise profits, and result in a widening budget deficit; *and* the expectations of a turnaround in the declining living standards will likely continue to be frustrated. Meanwhile, the Czech Republic (and even more so Slovakia) may experience workers' efforts to reverse the real wage decline, which may initiate a wage-price spiral.

Demand-Friendly Stabilization and Supply-Friendly Liberalization: An Imperfectly Coordinated Growth-Oriented Approach

With depflation ravaging the economies of CEE and the former Soviet Union and threatening the sustainability of the reform process, the overarching policy challenge is: Can the transition strategy be redesigned so that it can bring inflation down to low levels, jump-start economic recovery, maintain the low-inflationary growth, sustain the reform process, *and* accomplish all this without significantly slowing down the march toward marketization? The short answer is that this is a tall order and there exists no perfect and single response to this challenge. The longer answer is that yes, there are superior ways of reorganizing and coordinating the four core components of the conventional strategy; but while a few general principles can guide the alternative approach, the policy package must be tailored according to the specific economic and political conditions of individual economies. For example, the unique and complex conditions of Russia and other successor states of the Soviet Union call for significant modifications and extensions of the alternative strategy, especially at the stage of formulating concrete steps and implementing them.

The strategy rests on four major premises. First, the road to capitalism cannot be built on a "valley of tears" too long and too deep. While the state-enterprise sector should continue to shrink, overall economic growth must be restored soon. One cannot marketize an economy when the existing "market" is shrinking fast. It is also instructive to stand Milton Friedman's dictum that "inflation causes recession" on its head: *recession causes inflation, especially in a postcommand economy.* Second, as mentioned earlier, a more productive way to correct the speed mismatch problem is to soften and selectively slow down stabilization and liberalization measures rather than trying to do the impossible—significantly accelerate privatization of large SOEs.

Third, the weight of the collective wisdom of most Western economists notwithstanding, sector-blindness can be hazardous to the healthy capitalist development of a postcommand economy. At a very aggregate level, it is useful to categorize the enterprises (I am ignoring the agriculture sector, as I have done throughout) into three major groups: controlled, liberalized and newly emerging private.[36] The controlled sector is all state-owned, and this is where, along with natural monopolies, the bulk of the nonviable enterprises (the bad and the ugly) should belong. The liberalized sector will typically consist of SOEs, as well as those that have been privatized. State-owned liberalized enterprises should include largely viable enterprises and candidates for privatization. The emerging private sector is made up largely of newly established small enterprises in the form of limited liability companies, joint ventures, fully foreign-owned companies, partnerships, and single-owner firms. The privatized former SOEs and the newly established private firms are the two components of the productive (output-producing) private sector (privatization of the existing housing stock creates private wealth, but no output-producing enterprises).

Finally, we need to add one more critical dimension to the analysis of sequencing, stress, speed, and sectoralism: in the first few years, value-producing activities, preferably with strong economywide demand-expanding spillover effects, should get greater priority and governmental support than demand-depressing liberalization, restructuring, and liquidation. Once economic recovery is under way, with the private sector increasingly able to compensate for the decline in output and employment, the focus can shift the other way. A sweeping decontrolling of the command economy and an abrupt exposure to world prices can lead to suicidal waves of "destructive competition" rather than the Schumpetarian gales of "creative destruction."

Without trying to outline a full policy package, I shall highlight some of the main features of the alternative strategy by illustrating how it alters the design and the implementation of the four components of the conventional approach. I begin with liberalization because more than any other, this critical element of the conventional strategy intended to accelerate the transition to a market economy appears to be accomplishing the opposite by ultimately jeopardizing the sustainability of the reform process. To begin with, while a strong overall reform program—to be carried out immediately and later—should be announced on day one to signal a credible regime change, the actual implementation of liberalization measures should be phased in over a period of years, and it should be flexible and sector-sensitive. For example, while some prices should be decontrolled immediately, others (e.g., energy prices in Russia) should be freed up gradually, in steps. An abrupt sharp increase in an input price constitutes an adverse supply-and-demand shock, and in an inflationary environment, it can make the anti-inflation task of stabilization measures much tougher to accomplish. The OPEC shock's stagflationary effects on market economies is a lesson that should not be lost when it comes to reforming the command economies.

Regarding trade liberalization, all quotas should be transformed into equivalent tariffs, but there is a case for a *gradual elimination of tariffs* for sectors that need breathing time for restructuring, as well as for those enterprises that cannot be liquidated soon. While these tariffs should not be eliminated immediately, a timetable for phasing them out should be announced. This is standard practice in the market economies. Trade liberalizations undertaken in various free trade agreements, including past GATT rounds and the recently signed North American Free Trade Agreement (NAFTA), have taken this form. In the developing world the widely cited case of rapid trade liberalization took place in Chile during the 1970s. In 1973 the government replaced quantitative restrictions (QRs, or quotas) with average tariffs of about 100 percent (the highest tariff rate was over 500 percent) and it took six years to bring them down to a uniform rate of 10 percent.[37] The argument that you need a sledgehammer approach to create a market economy out of a centrally planned one infested with huge monopolies and a plan-obsessed "apparatchik" is faulty; as mentioned earlier, the consequences could in fact be counterproductive by raising the social costs of transition beyond the level of popular tolerance.

The final point involves the role of the liberalization policy in promoting economic recovery *and* modernizing and restructuring the industrial sector, making it increasingly competitive in the world market. The temporary protective walls of tariffs, as well as *direct* budgetary subsidies (not explicit or implicit input subsidies), can support the potential pockets of growth in the emerging private sector, as well as the existing SOEs that appear viable with necessary restructuring. An outward-looking approach based on the principle of dynamic comparative advantage should be pursued. Vigorous *domestic competition* should be encouraged by breaking up monopolies into several firms supplying the same product, while temporarily protecting these fledgling firms from *global competition*. The philosophy of "the survival of the fittest" should be pursued first at the national level, and the survivors should then be gradually exposed to foreign competition as they increasingly become "fitter." This two-step economic Darwinism is the model that Japan and the Asian newly industrialized economies (NIEs) pursued so successfully in their industrialization and overall economic development.[38] Incredibly, the 1989 trade-weighted average tariff rate in Poland (9 percent) was only slightly higher than in the United States (5 percent), and while Washington maintained quantitative restrictions on almost forty food and agricultural items in 1990 and 9 percent of U.S imports was affected by "voluntary export restraints," quotas and other non-tariff barriers are virtually non-existent in Poland.[39]

But there is a problem: Poland is no South Korea, and Russia is certainly no Japan. In other words, how do we deal with the dilemma that if the bureaucrats used to running a command economy are responsible for making these decisions, they will instinctively pursue an anticompetitive and antimarket industrial policy? Two responses are in order. First, the transitional economies are already running and will continue to run a de facto industrial policy. It is best to recognize this reality and try to make it as promarket and procompetition as possible.

Second, one possible way to impose an "industrial policy conditionality" is to form a "Foreign Economic Advisory Committee" for each country. This is especially critical for Russia; if this approach is successful, other countries can follow the same path. The advisory committee should consist of a top government official and a top businessman from the G-3 countries and South Korea, and one high official each from the World Bank and International Monetary Fund. So the committee will consist of ten individuals supported by a staff of economists, industry specialists, and bureaucrats from the ministries of the participating countries. This committee can judiciously guide the industrial policy of the transitional economy with the carrot and the stick of *official* funds approved by the World Bank, the EBRD, and other government agencies.

With regard to stabilization measures, the top priority should be inflation control. If sector-specific protection through tariffs and subsidies, as well as state support for investment by the private sector and the restructuring SOEs, can generate an economic recovery, or at least halt the persistent decline in demand and output, most of the deficit problem is likely to disappear. Tax reform to replace the old implicit taxation through appropriation of enterprise surplus accompanied by vigorous efforts at collection can also help. Money and credit growth will be a lot easier to control if loss-making and apparently nonviable *state-controlled* SOEs receive direct budgetary subsidies, but no credit from the banking system or other enterprises. With these reforms in place, and with liberalization measures and currency devaluations sensitive to the inflationary consequences, tight monetary policy has a much better chance of controlling inflation.

Finally, to improve the supply-side response and to get a better handle on monetary control, the growing problem of enterprise debts must be addressed immediately. State-owned banks should be recapitalized by replacing their bad loans with the government securities. These recapitalized banks should be allowed to lend only to *creditworthy* private and liberalized SOEs.[40] The government can get rid of these bad debts over time as it liquidates, restructures, and privatizes the debtor enterprises.

This "evolutionary model"—a growth-oriented, sector-sensitive, and, if you like, gradualist approach—has a much better chance at controlling inflation, promoting recovery, and putting the transitional economies on a sustainable path toward capitalism than the "creationist model" being tried currently. This evolutionary model appears best equipped to deal effectively with the ultimate paradox: a strong state with a coherent plan is precisely what a command economy needs to free itself from the strangling grip of the state. Indeed, effective design and implementation of the four components of the transformation package—stabilization, liberalization, privatization, and institution-building—require nothing short of a strong hand of the state.

Capitalism in today's most advanced industrialized countries took centuries to develop, and even then the state always remained intimately involved in shaping its evolution and ensuring its survival. The creationist model of *laissez faire* capitalism is an appealing, but abstract ideology: It was neither created instantly anywhere with a big bang, nor does it have much in common with the *modus vivendi* of advanced capitalist economies. True believers may cling to the creationist approach now in vogue in the transitional economies, but the weight of history and experience appears to favor the alternative.

Notes

1. Incomes policy normally means some measure to restrain wage inflation—for example, taxing enterprises that approve wage increases.
2. It appears that by the time this volume gets into the hands of the readers, CSFR will have already separated into two independent nations: Czech Republic and Slovakia. CEE-3 will then consist of Poland, Hungary, and Czech Republic.
3. See, for example, Richard Portes' chapter in this book; Andrew Berg and Jeffrey Sachs, "Structural Adjustment and International Trade in Eastern Europe: The Case of Poland," *Economic Policy: Eastern Europe* 14 (April 1992); and Andrew Berg, "A Critique of Official Data" (Paper presented at the IMF/World Bank Conference on the Macroeconomic Situation in Eastern Europe, Washington, D.C., 1992).
4. Ibid.
5. See Berg and Sachs, "Structural Adjustment and International Trade in Eastern Europe"; and Dani Rodrik, "Making Sense of the Soviet Trade Shock in Eastern Europe: A Framework and Some Estimates," National Bureau of Economic Research Working Paper, no. 4112 (Cambridge, Mass., 1992).
6. Rodrik, in "Making Sense of the Soviet Trade Shock in Eastern Europe," estimates that the trade shock caused the gross domestic product to decline by 3–4 percent in Poland and 7–8 percent in Hungary and Czechoslovakia.
7. Stanley Fischer and Alan Gelb, "The Process of Socialist Economic Transformation," *Journal of Economic Perspectives*, vol. 5, no. 4 (1991), p. 101.
8. International Monetary Fund, World Bank, Organization for Economic Cooperation and Development, and European Bank for Reconstruction and Development, *A Study of the Soviet Economy* (Paris: International Monetary Fund, 1990), pp. 18–19.
9. The Hungarian economist Janos Kornai has made the same point in an interview: "I hate the phrase 'shock therapy.' We don't apply the therapy for the sake of the shock. The shock is an inevitable side effect." See Robert

Kuttner, "The Dustbin of Economics," *The New Republic* (February 25, 1991).

10. "Eastern Europe Hesitates," *The Economist*, May 16, 1992, pp. 13–14.
11. See page 79 of this volume.
12. Fischer and Gelb, "The Process of Socialist Economic Transformation," p. 100.
13. See page 30 of this volume.
14. See, for example, Susan M. Collins and Dani Rodrik, "Eastern Europe and the Soviet Union in the World Economy," *Policy Analyses in International Economics*, no. 32 (Washington: Institute for International Economics, 1991), p. 11; Guillermo de la Dehesa, "Privatization in Eastern and Central Europe," Group of 30 Occasional Paper, no. 34 (Washington, D.C., 1991); and *The Economist*, September 21, 1991, survey, p. 26.
15. Alan Gelb and Cheryl Gray, "The Transformation of Economies in Central and Eastern Europe: Issues, Progress and Prospects," World Bank Policy Research Paper, no. 17 (Washington, D.C., 1991).
16. See also Fischer and Gelb, "The Process of Socialist Economic Transformation," pp. 101–104.
17. See Alan Gelb, "Socialist Transformations: An Overview of Eastern Europe and Some Comparators," unpublished manuscript, World Bank, June 1992, p. 24. He argues that "the choice is usually constrained, for a given country, by macroeconomic stresses and the nature of political conditions." For a normative analysis of the choice of strategy, see Fischer and Gelb, "The Process of Socialist Economic Transformation."
18. Jeffrey Sachs, "Accelerating Privatization in Eastern Europe" (Paper prepared for the World Bank's Annual Conference on Development Economies, April 1991).
19. This discussion draws heavily from Sanjay Dhar, "Enterprise Viability and the Transition to a Market Economy," World Bank Internal Discussion Paper, no. 113 (Washington, D.C., 1992). See also Ronald McKinnon, *The Order of Economic Liberalization: Financial Control in the Transition to a Market Economy* (Baltimore: Johns Hopkins University Press, 1991); and McKinnon, "Financial Control in the Transition from Classical Socialism to a Market Economy," *Journal of Economic Perspectives*, vol. 5, no. 4 (1991).
20. *The Economist*, "A Survey on Business in Eastern Europe," September 26, 1991, p. 10.
21. Michal Mejstrik and James Burger, "On the Brink: CSFR Privatization Readies for the Start of the First Round," *Privatization Newsletter of Czechoslovakia*, no. 6, May 1992.
22. An unprofitable (loss-making) enterprise is producing negative value-added output when the enterprise would be unprofitable even if it paid nothing to the workers. See Gordon Hughes and Paul Hare, "Competitiveness and Industrial Restructuring in Czechoslovakia, Hungary and Poland," *European Economy*, special issue, no. 2, June 1991.
23. In the former Soviet Union, the enterprise debt problem is even more complicated: The ruble debts could be owed to banks and enterprises of different republics (now independent nations). The foreign-currency debts of the former Union government have been allocated to various successor states according to a mechanical formula. But the legal condition

imposed by the Group of 7 governments (before the breakup of the Soviet Union) that each republic is "jointly and severally" responsible for all the Union debt to foreigners is still a stumbling block for the governments of former republics desperately seeking an International Monetary Fund program. At the time of this writing, Russia is the only post-Soviet country that confronts this problem, as it engages in seemingly endless negotiations with the Fund to become eligible to receive the $24 billion loan package that was announced with much fanfare on April Fool's Day in 1992.

24. Dhar, "Enterprise Viability and the Transition to a Market Economy."

25. *The Economist*, May 1992, p. 8.

26. Ibid.

27. See *Facts on File: Weekly World News Digest*, June 9, 1989, November 14, 1991.

28. *The Economist*, "A Survey on Business in Eastern Europe," p. 28.

29. Dhar, "Enterprise Viability and the Transition to a Market Economy."

30. *The Economist*, "A Survey on Business in Eastern Europe," p. 30.

31. For an analysis of how privately owned creditor banks and enterprises display similar behavior, see David Begg and Richard Portes, "Enterprise Debt and Economic Transformation: Financial Restructuring of the State Sector in Central and Eastern Europe," Centre for Economic Policy Research Discussion Paper, no. 695 (London, 1992).

32. For more details, see Begg and Portes, "Enterprise Debt and Economic Transformation."

33. See, for example, United Nations, "Dilemmas of Macroeconomic Management: Stabilization and Adjustment in Developing Countries," *Supplement to World Economic Survey 1990–1991* (New York, 1992); Miguel Kiguel and Nissan Liviatan, "Inflationary Rigidities and Orthodox Stabilization Policies: Lessons from Latin America," *World Bank Economic Review*, vol. 2, no. 3 (1988); and Miguel Kiguel and Nissan Liviatan, "Lessons from Heterodox Stabilization," World Bank Working Paper, no. 671 (Washington, 1991).

34. As pointed out earlier, Portes (in this volume) argues that the "excessive" 1990 devaluation of the Polish zloty had exactly this result. Berg and Sachs, in "Structural Adjustment and International Trade in Eastern Europe," strongly disagree.

35. Simon Johnson, "Private Business in Eastern Europe," in O. Blanchard, K. Froot, and J. Sachs, eds., *Transition in Eastern Europe*, University of Chicago Press (forthcoming 1993).

36. This analysis owes its origin to McKinnon, "Financial Control in the Transition from Classical Socialism to a Market Economy."

37. Dhar, "Enterprise Viability and the Transition to a Market Economy."

38. See Saburo Okita, "Transition to a Market Economy" (Paper prepared for the United Nations Development Programme Conference on Global Change, Bucharest, September 4–6, 1992); and Yukitsugu Nakagawa, "Reflections on Restoring the Former Soviet Union: Can the Japanese Experience Help?" International Institute for Global Peace Policy Paper, no. 92E (Tokyo, 1992).

39. General Agreement on Tariffs and Trade, *Trade Policy Review: United States*, Vol. 1, Geneva, April 1992; and Dani Rodrik, "Foreign Trade in

Eastern Europe's Transition: Early Results," in O. Blanchard, K. Froot, and J. Sachs, eds., *Transition in Eastern Europe*, University of Chicago Press (forthcoming 1993). Sweeping trade liberalization in a transitional economy, however, may turn out unsustainable: in August 1991, Poland introduced a new tariff schedule raising the average tariff rate to 14 percent.

40. See Begg and Portes, "Enterprise Debt and Economic Transformation."

Appendix

Symposium on
Making Markets: Economic Transformation in
Eastern Europe and the Post-Soviet Republics
February 12–13, 1992

Chairman: Robert Hormats—Goldman Sachs International
Authors: Robert Campbell—Indiana University
    Paul Marer—Indiana University
    Richard Portes—Center for Economic Policy
    Research
    Jeffrey Sachs—Harvard University
Directors: Shafiqul Islam—Council on Foreign Relations
    Michael Mandelbaum—Council on Foreign
    Relations
Coordinators: Radha Muthiah—Council on Foreign Relations
    Theresa Weber—Council on Foreign Relations
Rapporteurs: Audrey McInerney—Council on Foreign Relations
    Scott Monje—Columbia University

Paul Balaran—Ford Foundation
Lawrence Brainard—Goldman Sachs and Company
Aurel Braun—University of Toronto
Richard Debs—Morgan Stanley
Andrew Gaspar—Central European Development Corporation
Alan Gelb—The World Bank
Marshall Goldman—Harvard University
Donald Green—PlanEcon Capital Group
John Holsen—The World Bank
Robert Kahn—Federal Reserve Board
Uner Kirdar—United Nations Development Programme

Ivo John Lederer—A.T. Kearney
Robert Macy—Management Investment Partners
Alexander Motyl—Columbia University
Roman Pipko—Paul Weiss Rifkind
Paul Sacks—Multinational Strategies, Inc.
Enid Schoettle—Council on Foreign Relations
Mihaly Simai—U.S. Institute of Peace
Michelle Siren—Price Waterhouse
Dorothy Sobol—Federal Reserve Bank of New York
Anthony Solomon—Institute for East-West Security Studies
John Temple Swing—Council on Foreign Relations
Peter Tarnoff—Council on Foreign Relations
Jozef Van Brabant—United Nations
Jane Wales—Carnegie Corporation of New York
Michael Weinstein—*The New York Times*
Malcolm Wiener—The Millburn Corporation

Index

Abalkin, Leonid, 114
Academy of Sciences, 118
Adaptation, 9
Adenauer, Konrad, 149, 178n.6
Aganbegian, Abel, 115
Agriculture: Armenia, 138; European Community (EC), 37; Hungary, 58; Macedonia, 93; People's Republic of China, 117; Poland, 66; Russia, 31; Soviet Union, 20, 117–18; successor states of Soviet Union, 109; transfer of labor into services, 44; Ukraine, 138
Agroprombank, 139n.7
Aid from Western countries: forms of, 14. *See also* Financial assistance to Russia by Western countries
Airlines: successor states and the Soviet Union, 141n.32
Albania: debt rescheduling, 69; economic transformation, 94; progress in economic transformation, 94
Anglo-American loan, 37
Antall, Jorzef, 13
ANT cooperative, 110
"Approximation of laws," 33
Argentina: loans to, 180n.19; stagnation, 87
Armenia: agriculture, 138; birth and death rates, 137; research and development (R&D), 130; work force, 137
Asia: Japan and, 210; ties to Russian Soviet Federated Socialist Republic (RSFSR), 132
Austria: consumerism, 73; gross national product (GNP), 156; Hungarian border, 64; international financial assistance, 159; post–World War I, 154–56
Autarky, 22, 90, 102
Authoritarian rule and central planning, 10
Azerbaijan: birth and death rates, 137; forecasting, 138; work force, 137–38

Baikonur, 134
Balance-of-payments: financial assistance to Russia by Western countries, 158–59; Russia, 162, 164–65, 167
Balcerowicz, Leszek, 126, 180n.23
Balkans: elected officials, 12; Western-style politics, 14
Baltic nations: autonomy, 119; currency, 128; elected officials, 12; progress in reform, 135; ties to RSFSR, 132; Western-style politics, 14
Banking Committee of the U.S. House of Representatives, 168
Bankruptcy: Hungary, 58; laws regarding, 196
Banks and banking: Hungary, 58; Poland, 71, 162; recapitalization, 211; Russia, 170; Russian Soviet Federated Socialist Republic (RSFSR), 119–20; state production establishment (SPE), Soviet Union, 101–103
Begg, David, 44
Belarus, 132, 138
Belgium: gross national product (GNP), 156

Glossary of Abbreviations and Acronyms

CEE   Central and Eastern Europe
CMEA   Council for Mutual Economic Asistance
CSFR   Federation of the Czech and Slovak Republics
EBRD   European Bank for Reconstruction and Development
EC   European Community
G-7   Group of 7 nations
G-8   Group of 8 nations
GAB   General Agreement to Borrow
GATT   General Agreement on Tariffs and Trade
GDP   Gross domestic product
GNP   Gross national product
IMF   International Monetary Fund
NEM   New Economic Mechanism
R&D   Research and development
RSFSR Russian Soviet Federated Socialist Republic
SOE   State-owned enterprises
SPA   State Poperty Agency
SPE   State production establishment

About the Authors

Robert Campbell is distinguished Professor of Economics at Indiana University, Bloomington. His graduate training in Soviet economics was at Harvard University where he received an M.A. in Soviet area studies and a Ph.D. in economics. He has held teaching positions at the University of Southern California, University of California at Berkeley, Stanford University, and Harvard University. His publications include general analyses of the Soviet economy, and numerous more specialized studies dealing with energy policy, research and development, economic reform, and military affairs in the USSR. His most recent research focuses on Soviet telecommunications as an infrastructure controlling the ability of the USSR to deal with the information revolution.

Shafiqul Islam is Senior Fellow for International Economics and Finance at the Council on Foreign Relations. He has a Ph.D. in economics from Harvard University. Before joining the Council, he was a Visiting Fellow at the Institute for International Economics (1986–1987) and Chief of the Industrial Economies Division at the Federal Reserve Bank of New York (1984–1986). He has published widely on international monetary and financial issues. Most recently he edited *Yen for Development: Japanese Foreign Aid and the Politics of Burden-Sharing* (1991).

Michael Mandelbaum is Director of the Project on East-West Relations at the Council on Foreign Relations and the Christian A. Herter Professor of American Foreign Policy at the Paul H.

Nitze School of Advanced International Studies of the Johns Hopkins University in Washington, D.C. He is also the Associate Director of the Aspen Institute's Project on American Relations with Central and Eastern Europe and a regular columnist on foreign affairs for *Newsday*. Professor Mandelbaum received an M.A. from King's College, Cambridge, and a Ph.D. from Harvard University where he taught in the Government department. He has also taught at Columbia University and the United States Naval Academy. He is the author or editor of eleven books, including *The Rise of Nations in the Soviet Union: American Foreign Policy and the Disintegration of the USSR* (1991); *The Fate of Nations: The Search for National Security in the 19th and 20th Centuries* (1988); with Seweryn Bialer, *The Global Rivals* (1988); and with Strobe Talbott, *Reagan and Gorbachev* (1987).

Paul Marer is Professor of International Business at the Indiana University School of Business. He has M.A. and Ph.D. degrees from the University of Pennsylvania. He has served as consulting editor and contributor to the Joint Economic Committee of the U.S. Congress on several of its triannual assessments of the economic and political situation in Eastern Europe and has given expert testimony before congressional committees. Dr. Marer has authored, edited, or co-edited thirteen books. He has served as a consultant to the World Bank and the OECD on the centrally planned economies and on their transition to market systems. On leave from Indiana University during 1989–1990, he co-directed the Joint Hungarian-International Blue Ribbon Commission, which developed an economic recovery and transformation program for Hungary. In 1990, Dr. Marer was appointed by President Bush as a trustee of the Hungarian-American Enterprise Fund, which sets policy on how to allocate the $60-million grant that the United States is giving to Hungary to promote private enterprise.

Richard Portes is Director of the Centre for Economic Policy Research in London; Professor of Economics at Birkbeck College, University of London; and Directeur d'Etudes at the Ecole des Hautes Etudes en Sciences Sociales in Paris. He was a Rhodes

Scholar and a Fellow of Balliol College, Oxford, and has taught at Princeton and Harvard (as a Guggenheim Fellow). Professor Portes is a Fellow of the Econometric Society, a member of the Council of the European Economic Association, and Secretary-General of the Royal Economic Society. He is also Co-Chairman of the Board and a Senior Editor of *Economic Policy*. He has written extensively on sovereign borrowing and debt, centrally planned economies, macroeconomic disequilibrium, and East-West economic relations. Professor Portes has also coordinated and edited for the European Commission two sets of studies on "The Economic Transformation of Hungary and Poland" (*European Economy*, March 1990) and "The Path of Reform in Central and Eastern Europe" (*European Economy*, Special Issue, July 1991).

Jeffrey Sachs is the Galen L. Stone Professor of International Trade at Harvard University and a Research Associate of the National Bureau of Economic Research. He received his M.A. and Ph.D. from Harvard University in 1978 and 1980 respectively. Professor Sachs currently serves as an economic adviser to several governments in Latin America and Eastern Europe and is one of the architects of the economic reform program introduced in Poland at the beginning of 1990. He is currently leading a team of economic advisers for Russian President Boris Yeltsin. He also directs a project on economic reform in the Soviet Republics and in Eastern Europe for the United Nations University, World Institute for Development Economics Research (WIDER), in Helsinki, Finland. Professor Sachs is a member of several organizations including the Harvard Society of Fellows, the Fellows of the World Econometric Society, Brookings Panel of Economists, and the Board of Advisers of the Congressional Budget Office. He has also been a consultant to the IMF, the World Bank, the OECD, and the United Nations Development Programme.